For Hugh Clark,
with best wishes,

E[signature]

Negro Political
Leadership
in the South

Negro Political Leadership in the South

By Everett Carll Ladd, Jr.

WITH A NEW PREFACE BY ANDREW HACKER

STUDIES IN AMERICAN NEGRO LIFE
August Meier, General Editor

ATHENEUM   *New York*

1969

Published by Atheneum
Reprinted by arrangement with Cornell University Press
Copyright © 1966 by Cornell University
Preface copyright © 1969 by Andrew Hacker
All rights reserved
Library of Congress catalog card number 69-13435
Manufactured in the United States of America by
Kingsport Press, Inc., Kingsport, Tennessee
Published in Canada by McClelland and Stewart Ltd.
First Atheneum Edition

To my wife, Cynthia

Preface to the Atheneum Edition

by *Andrew Hacker*

FOR well over a century the American South has done reluctant service as laboratory for social scientists. Numberless Northern scholars have descended upon the region, hoping to explain how and why its customs and culture stand at such variance from the nation to which it is uneasily appended. These academic carpetbaggers have all too often carried with them dubious preconceptions, one of which is that the South is the domestic equivalent of an "underdeveloped" country. With agriculture long dominating its economy, with a rigid system of castes and classes, with fundamentalist religion and a tradition of violence, it has been assumed that over time the only direction the South could take would be one of eventual "modernization." Usually implied in this assessment is the notion that the North, with its record of economic prosperity and political progress, would serve as the model for emulation and identification. Hence the assumption of many commentators that a Southern two-party system would come into being, that industrialization would create a moderate middle class, and that the Negro population would eventually enter political life along lines similar to those traveled by other ethnic groups in earlier generations.

Everett Ladd's study of Southern Negro leadership is burdened with no such biases; certainly he feels no obligation to see the region as lagging "behind" the North or that its destiny is to follow in Northern footsteps. He is rightly impressed with the obduracy of Southern history, seeing traditional patterns as persisting long after a more formal logic might have decreed that change was surely scheduled to occur. Ladd captures both the spirit and the structure of Southern politics, noting not only its power to resist transformation but also the unexpected opportunities for innovation offered by a system never noted for its hospitality to reform.

That Ladd can speak of "Negro political leadership" in the South is itself instructive. For the leadership he describes has, from the outset, held out the potential for becoming a genuinely independent enterprise. If its list of electoral accomplishments has been comparatively meager thus far, the fact remains that the efforts of Negroes to exercise power are remarkably autonomous endeavors. All this deserves consideration, for the emerging patterns described by Ladd stand in sharp contrast to those of Negro politics in the North.

Northern Negroes who hold party and public office are almost invariably satraps of the white organizations dominant in their area. For over a generation "downtown" machines of the Northern cities have had the good sense to colonize black ghettoes, giving positions and privileges and patronage to complaisant Negro officials who would deliver their ration of votes on primary or election day. In the North the typical Negro "leader" (and quotation marks are probably in order here) is a loyal but uninspired party regular. Beholden to the white organization for his position, only in exceptional cases will he have a personal following of any substantial proportions. For every Adam Clayton Powell or Carl Stokes or Richard Hatcher, there are literally hundreds of black councilmen and committeemen and commissioners with no talent other than an instinct for committing themselves to the white hierarchies. Throughout the greater part of the 1960's there have been half-a-dozen Negroes in the House of Representatives. Yet it is hard to recall the names of more than one or two of these lawmakers, and it is even more difficult to recollect any serious campaign for racial legislation they have made on behalf of their constituents.

Due to the fact that Southern Negroes did not have the vote

until very recently, white political leaders saw no need to establish arms of their organizations in black neighborhoods. Patronage served little purpose and tokens of power were seldom shared. But it is now too late in the political day for colonization on the Northern model. Not only are more and more Southern Negroes learning to use the ballot, but they are already producing leaders (this time without quotation marks) of their own choice and creation. Ladd depicts a process which is not always smooth, nor by any means always successful; yet in so doing he demonstrates one of the advantages of late entry to the political arena. For during the long decades of virtual disenfranchisement Southern Negroes were able to build up a community spirit and a leadership echelon of their own with little interference from an uncaring white power structure. Hence such "backward" constituencies as Georgia and Mississippi could produce a Julian Bond and a Charles Evers, who in ideology and ability have given better service to their followers than do the black machine-vassals of Philadelphia or Chicago. Ladd's book is an exciting prelude to a series of new and unanticipated developments in American political life. Black citizens of the South are devising their own methods and models, and Harlem may soon find itself learning some lessons from Hattiesburg.

A fairly recent analysis of the attitudes and aspirations of Southern Negroes, based on extensive interview-surveys, is contained in Donald R. Matthews and James W. Prothro, *Negroes and the New Southern Politics* (1966). For an imaginative and durable discussion of the personalities and principles in black politics, see Lewis Killian and Charles Grigg, *Racial Crisis in America: Leadership in Conflict* (1964). The best study of political life in Northern cities is James Q. Wilson's realistic and still relevant *Negro Politics: The Search for Leadership* (1960).

Acknowledgments

THE research for this volume was made possible by a Research Training Fellowship of the Social Science Research Council, held during the academic year 1962–1963, and by grants from the Cornell Social Science Research Center and the Cornell–Ford Public Affairs Research Committee.

The project has benefited from the advice and assistance of many people. I am indebted to the many citizens of Winston-Salem and Greenville, Negro and white, who took time from their busy lives to cooperate in the conduct of the research. I especially want to thank four good friends, the Reverend William R. Crawford and Samuel D. Harvey of Winston, and Donald James Sampson and Gil Rowland of Greenville. They introduced me to their cities and to the patterns of race relations in each. All four, on the front line of the civil rights struggle, gave time and assistance far beyond what I could reasonably have expected.

I want to thank Professors Donald Matthews and James Prothro of the University of North Carolina. They shared with me experiences and data from their own studies of Negro politics. The staffs of the national office of the National Association for the Advancement of Colored People, of the Southern Regional Office of the National Urban League, and of the Southern Regional Council gave valuable advice and information.

Thanks are also due Professor Theodore Lowi of the University of Chicago, and Professors Steven Muller, Mario

Einaudi, and Clinton Rossiter of Cornell University, for their help and guidance not only in this study but in the more general preparation for it. Professor Rossiter first encouraged me to undertake the research on which this volume is based.

I am happy to acknowledge my very special debt to Professor Andrew Hacker of Cornell. He has been a source of inspiration, constructive criticism, advice, and intellectual guidance. His own scholarship has set the very highest standard for me.

Finally, I want to thank two women. Mrs. Anne Lounsbery typed the preliminary drafts of the manuscript and was a source of editorial advice. My wife, Cynthia, typed the final manuscript while fulfilling her obligation as wife and mother. Certainly the project would not have been completed without her sacrifice and understanding, and above all her wise advice and counsel.

EVERETT CARLL LADD, JR.

Storrs, Connecticut
June 1965

Contents

CONTENTS

Negro Political
Leadership
in the South

Introduction

THERE is a tendency for those living in the midst of rapid and profound social change to be so caught up in day-to-day developments that the enormity of the overall change escapes them. Negro-white relations in the South are today undergoing this kind of change, and the common myopia has appeared. Since 1954 we have been presented with an uninterrupted stream of Negro race-advancement activity: school integration suits, bus boycotts, voter registration drives, freedom-rides, "package" integration demands, and the "ins" —sit-ins, kneel-ins, stand-ins, wade-ins, and finally sleep-ins. Negro Americans are attaining "firsts" on literally a daily basis: Leroy Johnson became in 1962 the first Negro to be elected to the Georgia Senate since Reconstruction, Henry Frye the first Negro Assistant U.S. District Attorney in North Carolina. Stores hire their first nonwhite clerks, schools take in their first nonwhite pupils, and a deep-South governor for the first time invites his Negro constituents to an inaugural barbecue. And quietly the Negro and white pastors of a deep-South city dine together for the first time as members of an integrated ministerial fellowship. Because of the rapidity of this change, and because it both springs from and precipitates expectations which at once cause it to appear shockingly inadequate, we often have difficulty assessing just what the last two decades have meant for black and white in the South. We are reminded sharply of this when reading Myrdal's *An American Dilemma*, published in 1944.[1] Although dazzled

---

[1] Gunnar Myrdal, *An American Dilemma* (New York, 1944).

by the magnitude and brilliance of the work, we find it of value now primarily as a historical document. We have to remind ourselves that the Southern Regional Council, so great an ally of racial justice in the South, in fact did not seek desegregation as a necessary part of its program to improve the educational position of Southern Negroes until after the *Brown* decision. In 1940 no more than 250,000–275,000 Negroes were registered voters in the states of the old Confederacy; today more than 2,000,000 are on the books. The sovereign state of South Carolina was spending $3.12 for each white child in its public schools twenty years ago for every $1.00 spent for Negro pupils in the state. In 1957 the figures were $1.34 for every $1.00. As late as 1960, the public facilities of the South, from city parks to hotels and restaurants, remained almost completely segregated. But protest activity—particularly that of 1963—and finally the 1964 Civil Rights Act shattered these barriers. By late 1964 most of the cities of the rim South were completely "open"—all major public facilities admitting Negroes—and compliance with the Civil Rights Act was swifter and more complete in deep-South cities like Jackson than many observers had expected. It is now but a few short years since a group of students from North Carolina Agricultural and Technical College sought service at a Woolworth's lunch counter in Greensboro and continued to sit in their seats after having been refused. But this magnificent instance of spontaneous rebellion now seems a chapter of history, so far and fast has the movement come since February 1, 1960.

These are scattered illustrations of a broad and pervasive change. The fabric of race relations in the American South has been torn by the developments of the last twenty years; the institutional and psychological structure of white supremacy is collapsing.

Negro political leadership necessarily has been caught up in this revolution in race relations, for the structure of race relations has always defined the essential features of race leadership. Ethnic group leadership exists because the ethnic group is conscious of itself in competition for certain scarce values with other ethnic groups. The sharper the competition and the greater the estrangement, rejection, and isolation of the ethnic group, the stronger its internal cohesion and its sense of identity. Negro Americans are an embattled ethnic group. Although one of the first such groups to arrive in the United States, it has been the least accepted. The most pressing needs and concerns of Negroes are racially defined. Their lives are race-ridden. No issue or problem can match the importance of racial problems. Leadership must reflect this racially defined predicament. Gunnar Myrdal was referring to this when he wrote in *An American Dilemma* that the pattern of Negro leadership has always been related to the pattern of race relations.[2] The goals Negro leaders pursue, the means they use, the difficulties they face, the resources at their command, have been linked historically and are still linked to the larger relationship of black and white.

This, then, is a study of Negro leadership in the South in a period of rapid and profound transition. In the last two decades a pattern of leadership which developed in the 1890's and then persisted for a half century has been swept away. In its place a new type of leadership has emerged, the essential characteristics of which are now distinguishable. Our task here is to describe these characteristics.

The questions, areas of interest, assumptions, and formally drawn hypotheses on which this study of southern Negro leadership was predicated all related to one or more of three central subject areas. First, we wanted to explore the meaning of *Negro leadership* in light of the changes in Negro political life and patterns of race relations. What does it mean to say that an individual is a Negro leader? We hypothesized that

[2] When we refer to Negro leadership it is to *political* leadership—concerned with the "authoritative allocation of values for the society"—rather than to "leaders" of Negro "society," business, and the like.

Negro leadership is issue leadership; or to put it another way, that in the absence of strong institutional bases, and given the intensity with which the cause of race advancement is held by Negroes, Negro leaders are particularly dependent upon popular approval of their handling of issues of race advancement. We assumed that because of this the position of race leaders should be especially vulnerable: they should have to run harder and faster than their white counterparts to keep up with the issue-orientation of their constituents and, hence, to maintain their position of leadership. We also expected that civic participation and reputation—at the local level—generally would not strengthen a claim to political leadership measurably. Little effort was made at the outset to develop any full and precise definition of Negro leadership, because the study as a whole is centrally concerned with defining it. But in general Negro leaders were thought of as persons able to make decisions affecting the choice of race objectives and/or the means utilized to realize these objectives.[3]

The second subject area includes an examination of the

[3] We disagree with the concept of leadership defined by, among others, Petrullo and Bass. Petrullo argued for "the concept of the leader, whether selected from above or below, as a freely followed person who is concerned with fulfilling the purposes of the group and the needs of the individuals in it. Such a leader is in contrast to a 'head man' who is appointed to carry out the objectives of those above him by directing or commanding." (*Leadership and Interpersonal Behavior* [New York, 1961], p. xvii.)

We agree with Easton when he observes that "both in the case where the legitimacy of the rulers is accepted and where the rulers are obeyed only because they possess a predominance of effective, violent sanctions, the rulers can be described as authorities." He rejects the argument that authority stands in contrast to coercion. There may be legitimate authority and nonlegitimate or coercive authority. (David Easton, "The Perception of Authority and Political Change," *Authority*, Carl J. Friedrich, ed. [Cambridge, Mass., 1958], p. 180.) We insist that a leader's position may be based simply on his ability to coerce. In fact, it is often difficult, if not impossible, to distinguish the

4

styles of race leadership in the South, and the continuum of leadership styles. What do Negro leaders want? How do they propose to get it? So much that is contradictory has been written about Uncle Toms, Conservatives, Militants, Radicals, Liberals, Moderates, Accommodationists, Race Men and Race Diplomats, and the various other typologies which have been developed, that there is a need to attempt to define the content and the limits of the leadership continuum in today's urban South. What are the major types or styles of race leadership? What factors determine the particular combination of leadership styles which form the pattern of Negro leadership in a given southern city? What kind of relationship exists between functions performed by Negro leaders and their style of leadership?

The third area involves the race-advancement organizations of the subcommunity. We wanted to examine the roles which they play; the extent of cooperation, competition, and conflict; the styles of leadership which characterize each; and the extent of community understanding and support of their performance. We were especially interested in developments in Negro electoral politics in the South. There has been an increase of 800 per cent in the number of registered Negroes in the South over the last two decades. The rate of increase in actual voting has probably been even higher. The expansion of the Negro electorate has, of course, occurred unevenly, and hence has assumed much greater importance in some areas than in others. We assumed that these developments in the area of electoral politics had added important new dimensions to the structure of race leadership. Is there in the South a group of Negro politicians for whom electoral politics is the main channel of race-advancement activity? Or has the

---

obeying of a command because one is afraid of the alternatives of not obeying, and the obeying of a command because it is considered legitimate.

vote remained simply another weapon in the hands of protest organization leaders? It was expected that the response in the leadership structure would be as varied as are opportunities for effective Negro participation in electoral politics. Extensive emphasis has been placed on "doing it yourself with a vote" by, among others, Justice Department officers and the leaders of all major Negro protest organizations. What in fact has the vote accomplished for southern Negroes thus far? What factors are operating to place limits on the effectiveness of Negro electoral activity? Is a high level of Negro activity in electoral politics simply an indication that the biracial system has been drastically modified in a given community and, hence, that emphasis on electoral activity in the absence of other changes may be abortive? What are the implications for the future of this electoral participation?

Finally, it must be emphasized that we study Negro political leadership to gain understanding of the characteristics of *Negro political life*. All the important elements of Negro political life are present—indeed, are focused—at the level of leadership. It is at that level that objectives are determined, resources committed, decisions made; it is at that level that tensions and trends become evident. The study of leadership here, then, is a bridge to a consideration of central features of Negro political life in the South.

Two community studies formed the nucleus of our research. One study dealt with an outer-South city, the other with a deep-South city. The choice of urban centers for an examination of the developing patterns of Negro political leadership was determined by the following. (1) Negro political activity has progressed much further in the cities than in the small towns and rural areas. Cities have brought large numbers of Negroes close enough together to make continuous communication possible. The anonymity of the ghetto provides the urban Negro with a buffer against white sanctions, a buffer absent in rural and small-town areas. Moreover, many leadership roles are open only to Negroes who are economically independent of whites, and only relatively large Negro communities are able to support significant numbers of businessmen and professional people —optometrists, dentists, lawyers, and college-educated ministers. The greater incidence of whites born outside the region, of non-WASPs (white Anglo-Saxon protestants), and the presence of more cosmopolitan members of the new corporate middle class in southern cities have made it easier for Negroes to find allies of sorts in these cities than in the more homogeneous rural and small-town South. (2) Negro political leaders recruited and trained for battles in the urban South have begun to filter out into the hinterland, along with colleagues from the North, encouraging their rural brethren. The tone of the new South is being created in its cities. If we are to gauge the speed, the intensity, and the direction of the Negro Revolt, it is to the urban South that we must look.

We selected an outer-South and a deep-South city, fully aware of the major differences among the cities of Virginia, North Carolina, Tennessee, Florida, Texas, and Arkansas— generally considered the states of the outer, or peripheral, South; and among the urban centers of Georgia, South Carolina, Alabama, Mississippi, and Louisiana—the deep South. Atlanta, for example, is a major exception to the pattern prevailing in the deep South. A somewhat more precise and finer distinction than that between the rim and the heartland of the region could have been utilized. H. D. Price developed a scale for ranking states from the most to the least southern.[4] On the basis of this he ranked Mississippi, Alabama, South Carolina, and Louisiana "most southern." Georgia and Arkansas were in the second group, followed by Virginia, North Carolina, and Florida in the third. Tennessee, because of its eastern two-thirds, and Texas were in effect relegated to the

[4] H. D. Price, *The Negro and Southern Politics* (New York, 1957), pp. 8–9.

7

rank of border states. One could easily devise a twenty-category classification, with counties rather than states the unit of reference. But every schema must conform to the demands of the inquiry it is serving. The task we set for ourselves was to deal broadly with the basic structure of race leadership in the South, with changes in this structure, and with the factors which shape and influence it. A preliminary analysis of the extensive literature on race relations in the South made it clear that concentration on one southern city would not be sufficient for this objective. The differences in race relations between the rim South and the heartland are too great. But the literature indicated that the *basic race relations structure* is essentially similar for most major rim-South cities, that Winston-Salem, Charlotte, Richmond, Jacksonville, Nashville, Little Rock, and Houston belong to the same "world" of race relations. The literature also suggested that many deep-South cities—from Columbia and Greenville to Montgomery to Jackson and Baton Rouge—share a common pattern of race relations.[5]

[5] This distinction between the structure of race relations in the outer South and the deep South will be developed in detail below. The literature describing the different patterns existing now and historically is extensive. See in particular M. Elaine Burgess, *Negro Leadership in a Southern City* (Chapel Hill, N.C., 1960), for a description of the pattern in Durham, North Carolina, in the late 1950's; also Daniel C. Thompson, *The Negro Leadership Class* (Englewood Cliffs, N.J., 1963), for New Orleans; H. D. Price, *op. cit.*, for excellent material on Florida; and Howard H. Quint, *Profile in Black and White* (Washington, D.C., 1958), for a discussion of race relations in South Carolina, historically and for the present. Key's description of the impact of race on the politics of the southern states is excellent and demonstrates from a different perspective major outer-South–deep-South differences. *Southern Politics in State and Nation* (New York, 1950). For differences in the historical development see John Hope Franklin's *From Slavery to Freedom: A History of American Negroes* (2nd ed.; New York, 1956).

8

The major determinant of the different patterns of race relations of the two subregions has been the much higher concentration of Negroes in the states of the deep South. As the data in Table 1 indicate, this difference in the concentration of Negroes has existed historically in much the same form as it exists today.

TABLE 1

PERCENTAGE OF THE TOTAL POPULATION WHICH IS NEGRO, DEEP-SOUTH AND OUTER-SOUTH STATES, 1910 AND 1960.*

	Range, 1910	Range, 1960	Mean, 1910	Mean, 1960
Deep-South states	42.5–56.2	28.6–42.5	47.8	32.6
Outer-South states	17.7–32.6	12.6–25.4	24.9	17.7

* Florida is not included in the figures for the outer-South states in 1910. The population development in that state over the last five decades—the settlement of the Peninsula—has completely altered the character of the state's political and economic life. In 1960 Florida clearly was a rim-South state. In 1910 the principal population concentration was in northern Florida and the state resembled its neighbors Georgia and Alabama. Source: *Negro Population 1790–1915*, and *U.S. Census of Population: 1960*.

To approach this another way, we agree with the reader who observes that in some respects each southern city is different from all others in race relations. We agree that the two subregions identified here are in no sense internally uniform. We agree, moreover, that for certain analytical purposes an outer-South–deep-South division would be quite useless, indeed would blur important differences. But we hypothesized at the outset of this study, after a careful examination of the literature, that two quite different "worlds" of race relations exist among the cities of the South, that the similarities of the cities in each "world" are important, indeed pivotal, and that these "worlds" generally can be identified

9

with the rim South and the heartland respectively. We incorporated into our research plan means for testing this hypothesis further. These are described in the Appendix. This hypothesis, defined precisely against our particular research interests here, was confirmed by our research.

Winston-Salem, North Carolina, and Greenville, South Carolina, were selected for detailed analysis, as cities broadly representative of the two basic patterns of race relations. Selection was made on the basis of a careful examination of census data on all major southern cities and of all available published materials, and after consultation with several scholars who had recently completed research on race relations in the region. In addition, the author had traveled extensively in the Southeast before undertaking this study, and hence had a basic if casual familiarity with patterns of race relations. Other considerations, particularly of size, contributed to the final choice of cities. The assumption was that comparisons would be facilitated if the two cities were of comparable size.

As the study went on, it seemed necessary to have a basis for distinguishing between those aspects of Negro leadership which are peculiar to Winston-Salem and Greenville and those which are common to other cities. What was needed was a firmer basis for generalization than the two community studies alone could afford. Consequently, trips were made to other regional cities and informants in each were consulted. Eleven major southern Negro newspapers were regularly reviewed and these provided a wealth of data on Negro leadership in the cities of publication. A number of published and unpublished accounts of Negro leadership in other southern cities were carefully re-examined. This effort to combine a broader frame of reference with the continuity and depth possible in the community study approach is described in more detail in the Appendix.

There is growing recognition of the utility of the community as a frame of reference within which to examine the location, structure, and functioning of political leadership.[6] The community is a laboratory for the social scientist. It furnishes opportunity for observation of the composition, goals, strategy—the whole structure of political leadership— with an attention to detail and in a much more systematic manner than is possible in a larger setting.

The author spent approximately three months in each of the cities, Winston-Salem and Greenville, selected for detailed analysis. These two cities are in the 100,000 population range, large enough to share patterns of urban politics, but manageable.[7] The researcher was able to get an overall view of race relations in a relatively short time, something much more difficult to do in a metropolis. Moreover, the "typical" urban life of the South is that of medium-sized as opposed to large cities.

Some 350 interviews were conducted with Negro and white leaders in the two cities. These ranged in length from thirty minutes to more than five hours, averaging approximately two hours. The selection of the leaders interviewed is described in detail in the Appendix. Here we need only mention that our objective was to identify and interview all Negroes in each community who, by virtue of their organizational position, their contact and association with other Negro

[6] See Floyd Hunter, *Community Power Structure* (Chapel Hill, N.C., 1953); Burgess, *op. cit.*; Thompson, *op. cit.*; Robert Dahl, *Who Governs?* (New Haven, 1961); and James Wilson, *Negro Politics: The Search for Leadership* (Glencoe, Ill., 1960).

[7] The 1960 census listed the population of Winston-Salem at 111,135. Greenville's population was 66,188. In fact, however, the cities are virtually identical in size. Annexation in Winston-Salem has meant that the formal boundaries roughly coincide with the actual dimensions of the city. In Greenville, in contrast, areas of high population concentration less than a mile from the center of the city have not been annexed. Greenville's *urban area* contains 126,887 people; Winston-Salem's, 128,176.

leaders, and/or their reputation in the community, were in a position to influence significantly the realization of race goals and activity designed to promote these goals. Two groups of white leaders were interviewed: (1) those who had had extensive contact with Negro leaders through biracial organizations and activities and in political campaigns, and (2) a sample representative of the spectrum of white leadership in each city. The former were interviewed to gain an "external" evaluation of Negro leadership, and to determine the level and content of interracial communication. The latter contributed to our understanding of the race relations of each city.

Interviews with white and Negro leaders were loosely structured. These were conducted only after background information on each city had been carefully compiled. For this preliminary work, informants were consulted and histories, population statistics over the past seventy years, and data on the economic life of each city were utilized. Particular attention was given to the newspapers published in each city. These were scanned on a day-by-day basis from 1954 through the present for stories on race relations, the activities of Negro leaders, and other race-related news.

A stratified areal sample survey was conducted in the Negro subcommunity of each city, using Negro interviewers. The survey, based initially on Negro residential areas,[8] was used to ascertain (1) which persons are recognized as leaders by the Negro population at large, and which segments of the leadership speak for which segments of the subcommunity; (2) whether there is a single leadership group recognized by all socioeconomic and geographic segments of the subcommunity; (3) the general level of political awareness of Negroes in the two cities; (4) the demands made on the leadership in terms of priorities assigned race goals (what

[8] Selection of the sample is discussed in the Appendix.

the rank and file want their leaders to work for immediately); and (5) subcommunity evaluation of the activities of the various race-advancement organizations.

The author was also present as an observer and on occasion as a participant-observer at meetings of race-advancement organizations, biracial committees, and political party organizations in each city.

Political leadership, of course, continually interacts with other elements in the situation or setting in which it is operating. Two aspects of the setting of race leadership are especially important in this connection and will be examined in Chapters I and II. First, we must describe the main elements of the Revolution in race relations in the American South and demonstrate how the present leadership structure is based upon this fundamental change of setting. This is done in Chapter I, "Negro Politics in the South: An Overview." Yet if the setting of race leadership can be viewed as changing with time over the entire South, it also can be seen as varying from place to place at any particular time. Race relations are different today in Winston-Salem than in Greenville, and patterns of leadership necessarily differ. In Chapter II, "Winston-Salem and Greenville: The Community Setting," an attempt will be made to isolate those variables which together determine the essential features of the structure of race leadership in a given southern city.

Part I

THE SETTING FOR

RACE LEADERSHIP

CHAPTER I

Negro Politics in the South: An Overview

In the South the Negro's person and property are practically subject to the whim of any white person who wishes to take advantage of him or to punish him for any real or fancied wrongdoing or 'insult.' A white man can steal from or maltreat a Negro in almost any way without fear of reprisal, because the Negro cannot claim the protection of the police or courts, and personal vengeance on the part of the offended Negro usually results in organized retaliation in the form of bodily injury (including lynching), home burning or banishment. . . . Physical violence and threats against personal security do not, of course, occur to every Negro every day. . . . But violence may occur at any time, and it is the fear of it as much as violence itself which creates the injustice and the insecurity.

Gunnar Myrdal, An American Dilemma [1]

THE one word which better than any other describes the position of Negro Americans in the South from the 1890's until the outbreak of World War II is *powerless*. In 1900 the

---

[1] New York, 1944, p. 530.

nearly eight million Negroes in the states of the old Confederacy had no voice in the important social, economic, and political decisions which affected them and the life and future of their region. And the South which Negro G.I.'s left in 1942 was not very different. The symptoms of this powerlessness were everywhere. Negroes were totally excluded from positions of decision making in all institutions which served the entire, as opposed to solely the Negro, population. All public facilities in the region, including city parks and playgrounds, theaters, hotels, and restaurants were rigidly segregated—as was, of course, the entire school system. The disenfranchisement of Negroes was virtually complete and was accomplished through such practices and vehicles as the white primary, the poll tax, a biased application of voting requirements, and a variety of pressures directed at discouraging Negroes from even attempting to participate in electoral politics.[2] When the United States entered World War II, only 5 per cent of her Negro citizens in the South were registered. In only a few localities—principally in cities of Tennessee, North Carolina, and Virginia—was voting by significant numbers of Negroes accepted. And even in these cities, local

[2] Since most of the South in this period was solidly Democratic, with the only genuine contests for public office occurring in the nominating primaries of that party, the exclusion of Negroes from membership in the Democratic party was a very convenient means of excluding them from politics. After two decades of litigation, the Supreme Court condemned finally the white primary in the landmark *Smith v. Allwright* decision. 321 U.S. 649 (1944). The Court ruled that the conduct of a primary election under no circumstances can be considered purely private activity. Because of the central position of primaries in the electoral process, state delegation to a party of the power to determine qualifications for primaries is the delegation of a state function, thus making the party's action state action. And the Fifteenth Amendment, of course, forbids the states to deny any citizen the right to vote "on account of race, color, or previous condition of servitude."

Negro organizations often played ball with the dominant white political organization as a price for the privilege of voting.[3] Or—as in Nashville, Charlotte, and Raleigh—the Negro vote lacked solidarity (primarily because no candidate would make any significant appeals or promises to it), and splintered much as the white electorate.[4]

The worst expression of this powerlessness, however, was the vulnerability of Negroes to assaults on their personal safety and well-being. The introductory quotation from Myrdal's *Dilemma* in no way exaggerates this vulnerability. Because in large parts of the region the Negro could not expect white law enforcement officials to protect him and because courts of law were in fact (as far as he was concerned) instruments for maintaining white supremacy, he frequently had to endure whatever harassments and brutalities which whites chose to mete out. At least 3,275 Negroes were lynched in the American South between 1882 and 1936.[5] We have no way of determining how many Negroes met other forms of violent death at the hands of whites in this period. And as Myrdal pointed out, although violence, intimidations, and frauds occurred only sporadically, the fears created were ever-present.

The old biracial system stood as full testimony to the powerlessness of southern Negroes. Encompassing all the elements cited above, and more, this was a pervasive pattern

[3] The late E. H. Crump, the political boss who ruled Memphis for more than a quarter of a century until his death in 1954, used the Negro vote to keep his candidates in office. V. O. Key notes that local outposts of the Byrd organization in certain Virginia cities used the Negro vote in a similar manner (*Southern Politics in State and Nation* [New York, 1950], p. 649).

[4] *Ibid.*, p. 649.

[5] E. Franklin Frazier, *The Negro in the United States* (New York, 1957), p. 160.

of discrimination, rooted in law and custom, and enforced by legal and extralegal violence. It assigned one position in society to whites, and another—distinctly subordinate and inferior—to Negroes. This biracial system is now disintegrating. Discrimination remains, but not the system which until two decades ago stood securely as part of the "southern way of life."

To understand what has happened, we must look to several central precipitating factors: changes in the definition(s) held by white Americans of the proper or legitimate pattern of race relations; changes in the expectations of Negro Americans and in certain basic demographic facts of southern Negro life; and, resulting from these, changes in the power position of southern Negroes.

Historically many white Americans have objected to the flagrant injustices within the old biracial system—lynchings, the appalling inferiority of Negro schools, economic exploitation. But until the last two decades the legitimacy of the system itself was not seriously challenged by any powerful segment of white America. The challenge has developed within the last twenty years, and it has two main bases: (1) that the biracial system is without intellectual or moral justification (the ideological basis), and (2) that however right or wrong it may be it is not expedient (the political basis). These obviously overlap and interact, but we will not attempt to untangle the "chicken or the egg" causality question.

Four factors seem to be particularly important in explaining the erosion of the ideological defense of segregation. White (and Negro) Americans were long treated to a view of Africa as one massive steaming jungle where naked black savages were regularly made fools of by one naked white man called Tarzan. This "Tarzan image" of the black man was widely disseminated, and it reinforced the biracial system. It strengthened the view of the Negro as little more than a beast, distinctly inferior to white *Bwanas*. And it made the forced move of Negroes from their homeland to the United States appear a distinctly liberating experience. But in the postwar period we have witnessed the emergence of independent black African nations. Whatever one thinks of Tshombe and Kenyatta, they obviously are quite above the savages Tarzan regularly outwitted and overpowered. They are *men*.

The falsity of the charge that Negroes are biologically inferior is now clearer than ever before. The Negro middle class is much larger. The accomplishments of Negro Americans are much more impressive and better publicized. Social prestige is affected by the roles which individuals play, and white America slowly is becoming accustomed to the performance of Negroes in roles far above those which have been theirs historically.

In addition, within the United States, the cumulative effect of social science research has been felt. As late as the 1920's, the biracial system was not seriously challenged by legitimate scholarship. The weight of the scholarship of the last three decades, however, has precluded any intellectually respectable defense of the system. Prejudices remain strong, of course, but they are now *known* as prejudices rather than as *facts*. Moreover, even among the less well educated there is recognition that the "environment" may have a good bit to do with the way people are. The popular statement of Social Darwinism—that the good guys will win, that the virtuous will be rewarded, that the industrious and talented will be served; and concomitantly, that those who are not getting along well are receiving their just deserts—clearly has been weakened, though certainly not replaced, by the social science based concept of social guilt or responsibility.

Finally—and this is a product of the first three factors—there is the factor of numbers. Two decades ago proponents of the old biracial system could be confident of the rightness of their stand. Who was questioning it? Today, they find themselves attacked on all sides—from other countries, by northern whites, by Negroes North and South, and even by a small but growing number of southern whites. The southern white majority is acutely sensitive to this, and we should not be deceived by all the brave talk that the rest of the world can be damned. We have only to note how hungrily the white South devoured Carleton Putnam's very meager offering, *Race and Reason: A Yankee View,* to see how starved for outside approbation it is. Beliefs are strongest when they are uncontradicted. The belief in Negro inferiority is being contradicted with constantly increasing power. For all these reasons, the white South is much less certain of the legitimacy of its cause than it was twenty years ago.

The old biracial system is also under attack for political reasons. Some Americans seem more sensitive to the charge that the system is "helping the Communists" than to the criticism of segregation as ethically wrong and intellectually unjustifiable. Our position as a world leader together with the challenge of Communism has made segregation a distinct embarrassment. But purely internal considerations are of much greater importance. The mass migration of Negroes to the urban North in the last five decades has helped persuade increasing numbers of northern politicians to be more solicitous of Negro interests.[6] More than 3.5 million Negroes were registered to vote outside the South in the 1964 presidential

[6] The scope and timing of the Negro migration is indicated by the percentage of the total Negro population of the United States living in the eleven states of the old Confederacy in selected years:

1830	92.8	1930	78.7
1870	90.6	1960	52.3
1920	85.2	1964 (est.)	49.0

election, and these voters were strategically concentrated in the major cities of the large industrial states:

California	550,000	Pennsylvania	412,000
Ohio	298,300	New Jersey	80,000
Illinois	540,000	Michigan	353,520 [7]
New York	580,000		

In 1960, the 6.2 million Negroes living in these states constituted 8.1 per cent of the total population of these states. Negroes make up at least 10 per cent of the population in fifty-seven congressional districts outside the South. The migration has, in brief, added enormously to the strategic distribution of the Negro population in the country, and must be considered in any explanation of the factors committing the federal government to a policy of eradicating certain forms of discriminatory treatment in the South.

And there have been important changes within the South. The establishment of branch plants of northern corporations and a consequent influx of Yankees, industrialization and urbanization of the region, and, again in a circular fashion, the increasing economic and political power of southern Negroes have brought the Negro a motley collection of allies.[8] Businessmen not infrequently have used their influence to bring about a limited accession to Negro demands, probably in no small part because continued resistance would mean racial tension—bad for business. Atlanta's experience remains the best illustration of this. Negro voting on a fairly large scale in some parts of the South has made it good politics for white politicians to avoid an anti-Negro position even if it is still bad politics to be identified as pro-Negro.

[7] These are estimates furnished by the NAACP in a report issued on October 9, 1964, and again—in somewhat revised form—on October 31, 1964.

[8] Northerners moving South with branch plants rarely crusade against "the southern way of life." Many, perhaps most, sympathize with the white southerners, but they are not wedded to the traditions,

The action of the United States Supreme Court represents a unique blend of the ideological and the political aspects of the challenge within white America to the legitimacy of the biracial system. The frontal assault by the Court in the last two decades on that system reflects the growing conviction that segregation is wrong. It is also true that the Court, a political institution, has responded to a new alignment of political power.

The Supreme Court has also contributed to the rise in Negro expectations. By placing the structure of American law against the institutions of white supremacy, the Court has encouraged large numbers of southern Negroes to expect that the American democracy can give them much more than they have been getting.

It seems safe to say that Negro Americans never regarded the old biracial system as right or natural. But it seems equally clear that until two decades ago few saw any possibility that things could be much different in the short run. Their expectations precluded any assault on the system. Negroes wore the mask of passivity to survive through a period in which no significant segment of white America gave aid and comfort to any attack on white supremacy. There has been, then, a revolution in expectations. In discussing the relationship of economic development to democracy, S. M. Lipset makes the point that "stable poverty" does not produce pressures for change. On the contrary, "individuals whose experience limits their significant communications and interactions to others on the same level as themselves will . . . be more conservative than people who may be better off but who have been exposed to

---

values, and style of the old biracial system. Confronted with the choice of obeying a court order or closing the schools, transplanted northerners generally favor the former. In this way they have become allies of sorts of southern Negroes. Some, of course, bring genuinely liberal attitudes.

the possibilities of securing a better way of life. The dynamic in the situation would seem to be *exposure to a better way of life*." [9] And Marx, with characteristic insight, observed:

A house may be large or small; as long as the surrounding houses are equally small it satisfies all social demands for a dwelling. But let a palace arise beside the little house, and it shrinks from a little house to a hut.[10]

Negro Americans have been exposed to the palace which is full acceptance in the American democracy. The central element in their exposure to a better way of life is not, of course, simply seeing it. The peasant in 1700 could *see* the palaces of the nobles. What he could not see was the possibility of the life therein *ever being his*. The "new Negro" expects to get some of the things which his father believed beyond reach.[11] All of the changes which have led a segment

[9] S. M. Lipset, *Political Man* (Garden City, N.Y., 1960), p. 63. The italics are mine.

[10] Karl Marx, "Wage-Labor and Capital," in Marx and Engels, *Selected Works* (Moscow, 1958), I, 93.

[11] See, for example, William Brink and Louis Harris, *The Negro Revolution in America* (New York, 1964), p. 238. They wanted to know whether Negroes expected to find their situation better, worse, or about the same five years from now.

	Total rank and file %	Leaders %
Pay		
Better off	67	81
Worse off	2	7
About the same	14	11
Not sure	17	1
Housing accommodations		
Better off	62	52
Worse off	2	4
About the same	24	44
Not sure	12	—

of white America to question and in some cases to actively oppose the old biracial system have increased Negro expectations that the system can and will be altered in their interest. The change in white attitudes has resulted in a weaker application of the sanctions—formal and informal, legal and extralegal—which sustained the system.

Accompanying these developments, and essential as a basis for the revolution, are certain long-term changes of a demographic nature. The level of those skills necessary for significant and continuous political participation has risen steadily in the southern Negro population. Specifically, southern Negroes have become better educated. The pool of leadership talent is bigger. Also, their economic position has been strengthened. Particularly important here is the creation of a Negro middle class economically independent of whites —dentists, optometrists, lawyers, and so on, in addition to ministers. The urbanization of the Negro population *within the South* has played a part. Certainly the revolution could never have occurred in the kind of scattered, rural population that southern Negroes formed in 1910. The importance of these developments is discussed at length in the next chapter.

Together, these factors—the ideological and political challenges within white America, the marked increase in Negro expectations, and the demographic changes—have served to extend and expand Negro political power. It should be clear, of course, that Negro political power itself has contributed to the establishment of the conditions which have furthered it: changes in each area set the stage for further changes in the others—a snowball effect. One does not need to spend many days in a southern city in which Negroes make up 25 per cent of the electorate—that is, of those registered and voting—to see that the behavior and to a lesser but still significant degree the attitudes of whites become more permissive when Negroes actually possess significant sanctions. (The result may be exactly the opposite when there is merely an unrealized potential for significant political power —as in Mississippi.) "Ideology," Mr. Dooley might have said, "follows th' iliction returns." This aside, the revolution in American race relations must finally be understood as a revolution in political power.

Evidence of a strengthened political position is everywhere. In September 1964 the Reverend K. L. Buford and Dr. Stanley Hugh Smith won positions on the Tuskegee, Alabama city council, and in doing so became the first Negroes elected to public office over white opponents in Alabama in almost a century. Three out of every ten registered voters in Winston-Salem are Negroes; and in three successive elections between 1957 and 1961, the victorious mayoralty candidate received a distinct minority of the white vote. Negroes throughout the South, pushed on by their fears of Goldwater, recorded impressive electoral advances in the 1964 elections. November 1964 saw election results in the South that were— from a civil rights standpoint—mixed, because a white backlash produced in some sections an unusually large and anti-Negro white vote. Turnout in the five states of the deep South increased from 2.5 million in 1960 to 3.5 million in 1964, and analysis makes it clear that Goldwater-supporting whites accounted for much of this increase. Still, it is also clear that Negroes themselves registered impressive gains in electoral participation. Between 1952 and 1962, Negro registration increased by only about 400,000, from a little more than 1,000,000 to 1,414,000. By the Fall of 1964, however, 2,250,000 Negroes were registered in the eleven states of the old Confederacy. And the largest part of this increase was recorded in the eight months preceding the November 1964 election. The rapidity of the expansion is indicated by the data in Table 2.

TABLE 2

EXPANSION AND DISTRIBUTION OF NEGRO REGISTRATION
IN ELEVEN SOUTHERN STATES *

State	Negroes of voting age	Negro † registration Feb. 1964	% of voting-age Negroes † registered Feb. 1964	Negro † registration Nov. 1964	% of voting-age Negroes † registered Nov. 1964
Texas	649,512	300,000	46.1	375,000	57.7
Tenn.	313,873	202,974	64.6	220,000	70.0
Florida	470,261	213,128	45.5	299,964	63.8
N.C.	550,929	233,773	42.3	276,000	50.1
Virginia	436,720	108,312	24.8	200,000	45.7
Arkansas	192,626	80,000	41.5	90,000	46.7
S.C.	371,104	111,628	30.0	181,050	48.7
Georgia	612,910	221,919	36.2	285,000	46.4
La.	514,589	162,084	31.4	184,000	35.7
Alabama	481,320	90,000	18.6	111,000	23.0
Miss.	422,256	28,000	6.6	28,000	6.6
Totals	5,016,100	1,751,813	34.9%	2,250,014	44.9

* Data on the voting-age population in each state are from the
U.S. Census of Population, 1960. The Southern Regional Council furnished the estimate of the number of Negroes registered as of February
1964. The estimates for November 1964 were released by the National
Association for the Advancement of Colored People. The Southern
Regional Council estimated that 2,164,200 Negroes were registered
for the November elections in the South, 86,000 less than the NAACP
estimate of 2,250,014 cited here. Precise figures, of course, are not
available, but these estimates are broadly reliable.

† The figures given for Texas are for "nonwhites" rather than
for Negroes.

It is clear that if all votes cast by Negroes were simply
subtracted, Johnson would have lost Florida, Virginia, Tennessee, and Arkansas. And the result in North Carolina would
have been very close. In Florida, for example, the Democratic
nominee won by only 37,800 votes, while an estimated

211,000 Negro voters gave him between 97 and 99 per cent of their votes. (It should be recognized, however, that if the race issue had been kept out of the campaign, Johnson probably would have won all eleven southern states by landslide majorities. The race issue was the one factor producing mass defections from the first southerner to occupy the White House in almost a century.)

The higher turnout of registered Negro voters was perhaps the most impressive single aspect of the generally heightened Negro political participation in 1964. Estimates of the number of Negroes voting November 3, 1964, necessarily are not precise, and state-by-state estimates vary greatly— more one suspects than actual performance—from a high of 86 per cent in Texas to a low (excluding Alabama and Mississippi) of 61 per cent in North Carolina. We do have *precise* data, however, for certain cities. In Winston-Salem, for example, over 80 per cent of the registered Negroes went to the polls and cast valid ballots for President, a turnout far in excess of the highest ever before achieved. At least 70 per cent of the 2.25 million Negro voters in the South cast valid ballots in the 1964 Presidential election.

Negro candidates have continued to have relatively little success winning elections. Only three were elected to southern state legislatures in 1964, two in Georgia (one the incumbent Leroy Johnson) and one in Tennessee (the first to serve in that state's legislature since Reconstruction). In Forsyth County, where Winston-Salem is located, a Negro candidate for the state legislature, the Reverend William Crawford, was defeated by a Republican opponent although his two white Democratic colleagues won by substantial margins. Crawford's defeat, discussed in Chapter V, is important because it illustrates the very great obstacles still confronting Negro candidates seeking city- or county-wide (to say nothing of state-wide) office in the South—Negro candidates, that is, who must win the votes of substantial numbers of whites. Although the elections of 1962, 1963, and 1964 saw for the first time a sizable scattering of Negro candidates for city councils, county school boards, and state legislatures, few won who had to depend on white support. With few exceptions, Negro office holders in the South represent the relatively few electoral districts which are overwhelmingly Negro.

The election of Negroes to public office in the old Confederacy is important and notable because for a full six decades from the 1890's to the 1950's almost *no* Negroes were elected. But the drama of the "first Negro elected" is deceiving. Certainly the most important results of the heightened participation in electoral politics lie elsewhere—in helping to defeat white candidates clearly anti-Negro, in making it good politics for white officials to meet at least some of the political demands of the Negro citizenry, and, more broadly, in changing the climate of race relations. A group with the kind of sanction which large scale voting provides generally will not be exploited to the same degree as one essentially powerless. Voting has meant that some streets in Negro neighborhoods have been paved, some Negro policemen have been appointed, schools in Negro areas have received more funds, recreational facilities in the ghetto have been improved, and the city fathers have shown somewhat more respect. There have been few miracles, but substantial gains have and will continue to be recorded. As the Southern Regional Council put it in a recent report:

Effective Negro registration and participation in elections is the best assurance that race will be eliminated as a politically profittable issue . . . and that all the southern states will be freed from the demagogic appeals to racism.[12]

Gains in Negro registration and voting have occurred unevenly. The concerted efforts of civil rights workers in the

[12] Report released November 15, 1964: "What Happened in the South?"

Mississippi "Freedom Summer" project of 1964 added few Negro voters to the rolls in that state. But this failure must be put in perspective. Wiley Branton, director of the Voter Education Project of the Southern Regional Council, reported that voter registration efforts for the twenty-one months up to December 31, 1963, succeeded in expanding the Negro electorate in Mississippi by only 3,228. Twenty-eight thousand Negroes were registered in Mississippi for the 1964 elections, only a few thousand more than were on the books in 1960. Mississippi, in short, has successfully resisted all attempts to build a substantial Negro electorate out of the state's 422,000 voting-age Negroes—who make up 36 per cent of the total number meeting the age requirement for voting.

Registration efforts have been far more successful in urban areas than in the rural South, both in terms of the numbers registered and the uses to which the registered electorate is put. The Director of the Voter Education Project estimated that 90 per cent of the 265,000 Negroes who registered between April 1962 and December 1963 were urban dwellers.[13] Sixty thousand Negroes are on the rolls in Memphis, Tennessee, and are an important force in the city's politics. But efforts to register Negroes in the nearby rural Tennessee counties of Fayette and Haywood have met determined resistance.[14] While it should be noted that these Western Tennessee counties border on Mississippi and have Negro majori-

[13] *New York Times*, Feb. 17, 1964.

[14] In May 1959 only 58 Negroes were registered in Fayette county. Shortly thereafter, however, 1,500 Negroes were registered as a result of a local drive and the intervention under the 1957 civil rights act by the Justice Department. Whites then retaliated. Many Negroes lost their jobs. A list of those who had registered was circulated, and those on the list found their credit cut off, loans called. The "offending" Negroes found themselves unable to buy even the necessities of life. These retaliatory actions were ended only when the Justice Department intervened vigorously. The situation was the same in Haywood County.

ties (Fayette is 68 per cent Negro, Haywood 61 per cent) and hence that white resistance is particularly strong, Negroes throughout the rural South are far more vulnerable to economic sanctions and to threats to life and liberty. Rural Negro populations are more widely dispersed and hence harder to organize. They are poorer. And, in general, they have been drained of their most talented and best educated members, and hence do not have human resources comparable to those of urban populations. Once registered, Negroes in rural areas have a much more difficult task making their votes count.

We can profitably examine the basic demographic facts of life of Fayette County Negroes, because they unfortunately are essentially similar to those of rural Negro populations throughout the South.[15] The median age of Fayette's Negro males in 1960 was 16.3 years, against 27.4 for white males in the county, 28.0 for all Tennessee residents, and 33.1 for New York residents. This indicates, of course, the extent to which Negroes are fleeing the rural Tennessee county. In 1959, when the median family income for the United States as a whole was $5,660, for Tennessee $3,949, and for Memphis Negroes $2,666, the median family income of Fayette Negroes was $854. More than two-thirds (72.7 per cent) of all Negro-occupied housing units in the county were described by the 1960 *Census of Housing* as either *deteriorating* or *dilapidated*. Only 10.4 per cent of the units had all plumbing facilities. Fayette Negroes are particularly disadvantaged in their educational background. The chasm between Charlotte, North Carolina, Negroes, 9.1 per cent of whom in 1960 had some college education and half of whom had at least an eighth-grade education—close to the average for the urban South—and Fayette Negroes, only 2.3 per cent of whom ever attended anything called a college and half of whom had

[15] The source for the data which follows is the *U.S. Census of Population, 1960*.

a fifth grade education or less (and that in one-room Negro schools) is wide indeed. And these figures become even more striking when one remembers that urban-South Negroes themselves are seriously disadvantaged. Add to these grinding deprivations the wide dispersal of Fayette Negroes throughout the county, the relative lack of transportation, the absence of the anonymity which the ghetto provides, and the greater strength of virulently anti-Negro attitudes in the county's homogeneous white population, and one has gone far toward explaining the fact that despite concerted efforts to register Negroes between 1959 and 1964, only 2,000—fewer than 30 per cent of those of voting age—were on the rolls for the 1964 county election. After five years of continuous work in a county in which nearly 70 per cent of the population is Negro, the candidates for county office supported by the Negro citizenry were defeated in August 1964 by 2–1 margins. Such are the political problems of Negroes in much of the rural South.

The cities, and particularly those of the rim-South, are a different political world. Attaching Negro support to a candidate in Winston-Salem or Jacksonville is not automatically a "kiss of death." The "Negroes' candidate" will lose white support as a result of his association with Negro interests, but he will gain votes as well. Whether he will be damaged or helped depends on other aspects of his base of support, his personal attractiveness, and the specific time and setting for his candidacy. But certainly being anti-Negro is not a magical formula with which a candidate can automatically gain victory.

Negro voting in the South frequently has been bloc voting, with landslide proportions going to the favored candidate. We should not be surprised, given the overriding importance of race advancement, that when one candidate can be readily identified as more responsive to the interests of Negroes, large numbers of Negro voters will support him. The Negro voter cannot afford the luxury of being cross-pressured. There is no *series* of issues and orientations to make conflicting demands on his loyalties. What will the candidate do for the race? All else can and must be subordinated to this. Still, the cohesion frequently attained is impressive, and particularly so because of the fairly low level of political awareness of many Negro voters. Richard Bolling, the liberal Missouri Congressman, was opposed in his district's 1964 Democratic primary by a coalition of several Kansas City Democratic party factions. Bolling's district is 17.4 per cent Negro. A number of influential Negro ward and precinct leaders in Kansas City were allied with the anti-Bolling factions. They believed—as have Congressman William Dawson and members of his Negro Democratic organization in Chicago—that they had a stake in the success of the party "machine." [16] But although Negro voters followed these ward leaders in local races, they voted overwhelmingly for Bolling. The heavily Negro 14th ward was carried by Mr. Bolling, 2,924 votes to 426. In short, Negro voters would not follow their politicians in rejecting a Congressman whose record as a supporter of civil rights and social welfare legislation was so strong.[17] The opposition of Negro ward and precinct leaders did not significantly reduce Bolling's strength in Negro areas, to say nothing of defeating him.

When Negro leaders are united behind a man with a good civil rights record, the cohesion of the Negro electorate approaches unanimity. Dan Moore and Richardson Preyer

[16] This development—Negro politicians who are at times willing to subordinate immediate race interests to strengthen their positions in the party organization—is an important one. Thus far it is confined largely to northern and border-state cities, although as we shall see in Chapter V, it can now be found in embryonic form in certain southern cities.

[17] *New York Times,* August 6, 1964.

faced each other in the second, or runoff, Democratic primary in North Carolina in June 1964. Preyer's civil rights position from the viewpoint of Negro voters was good, that of Moore very bad. Preyer carried the Negro precincts of Winston-Salem by such margins as 778 to 1, 1,883 to 2 and 1,581 to 13.[18]

This cohesion of the Negro electorate, however, is a source of weakness as well as of strength. Politicians are able to exploit fears of Negro "bloc voting," and candidates can suffer badly in white hands when they are clearly the recipients of the "bloc" support. Richardson Preyer, although backed by Governor Terry Sanford and a fairly efficient organization, was overwhelmingly defeated by Dan Moore in the 1964 North Carolina runoff primary. I. Beverly Lake, an extreme segregationist, had been eliminated in the first primary. Preyer lost in the second because he was identified as the Negro-supported "racial liberal," while Moore wore the mantle (in the eyes of North Carolina whites) of the moderate. Negro voters, an embattled minority, necessarily and properly demonstrate cohesion. Yet the cohesion which makes them a balance of power in some races produces greater white cohesion against their favored candidates in others.

The Negro vote in the South now is largely a Democratic vote. At precisely the time Negroes are being driven from positions which they traditionally have held in southern state Republican parties they are entering in large numbers the organizational hierarchy of the Democratic party, from which historically they have been excluded throughout much of the South. Many "new" Republicans in the South, Goldwater Republicans, want a white man's party. They are not violently anti-Negro on the model of "Pitchfork Ben" Tillman or Theodore Bilbo. But they see a bright future for the Republican party in offering an alternative to Democrats unhappy about the direction of their party in recent years—particularly

[18] *Winston-Salem Journal*, June 28, 1964.

the direction in civil rights.[19] There are many exceptions to this. Some southern Republicans diligently court Negro support. But looking to the South as a whole, Negroes have been pushed still further into the Democratic camp by the rise of the "new" Republicans.

The Negro electorate in the South is not irrevocably Democratic, however; but rather potentially is highly fluid. It can be captured by any candidate who is demonstrably "better" on civil rights issues than is his opponent. Indeed, the Negro vote appears to be potentially less stable than that of virtually any other demographic group. White voters, of course, will leave their party for another if they become convinced that their interests are not finding expression. Senator Barry Goldwater, as the Republican nominee in 1964, carried 87 per cent of the vote in Mississippi—so strong was the white reaction in that state to the civil rights movement and the identification of the national Democratic party with the movement. But the "embattled" psychology of Mississippi whites is exceptional. Given the strength and persistence of party identification, it takes a crisis of major proportions to push many voters from their party home; and such crises for white voters in affluent America are few.[20] But the Negro vote exists in a state of perpetual crisis. Race advancement necessarily dominates Negro electoral participation as no issue dominates the participation of white voters. No other group ever has had to look to government for so much assist-

[19] A number of Republican leaders in North and South Carolina were interviewed in late 1962 and in 1963.

[20] Bone and Ranney concluded that "party identification is one of the most stable of all forces in American politics. The evidence of history is that large masses of voters switch their basic loyalties only in times of great crisis" (*Politics and Voters* [New York, 1963], p. 10). Campbell *et al.* found that 85 per cent of the "Strong Democrats" stayed with Stevenson in 1956, as did 63 per cent of the "Weak Democrats" (*The American Voter* [New York, 1960], p. 160).

36

ance affecting such vital interests as Negro Americans must at present.

Some observers have equated Negro loyalty to the Democratic party with that shown by "newer" ethnic groups such as Polish Americans. In fact, with the exception of a few large northern cities like Chicago, where Negro voters are thoroughly enmeshed in a Democratic electoral machine and where ghetto politics resembles that of other ethnic minorities at a similar point in their trek along what Samuel Lubell has called the "tenement trail," Negro voters are much less firmly attached to the Democratic coalition. Louis Gerson chronicled the continued efforts of Republicans in the first decade after World War II to find issues—for example, the 1952 platform promise to "repudiate all commitments contained in secret understandings such as those of Yalta which aid Communist enslavements"—that could win over Americans of east European ancestry.[21] He concluded that these efforts were largely unsuccessful. The most significant ethnic defections of the last two decades appear to be products of slow demographic changes—such as the movement to the suburbs and middle-class respectability—rather than of success in manipulating an issue. The Negro American differs from other hyphenates, then, in that he is continually involved with an issue strong enough to produce defections.

The fluidity inherent in a vote so completely dominated by a single issue of transcendent importance to the group occasionally produces very dramatic shifts in voting. Lyndon Johnson carried Negro precincts in Pine Bluff, Arkansas, with 97.8 per cent of the total vote. But Orval Faubus, the Democratic gubernatorial candidate, received only 11.5 per cent of the vote in these precincts even though he and his

[21] Louis Gerson, *The Hyphenate in Recent American Politics and Diplomacy* (Lawrence, Kans., 1964), pp. 178–220.

supporters had made some effort in this campaign to secure Negro support. Faubus' anti-Negro image had been too firmly established, while the record of his opponent (Winthrop Rockefeller) in support of Negro aspirations was generally good. In 1956 Dwight Eisenhower carried Forsyth county, North Carolina, with 64 per cent of the two-party vote. Eight years later Senator Goldwater lost the county by a narrow margin, gaining 49 per cent of the vote. The Democratic share of the county vote was 15 per cent higher in 1964 than in 1956—51 per cent as opposed to 36 per cent. Voting by whites was remarkably stable over the 1956, 1960, and 1964 elections, fluctuating from 34 per cent Democratic in 1956 and 1960 to approximately 40 per cent Democratic in 1964. But though Eisenhower received 47 per cent of the Negro vote in the county in 1956, Goldwater's share of this vote in 1964 was about 1 per cent.[22]

The Negro vote in recent elections has been faithfully Democratic, and certainly a large majority of Negro Americans vote for Democratic candidates when they are unable to see a decisive difference on racial questions. "Other things being equal," most Negro voters support Democrats. But Republicans who wish to tap the Negro vote, and who find it politically feasible to make a clear appeal for Negro electoral support, can get it. We should expect the southern Negro electorate to remain overwhelmingly Democratic in its voting habits, because many "new" Republicans in the South have little interest in making their party a home for the Negro. Many are committed to building a party which appeals to white disenchantment with the Negro revolution. But with

[22] The Republican share of the two-party vote for President was much lower in 1964 than in 1956 in many parts of the country, of course; but as great as was the defection of white voters—Goldwater received only 44 per cent as many votes in New England as Eisenhower did in 1956—the *rate* of defection by whites did not approach that by Negroes.

a vote so responsive to even subtle differences in approach to racial questions—a vote so inherently fluid—we can expect occasional sharp fluctuations in the shares of the vote won by Republican and Democratic candidates.

The Negro electorate in the South has doubled in size, then, in the last decade. More than 40 per cent of the five million voting-age Negroes in Dixie were registered to vote in the November 1964 elections. The Negro electorate has become large enough and active enough to make itself felt in state politics—except in Alabama and Mississippi. It has become a significant electoral force in most of the urban South, if in only a few of the rural areas and small towns of the region. Expansion of this electorate will continue, although certainly at a slower rate in much of the rim-South as the core of nonregistrants is reduced to those severely disadvantaged in socioeconomic terms, and hence those who, quite apart from race, tend to be the least active and conscious politically.

The Negro's access to the ballot box is still very recent, and we can expect higher levels of participation as legal barriers fall and extralegal harassment and intimidation diminish: more Negroes seeking public office; more gaining appointment to governmental boards and commissions such as school boards; and more attaining lower- and middle-level positions in city, county, and state Democratic (and in certain areas Republican) party organizations. There will be more Negro voting organizations producing larger electorates, bargaining more effectively with white candidates.

Developments in electoral politics give ample basis for both optimism and pessimism. Certainly, the level of Negro participation has increased greatly in the last decade and particularly in the last three years, and important benefits have been realized. Two decades ago Negroes were a cipher in virtually all of the South; today they are a force to be considered. Nothing should obscure the revolutionary nature of this development. But at the same time, emphasis on what has been accomplished should not obscure the fact that the political position of Negroes in the South remains very weak, and that substantial obstacles confront any attempt to strengthen it. The rapid migration of Negroes from the South continues. Only 20 per cent of the voting-age population in the eleven states of the old Confederacy is Negro, and this figure will decline further before it stabilizes. There is little prospect that Negro voters will be able to enter into an effective and continuing coalition comparable to the one which, for example, Polish Americans entered into in the urban North three decades ago. It will remain bad politics for white politicians to become associated too closely with the political interests of Negro Americans.

The expansion of Negro electoral power, so dramatic in the last decade, has meant or will soon mean for much of the South an impressive change in the style of politics. The militantly segregationist politician is becoming a figure of the past. The Negro vote is entering an evolving balance as two-party politics becomes a reality in state and local, as well as presidential, elections. But the white South is waking from its long political stupor, and large numbers of white voters will continue to oppose candidates identified with the Negro's cause, and particularly Negro candidates. Relatively few positions can be won by the Negro vote alone, and the vigorous participation by Negroes will continue to produce reactions—the backlash—in favor of racially conservative candidates. Parts of the South already have left, and many more soon will leave, an era characterized by the powerlessness of Negroes. The Negro no longer is a cipher in southern politics—no longer merely a "threat" to be evoked or a thing to be exploited. But achievement of a position as an equal participant in the American democracy belongs to another era still far distant.

The increased political power of Negroes in the South

manifests itself in areas other than electoral politics. Race-advancement organizations, now infinitely better organized than two decades ago, have more members and possess a variety of techniques ranging from economic boycotts to direct action demonstrations with which to compel recognition of their interests. NAACP membership in the states of the old Confederacy has increased by 1800 per cent in the last twenty-five years. CORE chapters now are active throughout the South. The Southern Christian Leadership Conference has affiliates in many regional cities, such as the Danville (Virginia) Progressive Christian Association. Peak community organizations have been established in every southern state, and range from the very effective—such as Durham's Committee on Negro Affairs (CONA)—to the relatively weak and struggling—such as the Edenton (North Carolina) Movement or the Alabama Civic Affairs Association. The significance of the 1964 Freedom Summer in Mississippi is that the project was *possible at all*. The development observed in electoral politics has its parallel in all levels of political participation.

We have tried here to suggest something of what this revolution has meant for Negroes who must live their lives in Dixie. Comparison of the position of Negroes in Winston-Salem—a rim-South city in which Negroes are perhaps as strong politically as anywhere in the region—with that of their counterparts in Greenville—where Negroes remain far weaker politically—will provide us with a much more detailed picture of this development.

This expansion of Negro political power necessarily comes to a focus at the level of leadership, and the changes in southern Negro leadership are profound. We now hear much of a greater militancy of Negro leaders—a response viewed with both alarm and surprise by segregationists and with a curiosity tinged with concern by many other whites. But the cause of this new militancy should be obvious. Negroes now expect much more than they did two decades ago and their leaders have the power to do things which at that time would have been either impossible or highly dangerous. When we speak of a greater militancy of Negro leadership in the South we are in fact saying that within the last two decades the basis for leadership protest "outside the *status quo*" has been established. Charles Johnson was correct when he wrote in 1944 that southern Negro leadership, insofar as it protested against discrimination in work opportunities, schools, libraries, and other public facilities, did so within the "separate but equal" framework.[23] The change in the structure of race relations now permits the dominant thrust of southern Negro leadership to be against that principle and all its implications.

Negro leadership in the South from the end of Reconstruction to World War II was extremely weak. What influence Negro leaders had in this period was indirect, channeled through a white intermediary. They could not directly influence race relations. Since the Negro was not viewed as an immediate threat, Negro leaders at times enjoyed small successes with divided whites. Lewis describes the activity of Negro leaders in a small South Carolina town in the late 1940's in the appointment of a principal for a Negro school. A white school official favored one candidate, the Negroes backed another. Several Negroes spoke to influential whites in behalf of their candidate and the school official yielded. The attitude of some whites was indicated by the remarks of one: "I guess your preachers are satisfied now with the appointment." [24] But the important point is that in day-to-day activity Negro leaders in the South twenty years ago had *no other means* of attaining their objectives.

This was the period of the "Uncle Tom," the "handker-

[23] Charles Johnson, *Patterns of Negro Segregation* (New York, 1943), p. 251.
[24] Hylan Lewis, *Blackways of Kent* (Chapel Hill, 1955), p. 171.

chief head," the "white man's nigger." Whites wanted passive Negroes who would be faithful servants and efficient workers. They rewarded "good" Negroes who said the right things and who showed proper respect for the system of race relations. The rewards, as in the case described by Lewis, took the form of consulting with these "good" Negroes, listening to their appeals for help, and then channeling certain tangible benefits through to the Negro community.

In this way Negro leaders were "made." Negro communities accepted these white-designated leaders because they had no choice. They needed people who could talk to influential whites and secure from them certain goods and services, and who could obtain small favors and personal protection in a white-dominated society. Negroes also accepted this white-selected political leadership because, under the old biracial system, the white community had the preponderance of status-conferral power. The Negro with access to whites gained in status in his own community (and this, in turn, furthered his position with whites). Myrdal observed that

the Negro hates the Negro role in American society, and the Negro leader who acts out this role in public life becomes the symbol of what the Negro hates.[25]

Frazier, Myrdal, and others describe the hostility between the brown upper-strata Negroes who furnished the preponderance of accommodating leadership, and the black masses. Still, southern Negroes in this period were without political power. Recognition of this lack of power, together with the low level in skills necessary for political participation and low expectations about the possibility of change, produced inactivity and passivity, and a general acceptance of the "white man's nigger."

To summarize, and this is a generalization so broad that it necessarily admits exceptions, Negro political leadership in

[25] *Op. cit.*, p. 574.

the South in the last decades of the nineteenth century and the first four decades of the present century was not Negro-selected leadership. The ability of these leaders to effect the patterning of political behavior within their communities did not rest upon their control of institutional structures which in a major way affect social, political, and economic life; nor did it rest upon a charismatic relationship with the Negro masses or upon the adoption of positions on race-related issues that articulated the deep sense of frustration and hostility which southern Negroes felt. Crucial for the maintenance of a position of leadership was a favorable relationship with influential whites. The majority of southern Negroes, caught up in the biracial system, without effective political power, and without expectations that the system could be altered significantly in the near future, necessarily accepted those leaders able to gain the most within the system. This is *out-group based* leadership. The term does not imply that a group of influential whites would sit around a table in City X and decide who would be Negro leaders. Such a model would be ridiculously simplistic. There were only a limited number of Negroes with sufficient interest, time, skills, industry, and community respect to be leaders. But given the overwhelming preponderance of political, social, and economic power of the white majority, it is hardly surprising that the decision of influential whites as to which of the "eligible" Negroes were to be leaders was accepted by the Negroes themselves. The out-group determination thus was binding on the in-group. Whites had patronage (social, economic, and political) to bestow. White support of thoroughly disreputable and incompetent Negroes would not have given such people authority in their community. But this was not an issue. Whites wanted to reward "solid" Negroes of the Booker Washington model.

The rise over the last two decades in Negro skills and expectations, and above all in political power, has made possible a Negro leadership in the South whose effectiveness rests not on white support or tolerance, but on support within the Negro community. The significance of this shift from white-based to Negro-based leadership can hardly be overemphasized here. Southern Negroes no longer are political blanks. Their newly achieved ability to apply significant—though far from sufficient—sanctions has enabled them to sustain leadership responsive to their interests. This new leadership is issue-oriented, and the one issue that matters is race advancements. Its authority is dependent upon subcommunity approval of its promotion of race advancement.

This shift in the basis of authority of Negro leaders to something closer to the model of sustained popular selection and away from out-group selection has had important ramifications. Negroes who by their very proximity to whites had influence in the past frequently have lost it. Hylan Lewis in his South Carolina study observed that under the old system Negroes with intimate access to influential whites—certain cooks, for example—were looked upon as important people in the subcommunity. He quoted a Negro as saying: "You can get along all right just so you don't cross one of these white folks' cooks." [26] All this has changed.

More importantly, under out-group selection Negro leadership was splintered and fragmented. What reason was there for organization or unity? The maintenance of a leadership position demanded access to influential whites. Negroes who had achieved this had every reason to seek to exploit it and to handle matters individually and informally. The charge was often made by Negroes that they suffered from not "sticking together." But "sticking together" makes sense only when the group has sufficient political power to sustain leadership of its own choosing. With the transition to in-group selected leadership, an extremely self-conscious attempt has been made to bring disparate elements together for the great struggle. A new Negro leadership drawing its authority from

[26] *Op. cit.*, p. 168.

the support of the Negro masses has seen the necessity of attempting to weld together the entire community. There are few medium- or small-sized cities in the South in which an attempt has not been made in the last decade to create effective community-wide race-advancement organizations. Many of these attempts have failed, but the effort goes on.

That the objectives of Negroes and the means which they use have changed greatly can scarcely—in view of the developments sketched above—be considered surprising. The new goals-means orientation is simply testimony to the dramatic alteration of the position of southern Negro leaders. Twenty years ago the NAACP had a monopoly of Negro "radicalism"—radicalism meaning little more than keeping the flag of protest flying in the South while the slow assault on discriminations went on in the courts. Today, the Association is under attack for its "moderate and legalistic" approach to race relations.[27]

Today, Negro leadership in the South is emphasizing goals on which, historically, southern whites have been most sensitive. Myrdal observed in *An American Dilemma* that certain types of discrimination were "more important" to southern whites, and that the importance corresponded to the relationship to the "anti-amalgamation doctrine." Ranking just below opposition to sexual intercourse between Negro males and white females was opposition to "dancing, bathing, eating, drinking together; and social intercourse generally. . . . Thereafter follows the segregations and discriminations in the use of public facilities such as schools, churches and means of conveyance." After these came discrimination in voting, in courts of law, and by police and other public officials, and discrimination in securing land, jobs, and public relief.[28] The thrust of the activity of the major protest

[27] See, for example, Louis E. Lomax, *The Negro Revolt* (New York, 1962).

[28] Myrdal, *op. cit.*, pp. 60–61.

organizations is now aimed at goals which stand near the top of this "rank order of discriminations."

And the means so frequently used to promote these goals —direct action demonstrations, from sit-ins to picketing to freedom rides—are considered particularly objectionable by many whites, North and South. The physical confrontation, the physical defiance, the possibility of violence, the very invitation to mass involvement, have introduced into southern race relations a distinctly new element. Before that chilly December 5, 1955, when Mrs. Rosa Parks refused to give up her seat in the front of a bus to a white man and in so doing precipitated the Montgomery Movement, Negro leaders in the South had been limited in their promotion of race goals to one or more of three other means: (1) requests presented by individuals to whites considered not hostile, (2) requests presented by Negro organizations such as voting leagues with the implicit threat of "withholding" such support as the vote, and (3) the lawsuit. Direct action has been a major addition to the arsenal of race leaders, and together with the expansion of the franchise has provided them with the significant sanctions which they lacked previously. Although some proponents of the 1964 Civil Rights Act emphasized the need for such legislation to "get the civil rights struggle off the streets and into the courts," there is no indication that direct action will cease to be a major weapon, although the objectives for which it is used have changed and will continue to change.

The more specific developments in race leadership which will occupy our attention in the following chapters all are set in this profound change—revolution—in the structure of race relations in the American South. The old biracial system —based on and perpetuating the political powerlessness of southern Negroes—has been shattered. Negro leaders throughout Dixie are operating in the new and still evolving setting which this revolution has produced.

47

CHAPTER II

Winston-Salem and Greenville:

The Community Setting

FLOYD HUNTER'S "top leader," the Nazi Fuehrer, a successful street orator, and a primitive tribal chieftain are all leaders; but the basis of their authority, the scope, direction, and purpose of their leadership, and their means and techniques of leadership differ drastically. The phenomenon of leadership, then, cannot be understood apart from the larger setting in which it operates. In Chapter I we examined the changes in the position of the Negro which, over the last two decades, have affected the entire structure of race relations in the United States. These changes—products of the continuing breakdown of the biracial system—are national in scope and are part of a larger setting in which all Negro leaders are acting. Yet, as important as this basic trend in race relations is to the structure of race leadership, we must recognize that Negro leaders throughout the South confront markedly different situations. Sharp differences in the socioeconomic position of Negro communities, in white racial attitudes, in the level of political competition, and so on, have produced different patterns of race leadership.

Our focus shifts, then, from a general discussion of those forces which together are creating the revolution in race relations in the American South to a detailed consideration on the local level of that myriad of variables in the setting of race leadership that must be considered if the phenomenon of race leadership is to be understood. The leadership setting in the outer-South city is contrasted with that in the deep-South community.

We have referred to the *setting of race leadership*. The components of the setting important for understanding various styles of leadership differ. Here we are concerned with Negro political leadership in two southern cities. The parts of the total setting which will be identified will not all bear the same relationship to the leadership structure. Some will be related as both cause and effect. For example, data on the educational level of the Negro population indicate one facet of a pattern of race relations (e.g., the willingness of city officials to spend money for Negro education), the human resources which Negro leaders can manipulate in the interest of race advancement, and the success of Negro leaders in one area of race-advancement activity. White racial attitudes help determine the goals pursued by Negro leaders and define "legitimate" Negro political activity. Thus they influence the selection of race leadership. If Negro participation in electoral politics is considered illegitimate by whites in city X, we can predict that Negro school teachers will not be prominently associated with such activity. The structure of Negro political organization at once indicates the problems confronting Negro leadership, the tools with which it works, the kinds of sanctions which it can employ, and the potential effectiveness of the leadership in race-advancement activity. No attempt will be made to determine the precise relationship of each variable to Negro leadership in Winston-Salem and Greenville. Each, however, relates as cause and/or effect to the structure of race leadership in the two cities.

The variables introduced fall under three general categories: The demographic characteristics, principally of the

Negro community; the pattern of discriminatory treatment (including white racial attitudes); and the structure and level of Negro political organization.

THE DEMOGRAPHIC SETTING

Both Winston-Salem and Greenville are "new" southern cities, born in this century. They are children of the industrialization of the region. In 1880, when more than 90 per cent of Negro Americans lived in the eleven states of the old Confederacy, Winston and Greenville were small towns with between 4,000 and 6,000 people. Industrialization came earlier to Winston-Salem. In the first three decades of this century its population increased by 550 per cent, reaching a total of 75,000. In this same period Greenville's population only doubled and lagged far behind that of the North Carolina city. Up until 1940 Greenville's industries consisted for the most part of small textile mills. Then, between 1940 and 1960, rapid diversified industrialization produced a sharp expansion of the South Carolina city. Between 1940 and 1950, for example, when Winston-Salem's population was increasing by but 10 per cent, Greenville's increased by more than 67 per cent.

The form industrialization took is important for understanding political and economic differences in the two cities today. Three major industrial firms were established in Winston in the last years of the nineteenth century. By 1930 each was mature. Together these firms have dominated the economic and to a large extent the political life of the city, although other corporations have established branch plants in the last two decades. Each of the companies—R. J. Reynolds, Hanes Hosiery, and P. H. Hanes—is a leader in its field. (In 1965 a merger of Hanes Hosiery and P. H. Hanes was achieved, uniting the corporate expressions of the two branches of the Hanes family. But these corporations were independent throughout the period in which research was conducted.) The largest company, Reynolds, is a major national corporation. These firms, then, are home-grown industries. Their founding families and corporate executives appear to look upon Winston as a personal fief. In the sound tradition of *noblesse oblige*, it is in a sense *their* city and its problems *their* problems, and they have remained the dominant voice in the city's political life. The influx of young executives without a close identification with the city or indeed even with the South seems to have altered this relationship somewhat, and can be expected to change it further, but it remains strong.

Early industrialization in Greenville, we noted, was in relatively small textile mills. In the last twenty years a rapid expansion has broadened the industrial base and enabled Greenville to approach Winston-Salem as a southern industrial center. But where Winston's economic and political life has been dominated by three large firms, there has been a fragmentation of economic and political power in Greenville. From the early days when small textile mills and the surrounding cluster of company houses formed a belt around the city, until today, the old firms existing together with a number of new firms producing chemicals and machine tools, Greenville's political, economic, and social life has reflected an absence of the central direction found in Winston-Salem. Greenville's new industries are branch plants of large northern corporations like Maremont. Instead of the somewhat benevolent paternalism of a small group of economic dominants—closely knit, firmly established, and powerful—Greenville has suffered from the civic inaction of businessmen either too insecure economically to act effectively, or too new to the city to feel any common bond or close identification with it and its social problems except where economic activity is directly affected. Reynolds and Hanes are consumer-oriented industries selling highly publicized national brands, and they believe, correctly or incorrectly, that their products would suffer from any adverse publicity which their city might receive. Greenville's industrial enterprises either are not known for national brands sold on a mass consumer market or, like J. P. Stevens, are not really identified with Greenville.

IMMIGRATION AND RESIDENTIAL SEGREGATION

Winston-Salem's Negro population, 37 per cent of the total in 1960, came to the city principally in the three decades between 1900 and 1930 to furnish labor for R. J. Reynolds. Over these three decades the city's Negro population increased from 13 per cent of the 1960 population (in 1900), to 80 per cent of the 1960 population (in 1930). These Negroes emigrated from rural areas in eastern North Carolina and South Carolina. Several important developments resulted from their coming primarily to furnish labor for a single major corporation, Reynolds.[1] One was the influence on the pattern of residential segregation. Old-South cities like Charleston, South Carolina, had a "backyard" pattern, with the Negro population scattered fairly uniformly throughout the city. The homes of Negro servants, indentured and then free, were located in the back yards of the wealthy whites for whom they worked. Important changes in the occupational position of Negroes eroded this pattern to a certain extent. The newer residential areas surrounding the core of the old city are "lily white," but the accommodation to racial proximity has persisted.[2] The most common pattern in the urban South today is one which Johnson calls "urban clusters." [3] In this pattern most Negroes residing in the city live in one to

[1] In 1930, 52 per cent of all Negroes gainfully employed in Winston-Salem worked for Reynolds. This was computed from data in the U.S. Bureau of the Census publication, *Negroes in the United States, 1920–32.*

[2] Charles S. Johnson, *Patterns of Negro Segregation* (New York, 1943), p. 9.

[3] *Ibid.*, p. 10.

three large clusters. Significant numbers, however, reside in smaller clusters—as many as twenty—scattered throughout the older parts of the city. This urban cluster pattern varies from city to city in the extent of the dispersion of the Negro population. The clusters in Greenville, for example, show very high dispersion. The fact that 60.8 per cent of the white population of Greenville lives in census tracts which are at least 10 per cent Negro indicates this. A much smaller percentage of the white population lives in tracts 10 per cent or more Negro in cities having a more typical urban cluster pattern.[4] (The figures for Durham, Jacksonville, and Richmond, for example, are 26.2 per cent, 29.2 per cent, and 23.9 per cent, respectively.)

In Winston-Salem, the concentration is so intense that the pattern can no longer be called urban clusters. As in a number of northern cities, most Negroes live in a single residential area. There is a *ghetto*. One can drive by the vast majority of Negro homes in Winston-Salem without ever entering an area where whites live. Figure 1 shows Negro residential areas in Winston. At least 10 per cent of the

[4] It would be possible, of course, to have a very high percentage of whites living in tracts 10 per cent or more Negro and still have relatively little population dispersion, but this in fact does not occur. Census tracts are relatively small and in order to get a majority of whites living in tracts with significant numbers of Negroes there must be a high degree of dispersion of the Negro population. Census tracts are small areas into which large cities and their adjacent areas have been divided. The average tract has about 4,000 residents. Basic demographic data is thus provided for relatively small sections of major cities as well as for the city as a whole. Other data, principally on housing, is provided for a still smaller unit, the block. The block is usually a rectangular piece of land bounded by streets. The population of a block ranges from zero (no residential units) to several thousand. The typical block in Winston-Salem and Greenville has between fifty and three hundred persons. This data on residential segregation has been computed from the *U.S. Census of Housing: 1960.*

living units in the blocks in the shaded areas are occupied by Negroes.[5]

Negroes came to Winston-Salem in the big expansion of the first three decades of this century, then, and settled around the Reynolds factories, principally in the north and east of the city. As more Negroes came, and later as a Negro middle class developed, the ghetto pushed further to the north, northwest, and south, but contiguity was always maintained. Negroes would move into blocks on the periphery of the ghetto, whites would move out, and the section would become all-Negro. Today the only areas in which Negro and white live side by side are those on the very periphery of the ghetto, and those in the northeastern section of the city where the ghetto has pushed out rapidly, isolating white families. A few of these, often older couples, have chosen not to leave their homes.

Greenville's Negro population, 30 per cent of the total in 1960, has expanded at a fairly steady rate throughout this century. Unlike Winston's Negroes, who came to the city in waves in the first three decades of the century to serve as laborers and operatives in a major industry and settled as a consequence around the mills, Greenville's Negroes have been employed for the most part as manual laborers and servants. One-half of the Negro labor force in Winston in 1930 found employment in tobacco mills. Only 5 per cent of Greenville's Negro workers at that time were employed in textiles, the city's major industry, and even here there was a proliferation of smaller firms. Of the Negro women employed in Winston-Salem in 1930 28 per cent worked as domestics; 60 per cent worked in the tobacco industry. But in Greenville in 1930 79 per cent of the Negro female labor force did domestic work. A quite different residential pattern necessarily resulted.

[5] The number of Negroes living outside these blocks is negligible.

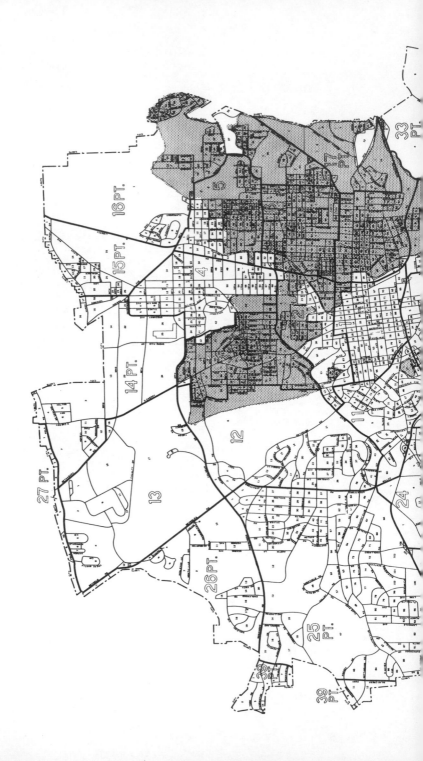

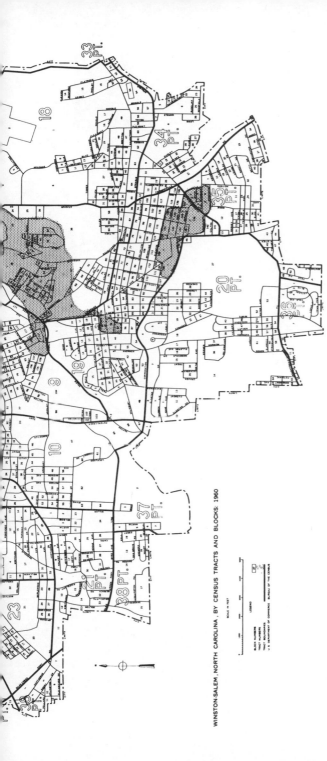

WINSTON-SALEM, NORTH CAROLINA, BY CENSUS TRACTS AND BLOCKS: 1960

SCALE IN FEET

LEGEND

BLOCK NUMBERS
TRACT NUMBERS
TRACT BOUNDARIES

U.S. DEPARTMENT OF COMMERCE BUREAU OF THE CENSUS

FIGURE 1. WINSTON-SALEM, N.C. SHADED AREAS INDICATE BLOCKS IN WHICH NEGROES CONSTITUTE 10 PER CENT OR MORE OF THE TOTAL POPULATION.

Lacking the magnet of a central employer of Negroes, but at the same time being formed too late to permit the old back-street pattern to develop, Greenville's Negro residential areas formed a dispersed cluster pattern. Today the city's Negro population is interspersed throughout the older residential sections in a series of clusters. The largest contains more than sixty city blocks; the smallest only a few dwelling units. The largest clusters, moreover, are elongated affairs threading in serpentine fashion throughout the older residential areas of the city. Figure 2 shows this. Newer residential sections are wholly white and generally are far removed from the Negro clusters.

In those blocks at least 10 per cent Negro, 21 per cent of all the occupied dwelling units are inhabited by whites. In contrast, only 8 per cent of the housing in comparable blocks in Winston-Salem are occupied by whites. This greater dispersion in Greenville is better illustrated by reference to larger units, or tracts. Comparing those tracts in the two cities which are 10 per cent or more Negro, we arrive at the data in Table 3.

TABLE 3

WHITE AND NEGRO POPULATION IN CENSUS TRACTS 10 PER CENT OR MORE NEGRO, WINSTON-SALEM AND GREENVILLE, 1960*

	Winston-Salem	Greenville
Percentage of the total city white population residing in these tracts	13.9	60.8
Number of whites for each 100 Negroes in these tracts	24.6	147.8

* Source: *U.S. Census of Population: 1960.*

The above should not be interpreted as indicating less residential segregation in Greenville. In fact as late as December 1962 Greenville was attempting to enforce an ordinance entitled "Colored Persons Not to Occupy Residences in White Block." Instead, the data presented above points to the fragmented nature of the Negro population of Greenville. This pattern of residential segregation, together with other factors which affect communication, has meant that Greenville contains not one but several Negro subcommunities.

OCCUPATION

Important occupational differences exist between the Negro populations of the two cities. Negroes came to Winston-Salem to furnish labor for the city's major industry, tobacco. The shortage of labor, and the heavy and unpleasant nature of much of the work in tobacco factories before World War II led Reynolds to turn to cheap Negro labor. The textile firms of Greenville never had to do this and the rule that Negroes would not be hired above the janitorial capacity in the city's textile mills soon became firmly established. The exclusion of Negroes from textile mills and their inclusion in tobacco factories are south-wide phenomena. Johnson noted that as early as 1880 the textile industry in the South drew all but its most menial labor from whites.[6] White and Negro workers in tobacco factories generally were segregated by buildings or sections of buildings, but at times the principle of racial separation was only symbolically preserved, and Negroes and whites worked in separate rows in the same room. And there were divisions of plants in Winston-Salem where Negroes and whites worked side by side as pickers, coppers, and stemmers. During the Christmas rush Negroes and whites regularly worked together in most of the mills.[7] In the big tobacco plants of Winston-Salem, Durham, and Richmond, Negroes performed most of the disagreeable, heavy work, but a few of them operated machines. Winston had Negro "making machine" operators from the very beginning.[8] This "camaraderie" of Negroes and whites in the

[6] *Op. cit.*, p. 84.   [7] *Ibid.*, p. 102.   [8] *Ibid.*, p. 100.

INSET

19 PT.

SCALE IN FEET

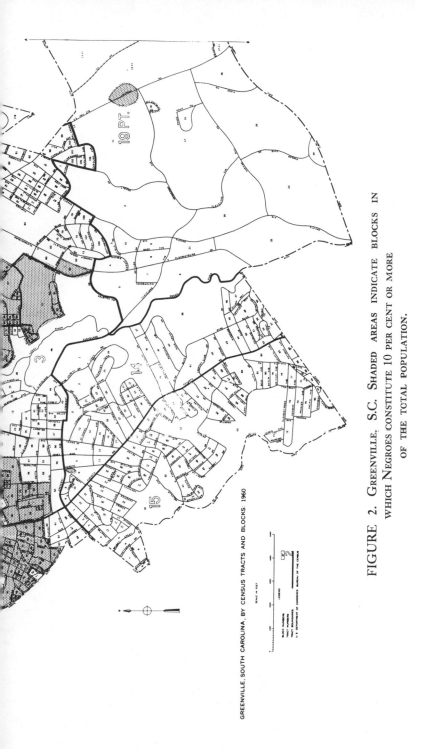

GREENVILLE, SOUTH CAROLINA, BY CENSUS TRACTS AND BLOCKS: 1960

FIGURE 2. GREENVILLE, S.C. SHADED AREAS INDICATE BLOCKS IN WHICH NEGROES CONSTITUTE 10 PER CENT OR MORE OF THE TOTAL POPULATION.

Reynolds plant was described in this way by one worker:

The poor whites and niggers is worked together, up at No. 2. They is using the poor whites to whip the nigger and the nigger to whip the poor whites. If the poor whites sort of get out of line, they fire them and put niggers in their jobs and they do the niggers the same way.[9]

Over the United States as a whole in 1930, 22.9 per cent of the workers in cigar and cigarette factories were Negroes; 2.2 per cent of the textile working force was Negro. This phenomenon can be explained in small part by the location of most tobacco plants in rim-South states while textile mills were more frequent in the states of the deep South. Textile mills in rim-South states, however, excluded Negroes to almost as great an extent as did those in the deep South. The nature of labor-force demands in the early periods of these two industries seems to have been more important. The tradition of Negroes working in tobacco factories was established at the outset. It never was established in textiles and a tradition of exclusion became inviolable.

By 1930 the typical Winston-Salem Negro was a factory worker. He was, to be sure, doing the heaviest work at the lowest wage, but he was nonetheless a factory worker. The Negro in Greenville was a domestic and a day laborer. The data in Table 4 indicate that this pattern has persisted, although with some erosion.

TABLE 4

PERCENTAGE OF NEGRO WORKING FORCE EMPLOYED IN CENSUS CATEGORIES CRAFTSMEN, FOREMEN AND KINDRED WORKERS, AND OPERATIVES AND KINDRED WORKERS *

City	1940	1960
Winston-Salem	44.0	36.0
Greenville	19.0	23.0

* Source: *U.S. Census of Population: 1940; 1960.*

[9] *Ibid.,* p. 102.

The greater fragmentation of the Negro labor force in Greenville seems to have retarded political consciousness and activity. Unionization of Negro workers in Greenville has been totally impossible. It would have been extremely difficult, to be sure, under any employment conditions, considering the deep-South attitude toward unionization in general and the unionization of Negroes in particular. But it is more than difficult, it is impossible, to unionize Negro domestics and day laborers. In contrast, the employment of some 5,000 Negroes by a single company created the basis for a fairly high level of political organization in the Winston-Salem Negro subcommunity. Specifically, the Negro employees of Reynolds presented an appealing target for unionization attempts. These workers were in fact unionized in the 1940's. The "saga of Local 22" will be discussed in some detail here because the activity of the union was a central factor structuring the pattern of race relations which exists today.

Active efforts to unionize the employees of R. J. Reynolds began in the summer of 1943.[10] Before that a Negro union organizer, the Reverend Carl Watson, had spent a year in Winston-Salem. He had made contact with most of the Negro ministers in the city and succeeded in enlisting the support of a number of them. One, the Reverend R. M. Pitts, is still a prominent Negro leader in the city.

From the outset the unionization drive used a strong racial appeal. Negro workers were told that joining the union would eliminate racial barriers to the use of restaurants, hotels, theaters, and public gathering places, and to the attendance at white schools. Ministers urged their flocks from the pulpit to support the unionization drive. Large numbers of Negroes attended mass meetings. Workers refusing to join the union found themselves labeled sinners (and worse).

[10] The union making the attempt was the Food, Tobacco, Agricultural and Allied Workers Union (CIO).

The drive succeeded in enrolling about 5,000 Negro employees of Reynolds in the union. Given the racial appeal used by the organizers of Local 22, it is hardly surprising that few white workers (no more than fifty) joined the union. But the Negro workers were a majority at Reynolds, and in January 1944 Local 22 won certification as the sole bargaining agent for all production and maintenance employees of the R. J. Reynolds Company.

The local's life was a stormy one. Indeed, the life of an all-Negro local in a southern city in the 1940's could hardly have been other than stormy. Union Negroes and nonunion whites regularly fought on the streets around the mills. Interracial parties sponsored by Local 22 brought sharp attack. Then, in the spring of 1947, the big strike began. When certain demands were not met, the overwhelming majority of Reynolds' Negro workers observed a strike call. Virtually all of the white workers and a good number of Negroes continued to work, however, and Reynolds remained open. With the strike, major interracial strife came to Winston-Salem. Certain parties initiated a wave of terrorism against non-striking Negroes. This grew nightly in intensity, and conditions in some Negro residential areas completely degenerated. Police entering the ghetto were greeted by a barrage of rocks and garbage. Negroes charged police brutality. Then in the midst of the strike the *Winston-Salem Journal* dramatically revealed that it had affidavits from three persons who were or who had been officials of the union stating that the strike was being prolonged and intensified by Communist agitators. These persons further claimed that the Communist Party had captured Local 22 "lock, stock and barrel." The revelation was all the more dramatic because one of the affidavit-signers had also been district treasurer of the CPUSA. A House Un-American Activities Committee investigator arrived in Winston and began an investigation of Communist activity in the strike. This charge of Communist infiltration demoralized the strikers, particularly since the charge was not denied, and the strike was settled on company terms after thirty-eight days. In the subsequent HUAC investigation it was established that the top leaders of the parent international (subsequently expelled from the CIO) and of Local 22 were indeed members of the CPUSA. It was also clearly established that only a very small number of those associated with Local 22 ever had had any association with the Party. The interest of the Negro members was solely in getting better working conditions and generally fairer treatment. In large part because of the revelation of Communist control of the Local and the subsequent red-baiting of members and supporters, opposition to the union increased and in 1950 Local 22 lost certification.

The source of the popularity of Local 22 in its first years is not hard to find. The union leaders made it their business to seek to eliminate the abuses to which Negro workers were subjected. Working conditions at Reynolds for Negro employees were bad: low wages, heavy work, and, in some ways hardest of all, the verbal and physical harassment by white foremen. To a certain extent the union succeeded in remedying those conditions. The union leadership, aware that the bonds of racial discrimination followed the Negro workers home, also demanded that the city government of Winston-Salem repeal zoning ordinances relating to Negroes living in certain portions of the city, and establish free access to all public facilities. Perhaps most successful was the drive to register Negro voters, a drive carried out under the aegis of the union leadership. Coming on the heels of the *Smith v. Allwright* (1944) decision outlawing the white primary, the drive increased Negro registration from 300 to 3,000 in two years. The union was instrumental in securing the election of a Negro to the Board of Aldermen in 1947. The Reverend Kenneth Williams was the first Negro to gain such a position in North Carolina since Reconstruction. More important than any single action was the change effected in the tone of race relations in the city. The activity of the union leadership between 1944 and 1948 contributed to the transformation of Negroes from "blanks" to participants in city politics. The unionization struggle dramatically increased Negro expectations and provided the first mass organization. Even amid the disillusionment which surrounded the collapse of Local 22 between 1948 and 1950, the gains remained. Today there is widespread agreement among Negroes in Winston—friend and foe alike—that Local 22 lost the battle but won the war. There are debits, however. Many Negro workers came to feel that they had been "used" by the leadership of the union, and it has since been hard to generate enthusiasm for unionization among them. Local 22 inflicted deep wounds in the Negro community, and these wounds have healed slowly. Recriminations are still heard relating to the position which so-and-so took during the strike. Winston-Salem Negroes can ill afford this. Most serious of all, at least for those immediately affected, was the loss of jobs by Negro workers. Reynolds speeded up the introduction of labor-saving machinery, and white workers were recruited from surrounding counties. Whole departments with Negro workers were dropped. Between 1940 and 1960 the percentage of the Negro labor force in manufacturing dropped from 44 per cent to 36 per cent. Even this, however, was not solely a debit. Partly to avoid further unionization attempts Reynolds did improve dramatically the conditions of work of all its employees. Though many Negroes lost their jobs, the mechanization of much of the very heavy, dirty work has resulted in better jobs requiring greater skills for the several thousand Negroes now in the employ of the company.

The above points to a second result of the comparative absence of Greenville Negroes from positions in industry. The drive for employment advances for southern Negroes has emphasized on the one hand white-collar jobs, and on the other semiskilled and skilled industrial work. Progress in getting the former comes slowly. In the short run, the economic position of the southern Negro can be significantly improved only by bringing him into industry on a salary parity with white workers. Attempts to bring Negroes into Greenville industrial firms have achieved only a token advance. The experience has been substantially the same in rim-South cities among businesses which historically have excluded Negroes. P. H. Hanes and Hanes Hosiery (textile firms) never employed Negroes above the level of janitors and maids. Not until 1963 did Gordon Hanes, president of Hanes Hosiery, announce to his colleagues on the Urban League Board that his company would hire Negroes as machine operators. Hanes is known in Winston-Salem as relatively liberal. His reputation among Negroes is good. Yet Hanes Hosiery with his "enlightened" management had not employed Negroes above the janitorial level. On the other hand, Reynolds, whose management in the past has been considered reactionary by Winston Negroes, in 1961 opened a new plant, its Whitaker Park Division, on an integrated basis. The 1900 white employees and the 600 Negro workers in that division are not segregated on the job, and they use the same cafeterias. In the older Reynolds plants, where whites and Negroes handled different operations in different mills, steps have been taken to integrate the other 2,800 Negroes and 7,700 whites. The Urban League was praising Hanes *for taking steps to hire a handful of Negroes,* and at the same time was praising Reynolds, already the employer of several thousand Negroes with a significant number in quite good jobs, *for further integrating its work force.* The struggle in one case was to hire, in the other to upgrade and integrate. These two companies at their inception had different labor needs, and different employment traditions developed. The Hanes management insists that it has been afraid its workers would not accept the hiring of Negroes. We need not be wholly convinced, of course, because businessmen have never been reluctant to do things opposed by their employees when they have deemed these to be in their economic interest. But it is true that patterns once set prove very resilient.

A congruence of factors only peripherally related to the pattern of race relations in our two cities, then, has produced major differences in the economic positions of the two Negro subcommunities. The chief industry of Greenville has been textiles. Wherever located in the South textile firms have not employed Negroes in any significant numbers. Winston-Salem's major industry has been a big employer of Negro labor and the problem of upgrading and integrating Negroes already in an industry has proved throughout the South a less serious one than trying to bring Negro workers into an industry in which they have never worked. Winston-Salem has one of the highest percentages of Negroes employed in manufacturing of any city in the South. It also has one of the highest Negro median family incomes in the region.

POTENTIAL POLITICAL PARTICIPANTS

Negro subcommunities in southern cities vary greatly in the level of skills required for political participation. The concept *potential political participants* will be used in describing these differences as they relate to the capacity for race-advancement activity.[11] It is hard to be precise, but those who

[11] There is general agreement that individuals with high educational, occupational, and income positions are more likely to participate in an active way in politics than are those at the bottom of the socioeconomic hierarchy. Edward Banfield describes in *The Moral Basis of a Backward Society* (Glencoe, Ill., 1958) the ways in which extreme poverty reduces the motivation to participate in political activity. It is probably true that the bottom fifth in income of the American population has no energy left from the struggle for existence to invest in political activity. Lipset observes that people at the bottom of the socioeconomic hierarchy frequently have little actual leisure time, or even more important, psychic leisure time free of anxieties to invest in nonpersonal political problems (S. M. Lipset, *Political Man* [Garden City, N.Y., 1960], p. 198). Both Knupfer and Lipset have noted that people in the lower strata are more deeply

by their skills and attitudes are equipped to provide continuous and rational political participation, are our *potential political participants*. To get at them through aggregate statistics, data on income, occupation, and education will be used. Income, occupational position, and education are, of course, only very rough indices. Aggregate data on these variables would tell us relatively little about the actual possibilities for political participation in groups of *white* Americans because the general level is so high. Very large numbers of white Americans have the skills, attitudes, and orientation necessary for active participation in electoral politics. But in such groups as the southern Negro, with low levels of the necessary political skills, relatively small differences in the number of potential political participants can be decisive for the content and level of political action. Increase at an arithmetic ratio in the size of the class of potential political participants may produce increases at a geometric ratio in certain facets of community participation such as voting, as the potential political participants stimulate their fellows.

---

isolated from extrafamily activities. They have fewer friends, a narrower range of contacts, read fewer books, and in general are more restricted to trivial aspects of life (Genevieve Knupfer, "Portrait of the Underdog," *Public Opinion Quarterly*, II, No. 1 [1947], 103–114). The "Yankee City" studies found that upper-strata people are more active in associations than are lower-strata people (W. L. Warner and Paul S. Lunt, *The Social Life of a Modern Community* [New Haven, 1941]). In short, differences in attitudes, values, needs, skills, and awareness are seen to separate the lower strata from the middle and upper in terms of level of participation. (Further evidence of this can be found in the voting studies.) We are saying here that the same variables used in aggregate data to indicate class or strata are also related to the levels of political participation. We will not refer, then, to strata and the participation of Negroes in politics. To do so would simply take us conceptually one step away. We prefer to use the term *potential political participants*, since our interest is in the level of those variables necessary for political participation.

Winston-Salem has a vastly greater store of potential political participants than does Greenville. Table 5 shows that Negro family income was $850 higher in Winston than in Greenville in 1959. More than twice the percentage of Negro families in Winston earned over $5,000 in that year. Greenville Negroes lag approximately one year in median years of school completed; and perhaps more significantly, the percentage of Negroes who have attended college is about twice as high in Winston-Salem as in Greenville (though it is very low in both cities). Negroes have been much more successful in gaining access to white collar employment in the North Carolina city. In summary, the data in Table 5 indicate that the Negro populations of both cities are seriously underprivileged in income, occupation, and education in comparison to the American population as a whole; but the socioeconomic position of Winston Negroes is much higher than that of their Greenville counterparts. The potential for active political participation in the North Carolina city is far greater.

TABLE 5

WINSTON-SALEM AND GREENVILLE NEGROES, U.S. NONWHITES, AND U.S. TOTAL POPULATION BY FIVE DEMOGRAPHIC VARIABLES, 1960 *

Variable	Winston-Salem Negroes	Greenville Negroes	U.S. nonwhites	U.S. total population
Median family income	$3254	$2410	$3161	$5660
Percentage of families earning over $5,000	22.0	9.0	27.2	58.1
Median years of school completed	7.8	6.8	8.2	10.6
Percentage with some college	8.9	5.1	7.7	16.4
Percentage of work force in white collar jobs	12.0	6.9	15.1	41.1

* Source: *U.S. Census of Population: 1960.*

Findings from several months of observation in each city confirm the picture indicated by the census data. The Negro community in Greenville suffers from a political paralysis brought on by a number of factors, not the least of which is the poverty, the low level of economic and political skills, and the limited political awareness. By contrast, Winston-Salem Negroes bring far greater human resources to the struggle for race advancement. No one-to-one relationship exists between the level of political activity and our indices of potential political participation, but possibilities and limitations of a general nature are indicated. It seems clear that very broad areas of political activity are precluded when a Negro community is below a certain level. Greenville Negroes lack sufficient potential political participants to sustain, by themselves, a high level of electoral or even protest activity. This does not mean that there can be no demonstrations, voting drives, and the like by Greenville's Negro citizens. It does mean that Greenville's Negro population will probably continue to lag behind Negroes in most southern cities in the level of political activity because of the scarcity of potential political participants.

Twenty-four southern cities have been ranked to determine the relative position of the Negro communities in each on these five income-education-occupation variables. The data is summarized in Table 6.[12] The striking aspect of the ranking

[12] The five variables are the same included in Table 5: median years of school completed (by those 25 years and older); percentage with some college; median family income; percentage of families earning over $5,000 per year; percentage (of the work force) in white collar jobs. We have also measured how Negroes in each city compare with the national figure (shown in Table 5) on each of these variables. This was done by determining the percentage which the Negro city population is of the total United States population for the variable. For example, the *median years of school completed* for Greensboro Negroes is 8.8; for the total U.S. population, 10.6; 8.8 is 83.0 per cent of 10.6. Finally, in Table 6, we have taken the average of

is that those cities with Negro subcommunities at the bottom of the socioeconomic ladder are without exception those in which race-advancement has proceeded at a very slow pace in voting, direct action, and related activity. Data collected from informants, newspaper reports, and the like on cities such as Gadsden, Columbus, Macon, and Augusta, as well as on Greenville, indicate that the Negro populations of these cities are too poor, and too lacking in skills necessary for political participation, to sustain a high level of political activity. We will return to this subject repeatedly with reference to Greenville. The census data is at least suggestive of the human resources which Negroes in each city are able to bring to bear. This data, it should be noted, will not tell us about the amount of integration but rather about one element (the human resources) needed for action. The capacity may exist in an area in which obstacles are so great that actual achievements are minimal.

Negro subcommunities in outer-South cities generally arc in a better position in terms of the resources indicated by our five variables than are those in deep-South cities, but there are important exceptions. Atlanta and Birmingham rank high. And both arc cities in which the Negro subcommunities have demonstrated relatively great internal resources for active participation in race-advancement activity in the context of urban American politics.

---

these five percentage figures which compare each Negro city population with the total U.S. population, and have called this mean of the five variables equally weighted the index of potential political participation. Median education, percentage with some college, median income, percentage earning over $5,000 per year, and percentage holding white collar jobs together provide a meaningful indication of the capacity for political participation. By representing the position of each Negro subcommunity on each of these variables by a percentage figure, with each percentage figure indicating a similar relationship to the national figure for each variable, relatively equal weighting was achieved. The source of this data is *U.S. Census of Population: 1960.*

TABLE 6

Negro populations of twenty-four southern cities by five education-occupation-income variables

City	Index of potential political participation	Medium years of school completed	% of U.S. total	% with some college	% of U.S. total
Greensboro	66.5	8.8	83.0	18.7	114.0
Raleigh	55.6	8.2	77.3	13.5	82.3
Richmond	55.6	8.0	75.4	7.6	46.3
Nashville	52.8	8.4	79.2	12.0	73.1
Winston-Salem	50.4	7.8	73.5	8.9	54.2
Birmingham	50.0	7.9	74.5	7.1	43.2
Durham	49.5	7.6	71.6	10.3	62.8
Atlanta	49.1	7.9	74.5	7.9	48.1
Charlotte	46.8	7.7	72.6	9.1	55.4
Columbia	45.7	7.7	72.6	10.7	65.2
Mobile	45.7	8.0	75.4	6.7	40.8
New Orleans	44.9	7.8	73.5	5.4	32.9
Jacksonville	44.5	7.8	73.5	5.7	34.7
Miami	44.1	8.2	77.3	5.3	32.3
Montgomery	43.2	7.6	71.6	9.0	54.8
Savannah	42.7	7.1	66.9	7.1	43.2
Baton Rouge	42.4	7.0	66.0	7.7	46.9
Tampa	40.6	7.4	69.8	5.0	30.4
Charleston	39.7	7.2	67.9	6.2	37.8
Columbus	38.9	6.7	63.2	5.8	35.3
Gadsden	36.0	7.1	66.9	3.5	21.3
Augusta	34.5	6.4	60.3	4.4	26.8
Greenville	33.0	6.8	64.1	5.1	21.0

City	% of workers holding white collar jobs	% of U.S. total	% of families earning over $5,000	% of U.S. total	Income in dollars	% of U.S. total
Greensboro	16.2	39.4	23.0	39.5	3,183	56.2
Raleigh	16.7	40.6	17.0	29.2	2,743	48.4
Richmond	21.8	53.0	25.4	43.7	3,387	59.8
Nashville	14.0	34.0	17.0	29.2	2,757	48.7
Winston–Salem	12.0	29.1	22.0	37.8	3,254	57.4
Birmingham	15.3	37.2	24.3	41.8	3,019	53.3
Durham	14.5	35.2	15.8	27.1	2,882	50.9
Atlanta	12.5	30.4	22.1	38.0	3,110	54.9
Charlotte	10.9	26.5	15.6	26.8	2,977	52.5
Columbia	13.3	32.3	11.6	19.9	2,197	38.8
Mobile	12.0	29.1	18.0	30.9	2,959	52.2
New Orleans	12.8	31.1	20.0	34.4	2,987	52.7
Jacksonville	11.7	28.4	18.8	32.3	3,048	53.8
Miami	8.2	19.9	19.2	33.0	3,310	58.4
Montgomery	12.0	29.1	11.0	18.9	2,349	41.5
Savannah	12.2	29.6	15.2	26.1	2,708	47.8
Baton Rouge	12.0	29.1	10.2	17.5	2,980	52.6
Tampa	8.3	20.1	18.0	30.9	2,946	52.0
Charleston	11.4	27.7	13.6	23.4	2,372	41.9
Columbus	11.0	26.7	13.9	23.9	2,596	45.8
Gadsden	8.1	19.7	14.3	24.6	2,694	47.5
Augusta	11.0	26.7	10.0	17.2	2,350	41.5
Greenville	6.9	16.7	9.0	15.4	2,410	42.5
Macon	8.7	21.1	11.4	19.6	2,504	44.2

Winston-Salem ranks near the top on each of these variables; Greenville at the bottom. Indeed, no major city in the United States had in 1954 as small a percentage of its Negro families earning $5,000 and over as Greenville, South Carolina. Almost three times as high a percentage of Negro families in Birmingham, Alabama, earned over $5,000 as in Greenville. And at this level such differences are of the very greatest significance. Among Negroes 25 years and older, one in twenty in Greenville had attended college; one in five in Greensboro had gone to college. It is not by chance that Columbus, Gadsden, Augusta, Greenville, and Macon are among the South's "forgotten cities."

The index of potential political participation is useful in demonstrating the extent to which the various urban-South Negro subcommunities differ in the human resources related to levels of political activity. The index for Winston-Salem (50.4) does not tell us anything more precise in relation to the 52.8 for Nashville and the 49.5 for Durham than that the Negro populations of these cities are in approximately the same socioeconomic position. Only in the extremes can there be confidence that the different index scores point to decisive differences in the capacity for political activity. The Negro subcommunities of Richmond (55.6) and Macon (33.6) are both "southern"; but the political participation resources of Macon Negroes are grossly inferior to those of their Richmond counterparts.

RELATIVE SIZE OF NEGRO POPULATION

Interestingly enough, in the variable frequently cited as a major correlate of the level of Negro political participation —the percentage of the total population Negro, at present and historically—Winston-Salem and Greenville closely resemble each other. The outer-South city with its vastly more permissive pattern of race relations has in fact a slightly higher concentration of Negroes. The small towns and rural areas of the outer-South are characterized by a lower concentration of Negroes than their counterparts in the deep-South. But there is little difference in the concentration of Negroes between the major cities of the two subregions. The late-blooming cities of the outer-South, fed not only from the rural areas and small towns of their own states but from the immigration of deep-South whites and Negroes, have Negro populations that in many cases are as large as or even larger than those of deep-South cities. Richmond (42 per cent Negro), Durham (36.3 per cent), and Nashville (37.9 per cent) match Birmingham (39.7 per cent), Jackson (37.7 per cent), and Columbia (30.4 per cent). This in no way challenges the thesis that the historically (and currently) greater percentage of Negroes in the deep South has contributed to a more rigid set of attitudes toward segregation among deep-South whites. Each city listed above is a child of the state in which it is located. Many of its white inhabitants have moved from rural and small-town areas in the state. Moreover, state boundary lines are potent factors in orienting political outlook.

Table 7 shows, by percentage, the size of the Negro populations of Winston-Salem and Greenville over the last

TABLE 7

PERCENTAGE NEGRO OF TOTAL POPULATION, WINSTON-SALEM AND GREENVILLE, 1900–1960*

Year	Winston-Salem	Greenville
1900	40.5	41.4
1910	39.8	40.1
1920	42.8	35.4
1930	43.3	37.3
1940	45.1	40.2
1950	41.8	27.7
1960	37.0	29.7

* Source: *Negro Population 1790–1915; Negroes in the United States, 1920–32; U.S. Census of Population: 1940, 1950, 1960.*

sixty years. There is, moreover, no marked difference in the racial composition of the surrounding rural areas. Both Winston-Salem and Greenville are cities of the industrial Piedmont. The surrounding rural areas have never approached black belt concentration, and in fact have had somewhat lower percentages of Negroes than have the cities.

The relationship between the concentration of Negroes and patterns of race relations in the South is one of the most carefully considered and documented subjects in the study of Negro politics.[13] We expected that the whites of Winston-Salem and Greenville would absorb many of the racial attitudes of their respective states. But we also expected that the white populations of these two cities located in areas with an historically lower concentration of Negroes would demonstrate more permissive attitudes on race relations than would whites in the more easterly cities of the respective subregions. In the case of Winston-Salem this expectation was confirmed. That city is generally and correctly considered to be somewhat more "progressive" in race relations than more easterly outer-South cities such as Raleigh and Norfolk. White racial attitudes in Winston-Salem are somewhat more permissive. Greenville, however, is considered by Negroes a "tougher" place than black belt deep-South cities such as Charleston and Savannah. In much the same way Gadsden, Alabama, is considered at least as oppressive as black belt Montgomery, and worse than Mobile down on the Gulf. This phenomenon is an interesting one. North Carolina piedmont cities are more "progressive" than eastern North Carolina cities where historically there has been a greater concentration of Negroes. But cities in the rolling hills or piedmont region of western

[13] See, for example, H. D. Price, *The Negro and Southern Politics* (New York, 1957), pp. 35–54; Donald Matthews and James W. Prothro, "Social and Economic Factors and Negro Voter Registration in the South," *The American Political Science Review* (March, 1963), pp. 28–32.

South Carolina (and in comparable sections of other deep-South states) often have biracial structures as unacceptable to Negroes as those of cities in the old slaveholding citadels, the black belt, of the deep South.

An explanation with respect to Greenville can only be suggested here. In the minds of its Negro citizens that city is a "cracker" town. It is located in a state historically convulsed by the race question. Its newness, the industrialization which brought in large numbers of low-status white laborers, and the absence of an established white upper-class—a so-called aristocracy, which is generally seen as imparting a certain tone of civility to race relations—have contributed to a pattern of race relations as rigidly discriminatory as that existing anywhere in the urban-South.[14] While the North

[14] There is ample evidence that the older sections of the deep South have been somewhat less rabid in their racism than the newer sections. South Carolina until 1900 had the highest percentage of Negroes of any state in the Union; since then it has been second only to Mississippi. Yet there is some basis for the argument that a certain pattern of "civility" can be detected in South Carolina racism, a "civility" absent from Mississippi and Alabama racism. In the late nineteenth century wealthy South Carolinians of cities such as Charleston —then a major city—were going North to Newport for summers. They were regularly associating on a social basis with wealthy northerners. At that time Mississippi didn't have a single city of any size. Its "new rich," managing the huge cotton "factories," were a frontier type of much less cosmopolitan nature. Mississippi had no figure paralleling South Carolina's Wade Hampton who sought to "conciliate the freed men, reconcile the races, and attract Negro voters to the support of his administration" (C. Vann Woodward, *The Strange Career of Jim Crow*, [New York, 1957], p. 30). The conservative philosophy which Vann Woodward describes as one of the "forgotten alternatives" to the comprehensive "Jim Crow" system was much stronger in the older southeastern areas. This conservatism was in its posture toward the Negro "an aristocratic philosophy of paternalism and *noblesse oblige*" (*ibid.*). South Carolina continued to resist much of the "Jim Crow" legislation after it had swept the more western deep-South states (*ibid.*, p. 49).

Carolina piedmont—by quite simple facts of geography, population, and economics which translate themselves into politics —is the dog wagging the "low country" tail, the South Carolina piedmont is the tail wagged by the "low country" dog. In the climate of prosperity, optimism, and dynamism which exists in Winston-Salem, a pattern of race relations somewhat more permissive than is found in a Norfolk or a Raleigh has developed; such cities have a closer proximity to higher concentrations of Negroes, and this has contributed a more "traditional" flavor to their race relations.

Greenville, despite its position in the South Carolina northwest where slaveholding never flourished and the percentage of Negroes in rural areas has always been low, cannot boast of a more permissive pattern of race relations than exists in Columbia or Charleston. The relationship of concentration of Negroes to white attitudes on race and race relations is not as simple as it is often thought to be.

Some Negro leaders have found their initial assumptions on race relations in Greenville, vis-à-vis the "low country" counties, proved incorrect. Two Negro professional men, both natives of "low country" counties, related why they initially decided to settle in Greenville.

"I thought things would be better up here. I thought Negroes would encounter less hostility than down around Charleston, but man this is a 'cracker' town."

"I expected things to be easier here, but Greenville is the toughest city in the state. Ten years ago, before I moved here, I wouldn't have believed it, but they have more integration in Charleston and Columbia than we do. Negroes can get to talk to the Mayor there [in Columbia] better than we can here. The white man uses the Negro as badly here as anywhere in the South."

Another Negro leader who had worked throughout the South agreed with this assessment. He said simply, "Greenville is a 'cracker' town."

These are the most important demographic characteristics of the Negro populations of Winston-Salem and Greenville relating to the structure of race leadership. The Greenville Negro subcommunity is fragmented. It is dispersed throughout the city in a crazy-quilt pattern which gives the worst of all possible worlds. Residential segregation exists along with a serpentine structure of Negro neighborhoods which retards intragroup communication. This is in large part the product of an occupational dispersal. Greenville Negroes rank low indeed in income, education, and job skills. In fact, the index of potential political participation shows Greenville below virtually every other major southern city, and in no major southern city is the Negro middle class smaller than it is in Greenville. Greenville is one of the South's forgotten cities in race-advancement activity, and the above demographic data goes far to explain why. In Winston-Salem the presence of a single major employer of Negro labor and the nuclear structure of the Negro residential area has furthered Negro community awareness and facilitated political communication. Winston Negroes have the resources to sustain a fairly high level of both electoral and protest activity. These differences translate themselves into quite different patterns of race leadership.

PATTERNS OF DISCRIMINATORY TREATMENT

In surveying the biracial structure of our two cities, we may now turn to the institutional patterns of segregation and other forms of discriminatory treatment in education and other community operated facilities and services, and in privately owned but publicly used facilities. This requires at the outset a brief consideration of the white racial opinions which are reflected in the patterns of discrimination.

The opinions of Winston-Salem whites on racial matters are those of urban-piedmont North Carolina. Those of Greenville whites are typical of urban South Carolina. These need not be discussed in depth here. Each represents the resolution of a whole series of factors: historical differences; differences in the socioeconomic position of the white and Negro populations; differences in the structure of political competition. In 1964 Negro participation in electoral politics was generally accepted as legitimate in Winston-Salem. In contrast, even voting by Negroes remains strongly suspect in Greenville. Winston-Salem newspapers editorialize against capital punishment (which in the South is largely the execution of Negroes); attack deep-South governors like Wallace and Barnett as morally wrong; censure a "low country" legislator who had tongue-lashed a Negro college president when the latter appeared before a legislative committee seeking funds for his college; and endorse (although with certain reservations) the 1964 civil rights legislation. Greenville newspapers, on the other hand, encourage resistance to integration on all fronts. Integration is headlined as "race mixing." Typical of the strongly anti-Negro flavor of these newspapers is an editorial entitled "Castro—You've Gone Too Far This Time." The editor purported to tell Castro that when his planes fired on an American fishing boat which happened to have two Negroes aboard he had at last done something Kennedy couldn't tolerate.[15]

A relatively high level of participation in politics by Winston-Salem Negroes over the last decade and a half has forced the city's white population into a number of sharply divergent responses. Negro leaders are able to recognize significant groups of white racial liberals, moderates, and conservatives. The relative weakness of the Negro community in Greenville has meant that thus far little pressure has been exerted on the city's white population to take a new posture toward Negroes. Differences in the intensity of anti-Negro feelings—which exist in Greenville as in every city—have not become public. If the white community were continu-

15 *Greenville Piedmont,* May 13, 1963.

ously confronted with a choice of making concessions or facing protest demonstrations, some division in approach would develop. In the absence of strong pressure from the Negro community Greenville's white population has continued to appear quite homogeneous on racial questions. The "Negro Problem" has not really been an issue. But in 1963 there were indications that whites soon would be forced to choose among different postures toward the Negro. The racial demonstrations which swept the South in 1963 seem in particular to have convinced many Greenville whites that their turn would soon come. The creation in 1963 of two biracial committees provided for Negro-white negotiations on behalf of certain limited integration goals. With this the kind of debate within the white community which in other cities has produced differentiation began. In this situation competing white groups vie for the lead in structuring the effective white racial opinions.[16]

[16] A survey of white racial opinions in the major cities of North Carolina probably would not reveal significant differences from city to city. The response of these white populations to race-advancement activity, however, differs in important respects; that is, the opinion structure actually controlling in specific interracial conflict does vary. This applies similarly to Greenville in relation to other South Carolina cities. Key has observed that "public opinion . . . may simply be taken to mean those opinions held by private persons which governments find it prudent to heed" (V. O. Key, *Public Opinion and American Democracy*, [New York, 1962], p. 14). And Blumer observed that "the character of public opinion in terms of meaningful operation must be sought in the array of views and positions which enter into the consideration of those who have to take action on public opinion" (Herbert Blumer, "Public Opinion and Public Polling," *The American Sociological Review*, XIII [1948], 545). This allows that although basic white racial opinions in the two cities are really quite fixed and will change slowly, the ways in which these are structured and made relevant for political decision-making permit great lateral movement on the continuum of responses to race advancement. In brief, an economic elite firmly in political control and committed to

SCHOOLS

The Winston-Salem school system was integrated in 1957. Greenville's public schools, in contrast, remained completely segregated, as did all public school systems with one exception in South Carolina, until 1964.[17]

Fear of court action and the constant prodding of the Negro member of the board caused the Winston-Salem school board in 1957 to grant one of four transfer requests which it had received from Negro students, and token integration was realized. This desegregation upon request for reassignment continued through the 1963–1964 school year. Three of eight requests received in 1958 were granted, and all which have been received since 1959 have been approved. Still, in the academic year 1962–1963 only nineteen Negro pupils attended previously all-white schools. More than 7,000 Negro children attend Winston-Salem public schools. The transfer policy permitted granting transfers only when the Negro pupil lived closer to a white school than to the Negro school he was attending. All white pupils attending an integrated school had the option of transferring out.

The decision to consolidate the city and county school systems—approved in January 1963—meant three important changes for Negroes in the area. First, the county school system (which included all pupils living outside the city of Winston-Salem) was integrated. The great geographic area of the county had created genuine hardships for Negro children above and beyond those associated with segregation in

---

racial peace as a necessary part of the city's progressive image; and a highly fragmented leadership structure in which "populist" leaders have been dominant, can produce differences in posture toward race and race relations greater than the actual differences in racial opinion. This has in fact been the case with Winston-Salem and Greenville.

[17] The Charleston school system represents the one exception. Negro pupils first entered previously all-white schools in Charleston in the fall of 1963.

the city. Second, the new city-county school board formed in July 1963 had three Negro members; Negro representation thus was one-quarter of the twelve-man board. This was the highest ratio of Negroes to whites on any major North Carolina governmental board or commission (other than advisory) and marked one of the few times Negro membership on such boards had gone beyond the token single-member stage. The newly constituted board then changed assignment policies to allow any pupil to attend the school nearest his home without special board approval. Then, on June 3, 1964, the board took the third and final step toward the neighborhood school pattern, approving the assignment of all first-graders to the schools nearest their homes, without regard to race. Thirteen of the forty-two elementary schools in the county were integrated in academic year 1964–1965.

Greenville schools first were integrated, on a token basis, in the fall of 1964, when fifty-five Negro students entered previously all-white schools. In addition to this lag in integrating schools, the gap in the quality of facilities available to Negroes and whites is much greater than in Winston.

GOVERNMENT-OPERATED PUBLIC FACILITIES

Winston-Salem city officials took the position in the late 1950's that the city could not *enforce* segregation of the various government-operated public facilities. Thus Negroes integrated a park and two swimming pools in the summer of 1963 without arrests. In contrast to nearby Greensboro, which closed its pools when Negroes sought admission to those used by whites, Winston continued to operate its pools despite a temporary reduction of white attendance. In September 1964, white voters had an opportunity to pass judgment on the continued operation of integrated public pools. At issue were referendum proposals permitting the use of tax funds for a supervised recreation program and of a million dollars in surplus funds for parks and swimming pools. The proposals carried by 2–1 margins, and received the support of a clear majority of whites. Rather than curtailing its recreation program in the face of integration, the city elected to expand it.

The Greenville response has been markedly different. An attempt to integrate a roller skating rink in the summer of 1962 led to the arrest of the demonstrators and to the closing of that rink along with a similar one operated in a Negro park. The manager of the "white" rink managed to find sufficient funds to build a private skating rink to meet the needs of the city's white population. Although the parks and the tennis courts therein are formally open to all, the city's swimming pools were closed in the face of integration demands. One pool has become a home for sea lions. Thus Greenville is the only city in the United States that provides swimming facilities for sea lions but not for its citizens. Confronted with the alternatives of accepting integration of various city-operated facilities or of closing the facilities, Greenville not infrequently has chosen the latter.

Until 1964 Winston-Salem operated two hospitals, one admitting only Negroes, the other only whites. The Negro hospital, the Kate Bitting Reynolds Memorial, provides somewhat lower rates and gives Negro physicians full authority. Reynolds, however, is an inferior hospital, seriously overcrowded and poorly equipped. The separate-hospital pattern made it virtually impossible for Negroes to get first-rate hospital facilities within Forsyth county. In 1964, however, a new county hospital was opened, and it admitted without contest all those who could afford the rates. Also in 1964, the city's Board of Aldermen gave preliminary approval for the construction of a new hospital in the Negro section, to replace the existing Negro facility.

The Greenville County Hospital admits both Negroes and whites, segregating them by ward and/or floor. In certain cases a given ward may be Negro at one time and white at another. Before 1951, no Negro physician had staff privileges.

Partial staff privileges were granted in 1951, and full privileges in 1954. One Negro physician maintains that the hospital director handles doctors on the basis of their competency, not race. Despite real inequities—the Negro surgical area is in the oldest part of the hospital and is not equal to the white facility, for example—Negro Greenvillians have found their medical needs fairly well met.

CITY GOVERNMENT EMPLOYMENT

Negroes have been excluded from city hall employment in both Winston and Greenville. This was broken in 1964 on only a token basis in Winston when a Negro secretary was hired in a city hall office. In other city employment Winston-Salem follows a pattern customary for rim-South cities: Negro policemen patrol Negro neighborhoods but have the authority to arrest white violators; Negro firemen staff a station in a Negro neighborhood; Negroes are supervisors at parks in Negro areas. Low-level positions in the fire and police departments are considered relatively low-status employment by most whites, but they are looked upon as highly desirable positions by many Negroes. Thus in Winston and many other southern cities, paradoxically, the level of education of Negro firemen and policemen is far higher than that of their white counterparts.

Greenville does not have Negro firemen and did not hire its first Negro policemen (special officers) until January 1964, even though the other major South Carolina cities, Charleston and Columbia, have employed Negroes in these capacities for some time. Greenville Negro leaders lament that in the area of city employment for Negroes Greenville lags behind many small "low country" counties. The employment of two Negro policemen was achieved only after lengthy consideration by a biracial committee and by the city council. The city's newspapers endorsed the idea of Negro policemen providing they could be completely isolated from the white police force. Even in an area of employment where the hiring of Negroes would remove some extremely unpleasant work from whites, Greenville's white leaders remained reluctant to change the traditional exclusion pattern.

LAW ENFORCEMENT

Impartial law enforcement is one of the most pressing needs of southern Negroes. Outer-South and deep-South states differ more sharply in this area, perhaps, than in any other. Winston-Salem Negroes expect and receive more verbal and occasionally more physical abuse from law enforcement officers than do the city's white citizens. Nevertheless, in Winston-Salem as in many rim-South cities, law enforcement officials do not for the most part look upon themselves as agents for enforcing white supremacy. In Greenville they do whenever racial lines are drawn. This is hardly surprising—it means only that the administration of justice is caught up in the prevailing biracial structure. The greater political power of Winston-Salem Negroes which has contributed to a higher level of integration in public facilities and to somewhat better employment opportunities in city-operated services is evident in the political role of police in interracial disputes as well as in the general treatment of Negroes who allegedly have violated the law.

In December 1962 a Negro woman in Winston-Salem complained to her alderman (a Negro) that she had received abusive treatment from two white policemen. The alderman raised the incident in an open city council meeting and demanded an investigation. The city manager assured the alderman that such actions were not condoned and that, although he doubted the incident had occurred, an investigation would be carried out. The investigation vindicated the policemen to the satisfaction of their chief and the city manager. There is little doubt, however, that the political power of the city's

Negroes which enabled their elected representative to demand and to obtain an investigation has tempered the behavior of white policemen toward Negroes. Both the channel and the political sanctions are absent in Greenville. It is clear that many whites and Negroes continue to see the city's police force as being committed to a defense of the interests of whites. Still, its record in its treatment of Negro violators must be considered good when compared to that of law enforcement agencies in many deep-South cities.

PRIVATELY OWNED PUBLIC FACILITIES

Sit-in demonstrations occurred in both Winston-Salem and Greenville in 1960. They succeeded in integrating lunch counters in the former city, but failed completely in Greenville. Lunch counters in the South Carolina city were not integrated until June 1963, and then through the work of a biracial committee, without demonstrations. Greenville Negro leaders agree that the impetus for the desegregation came not from Greenville at all, in fact, but from Greensboro, Durham, Charleston, and the many other southern cities where massive demonstrations occurred in the spring of 1963. By January 1964 Winston Salem was an "open city," those facilities refusing to serve Negroes being the exceptions. Most restaurants, motels, and other such facilities in Greenville remained closed to Negroes until Congress enacted the major civil rights legislation of 1964. Compliance with the public accommodations section of the 1964 Act in a purely formal sense was quick. But while Negroes in Winston-Salem have begun to use, beyond the token basis, their newly achieved access, many of the now formally integrated facilities in Greenville continue to be "off-limits" to Negroes. The two cities, in short, closely resemble sister cities in their respective states in the general patterns of segregation in privately owned public facilities.

LEVEL, STRUCTURE, AND CONTENT OF NEGRO POLITICAL PARTICIPATION

Negro participation in electoral politics is assuming greater importance throughout the states of the old Confederacy. Rates of Negro voting, the strength and degree of cohesiveness of the vote, Negro organization in electoral politics, and the position of the Negro in the larger structure of political competition are particularly important to this analysis both as a reflection of the prevailing patterns of race relations and as a causal factor shaping these patterns. Participation through the protest organizations will be similarly, though more briefly, considered.

ELECTORAL POLITICS

Negroes register and vote in Winston-Salem without restrictions and have done so for a decade and a half. The level of Negro participation in electoral politics in that city stands near one pole (maximum) for today's urban South. It is near the opposite pole in Greenville. There, the impediments raised to effective political participation by Negroes are formidable indeed. This is so even though qualified Negroes are not denied the right either to register or to vote. Winston-Salem Negroes are a major force in their city's electoral politics; their Greenville counterparts, despite efforts to bring about change, remain weak.

A comparative analysis of Negro participation in electoral politics in Winston-Salem and Greenville is, of course, part of a more general analysis of the conditions which determine the level and effectiveness of the Negro vote in the urban South. Four variables must be considered in this analysis: (1) legitimacy, (2) the political awareness and skills of the Negro population, (3) the size of the Negro electorate, and (4) Negro organization for electoral politics. These variables interact. More permissive racial attitudes (a broader definition of legitimate activity), for example, contribute to a larger electorate, which in turn makes it in the interest of white political leaders to extend still further the scope of "legitimate" activity. Together these four variables are of central importance in determining the level and effectiveness of Negro electoral activity. The first two were discussed above, and will be referred to here only briefly.

Legitimacy. Negro participation in electoral politics is recognized as legitimate in Winston-Salem; it is not in Greenville. No barriers stand before Negro registration and voting in the North Carolina city. Most Winston Negroes go to a Negro registrar to register; their votes are cast in precincts manned by Negro election officials. The time and place for registration make it not merely possible but convenient for Negroes to register. Negro leaders occupy middle-level positions in the local Democratic Party organization, and Negro support is not a "kiss of death" for white candidates. Winston-Salem certainly is not the best of all possible political worlds for Negro voters; but the basic legitimacy of participation by Negroes in electoral politics has been recognized.

Negroes register and vote in Greenville without the overt harassment characteristic of black belt rural counties. At 30 per cent of the population Greenville Negroes do not pose so serious a threat. Of those interviewed in a survey of Greenville's Negro subcommunity 8 per cent claimed that they had been subjected to certain discourtesies when attempting to register, but no one maintained he had been unjustly denied the opportunity to register or vote. Negro leaders agree that the literacy requirement has been applied so permissively that illiterates have been registered after limited instruction. The long-time registrar of Greenville County, a kindly woman in her sixties, seems to apply formal requirements quite impartially. Still, formidable barriers to effective participation by Negroes have been erected. The registrar once said, in the course of an interview at her office, that she treated everyone the same—that there was no discrimination in the registration procedure. Just at that moment a rather dark-skinned Negro entered her office. The registrar was heard to mutter under her breath to a fellow worker, "Ugh, there's another one!" The climate, then, is rather cold even though formally correct. All election officials in the county are white. Severe limitation of the period when registration is open, together with the requirement that registration must be effected in the county courthouse, has served to keep Negro registration low. Negroes do not hold positions of any importance in political party organization. And only the most circumscribed appeals to Greenville Negroes have been made by white politicians. Negroes thus frequently find themselves without incentive to vote. They feel—and rightly so—that it makes no difference whether they vote or not. In short, the Negro is not yet recognized as a citizen with a legitimate claim to participate in electoral politics in Greenville, and any overtures he makes are seen as intrusions.

Potential political participants. There are many more potential political participants among Negroes in Winston-Salem than in Greenville. We know that while political factors (application of election laws, the nature of party competition, the level of Negro organization, etc.) can greatly affect the level of participation in politics in general, and of registration and voting in particular, there are some persons who lack minimum skills and political awareness. Although it is difficult to be precise in these matters, it is clear that the potential Negro electorate in Greenville is much smaller than that in Winston-Salem, if the potential electorate is defined as those psychologically and intellectually equipped to be registered voters at this time.

Size of the Negro electorate. The effectiveness of Negroes in electoral politics is a direct product of the size and voting frequency of the Negro electorate in relation to the white electorate.

Table 8 compares Negro and white registration for Winston-Salem and Greenville. Winston-Salem Negroes—37 per cent of the population—constitute nearly 30 per cent of the potential electorate. In Greenville, although 30 per cent of the population, Negroes constitute less than 20 per cent of the potential electorate.[18] Only 26 per cent of the city's voting-age Negroes were registered before January 1, 1964; about half of the registered Negro voters in Greenville have been added to the books since then.

TABLE 8

NEGRO AND WHITE REGISTRATION, WINSTON-SALEM AND GREENVILLE, NOVEMBER 1964

	Winston-Salem	Greenville
Percentage of Negro voting-age population registered	62.0	52.4
Percentage of white voting-age population registered	78.0	75.1
Percentage of total electorate which is Negro	29.8	19.7

Figure 3 summarizes data on the percentage of the potential Negro electorate actually voting, the percentage of the potential white electorate voting, and the percentage of the total vote which was cast by Negroes in four mayoralty elections in Winston-Salem from 1957 through 1963. In each of the four elections Negro voters saw a clear-cut choice and delivered large majorities to the Democratic candidate. In each election a Republican seriously challenged the Democratic incumbent; and in two of these elections the victor received less than 53 per cent of the two-party vote. Figures for these elections do not distort Negro electoral strength.

[18] *Potential electorate* here refers to the number duly registered and hence eligible to vote in a given election. The *actual electorate* includes those who go to the polls election day.

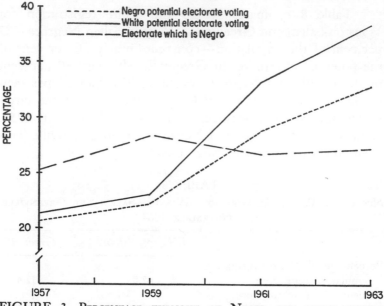

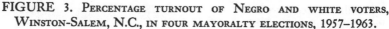

FIGURE 3. PERCENTAGE TURNOUT OF NEGRO AND WHITE VOTERS, WINSTON-SALEM, N.C., IN FOUR MAYORALTY ELECTIONS, 1957–1963.

For although the turnout of Negro voters has been numerically lower in elections in which Negroes find the stakes lower (e.g., elections to the county Board of Supervisors), so has the turnout of white voters. Thus the percentage of the total vote cast by Negroes has remained quite constant in elections over the past six years. This points to two important factors. First, there is in Winston a bloc of Negro voters who participate regularly in elections. There has not been an election since 1957 in which less than 20 per cent of the Negro electorate has turned out, although there have been elections in this period which aroused little interest in the Negro community. If the figure seems low it must be remembered that it does not compare unfavorably with the turnout of white voters. Second, those elections in which Negroes have found the racial stakes to be highest and for which they have there-

88

fore turned out in the greatest numbers, have also been *the most hotly contested elections* in which the turnout of white voters has been highest as well. This indicates that Winston-Salem has reached the position where important differences on racial questions inevitably force themselves into closely contested races. The nature of the white electorate and the size of the Negro electorate no longer permit candidates in such races (1) to differ merely on the question of who is the more intransigent where Negro demands are involved, or (2) to avoid race controversies and thus remain indistinguishable on racial questions to white and Negro voters alike. At the same time there is by no means so firm a consensus on the need for better treatment for Negroes that candidates are likely to compete to see who can make the most lavish promises to Negro voters. Race has taken its place with a number of other highly controversial issues which must be handled gingerly, for votes are to be lost whichever way the candidate turns.

The rate of turnout of Negro voters has followed the same curve as that of white voters, gradually increasing with each election. The birth and growth of an effective Republican Party in Winston has given the city more vigorously contested elections and—perhaps as important as the increase in the *degree* of competition—elections in which competition is more sharply *structured* than ever before. The increase in white voting can be attributed in large part to these factors. The increase in the rate of Negro voting represents a response to the same factors and also to greater organizational efforts, principally by white and Negro Democrats. There also is evidence of the gradual political maturation of Negro voters, who have exercised voting rights for little more than a decade and a half. And the increased voting rate indicates that the Negro voter sees a greater incentive to vote than ever before.

The higher rate of white voting means that the greatly expanded Negro vote (it increased by 71 per cent over the four elections) has remained between 25 and 30 per cent of the total vote in each election. Winston-Salem Negroes, constituting 37 per cent of the total population, 34 per cent of the voting-age population, and 30 per cent of the total number of registered voters, have cast an average of 27 per cent of the total votes cast in the last four mayoralty elections. The Negro vote has thus "held up" well—better in fact than one might have expected in view of the socioeconomic disadvantage of the Negro population. The greater stake Negroes see in political participation is a compensating factor.

There are few cities in the United States in which Negroes constitute a larger share of the actual electorate than Winston-Salem. Hence Winston-Salem is ideally suited for testing many of the assumptions on which the "do it yourself with the ballot" argument is based.

The rate of Negro voting in Greenville cannot be determined precisely. Negro dwelling units are so interspersed throughout the precincts and wards of the city that it is impossible to arrive at statistics comparable to those presented for Winston-Salem. But a fairly reliable estimate can be obtained by comparing the voting in the four Greenville precincts which contain significant concentrations of Negro voters with that in all-white precincts, and by correlating these data with the observations of Negro leaders and poll officials in precincts where most of the registered Negro voters are enrolled.

The Republican Party has not been a factor in local Greenville elections. Contests have been limited to Democratic primaries and the rate of turnout has been, almost without exception, extremely low. In the 1961 primary for city offices, a better than average turnout brought 27 per cent of the city's registered voters (16 per cent of those twenty-one years of age and over) to the polls. But in the ward with the highest concentration of Negro voters (42.2 per cent of the ward total) only 15 per cent of those registered voted. The population of this ward (the Fifth), both Negro and white, ranks lowest in the city for those socioeconomic variables correlated with voting rates; and this partially explains the lower turn-out. Information supplied by Negro leaders indicates, however, that many Negro voters chose to stay at home because they concluded the choice being offered was not, in terms of their political interests, a real one. The two candidates seeking the Democratic nomination were indistinguishable on race issues. Fewer than 10 per cent of the registered Negroes voted.[19]

Spirited election contests have occurred in some state and national elections. Greenville voters have shown no reluctance in the last decade to vote for "conservative" Republican candidates against "liberal" Democrats. In the 1960 presidential election Richard M. Nixon garnered 68.1 per cent of the vote cast in Greenville, and religion was only one factor contributing to his strength. The fact that he was the more conservative of the two candidates appears to be at least as important. A Republican, William Workman, challenged the incumbent Democratic Senator Johnston in 1962, and the parties' shares of the vote in Greenville were virtually the same as they were in the 1960 presidential election. Workman trounced Johnston in Greenville, gaining 68.2 per cent of the vote. These elections are of particular interest here because Negroes in each saw a genuine difference between the candidates. Kennedy wore the mantle of Roosevelt. Johnston was not a flam-

---

[19] The Democratic mayoralty nominee was not opposed, as usual, in the 1961 and 1963 general elections. Only thirty-three voters cast ballots in one mayoralty election a decade ago. Awareness of this provided fertile soil for a rumor started on the day of the 1961 general election. From sources unknown came the word that the NAACP was organizing a mass write-in effort to elect a Negro mayor, capitalizing on the extremely low rate of voting. The rumor spread throughout the city and in the afternoon polling stations were swamped as white voters responded to the call. An all-time high turnout for city general elections resulted. Fewer than fifty Negroes voted and there were no write-ins.

ing civil rights liberal; but beside Workman, the Columbia newspaper columnist who had made something of a reputation for himself as a staunch and articulate segregationist, and whose book, *The Case For The South*, could only alienate Negro voters, he looked quite good indeed. A greater percentage of Negroes voted in these two elections than in any other in Greenville up until 1964. A comparison of the two-party distribution in precincts having large numbers of Negroes with the distribution in all-white precincts gives us some indication of the patterns of Negro voting.[20]

TABLE 9

PERCENTAGE, BY PRECINCTS, OF THE TWO-PARTY VOTE CAST FOR DEMO-
CRATIC CANDIDATES IN THE PRESIDENTIAL ELECTION, 1960, AND IN THE
SENATORIAL ELECTION, 1962, GREENVILLE, S.C.

Precincts	For Kennedy	For Johnston
Group A precincts (Negroes 15% of registered voters, or more)	51.4	59.1
Group B precincts (Negroes 8%–15% of registered voters)	48.8	52.1
Group C precincts (Negroes 4% of registered voters or less)	29.6	28.7

There is no basis for assuming that in the precincts with a high concentration of Negroes the white vote divided itself between the two parties in the same way as it did in pre-

[20] We know that the white vote went heavily for Nixon and Workman respectively, and that the Negro vote went overwhelmingly for Kennedy and Johnston. The former can be seen in an examination of all-white precincts in the city. Discussion with Negro leaders in Greenville and an analysis of the vote in all-Negro precincts in Columbia and Charleston indicate that Negroes gave very large majorities to the Democratic candidates in each election. Greenville has no all-Negro precincts.

dominantly white precincts. On the contrary, we know that it did not. Nixon and Workman were strongest in the new middle-class areas of Greenville, where a desire to vote for the more conservative candidate rather than a sense of loyalty to the Democratic party was decisive. White voters in the older sections of the city and in rural areas outside the city, in contrast, apparently felt a stronger pull from traditional Democratic loyalties, and gave a larger measure of support to the Democratic candidates. And these older sections of Greenville happen to be those with pockets of Negro population, while the newer sections are all-white. Careful analysis of this data, together with data from other elections, from interviews with Negro and white leaders, and from a city-wide survey of Negro voters, indicates the following: (1) About 60 per cent of the registered Negro voters went to the polls in the 1960 presidential election, and Negroes made up approximately 11 to 12 per cent of the actual electorate. In the Johnston-Workman election they constituted less than 10 per cent of the actual electorate. (2) The Negro voting rate in most other elections up to 1964 was far lower. The general lack of competition on the local level, the loosely defined nature of such competition when it occurred, and the almost total absence of significant differences among competing white candidates on racial questions had produced an extremely low Negro vote in municipal elections, generally less than 10 per cent of the total. Registered Negroes were motivated to vote only in state and national elections, but even here the turnout was low, under 35 per cent of the registered voters (with the exception of the 1960 presidential and the 1962 senatorial elections). (3) In elections in which significant numbers have gone to the polls, Negro voting in Greenville has been bloc voting, with the preferred candidates receiving margins of 9 to 1 and better from Negro voters.[21] In Greenville as throughout the

[21] The relative importance of organization, communication, and coincidence of interest in creating this cohesion will be discussed in Chapter V.

South, Negro voters demonstrate an awareness of even the most minute differences in the positions of candidates on racial questions.

The year 1964 brought important changes to the pattern of Negro electoral participation in Greenville. First the number of registered Negroes in the city was doubled, largely through the efforts of the Greenville City and County Voters Crusade. The Greenville project was part of a South-wide campaign, directed by the NAACP, to register Negroes. For the first time, then, Negroes were numerically significant in electoral politics. Then in June 1964, a Negro attorney sought the Democratic nomination for one of the eleven state house seats from Greenville county. He ran last in a field of eighteen, and his 3,487 votes were nearly 7,000 fewer than the total of the last successful candidate. Analysis indicates that about one white voter in ten gave the Negro candidate a vote, and that this accounted for nearly half of his total vote. Only 25 per cent of the registered Negroes cast *valid* ballots. But this is not a fair indication of Negro participation, for many ballots cast by Negroes were invalidated by the South Carolina "full slate" law. In multimember constituencies, a voter must use all his votes—must, that is, cast a vote for each seat—or have his ballot thrown out. In this election, Negroes were, in effect, required to give ten votes to white men to have one vote count for their candidate. Many voted only for the Negro candidate and hence their ballots were thrown out. Between 1,800 and 2,000 ballots cast by Negroes were thus invalidated. In one precinct, the Negro candidate lost 51 of the 52 votes cast for him, in this manner.

The results of the November 3, 1964, voting give us a clearer picture of the level of participation which Greenville Negroes can now sustain. Greenville's Negro voters—as a result of realignment in late 1963—are concentrated in seven precincts. They constitute at least 40 per cent of the total in each precinct, but there are substantial numbers of whites in all seven. The remaining thirteen precincts are all-white or very nearly all-white. Comparison of voting in these two groups of precincts, together with the knowledge that no Negro leader in Greenville publicly endorsed Goldwater and that the several all-Negro precincts in the state went for Johnson by margins of between 20 and 40 to 1 (one Negro precinct in Atlanta surpassed this, voting against Goldwater 4000 to 4) enables us to determine fairly precisely the level of Negro voting. Probably between 3,200 and 3,400 Negroes —about 60 per cent of those eligible to vote—cast valid

TABLE 10

PERCENTAGE OF THE VOTE CAST FOR JOHNSON AND GOLDWATER, 1964 PRESIDENTIAL ELECTION, GREENVILLE, S.C.

Precincts	For Johnson	For Goldwater
Group X precincts (Negroes 6% of registered voters or less)	24.9	75.1
Group Y precincts Negroes 40% of registered voters or more)	82.2	17.8

ballots. Negroes thus comprised between 17 and 19 per cent of the actual electorate. Had their votes simply been subtracted, at least three Democratic candidates for the state house of representatives would have been defeated by Republican opponents. Had Negroes voted as solidly Republican in the state house contests as they did Democratic, the entire delegation would have been Republican. This was the first election in which Negro voters in Greenville could claim a balance-of-power role. Although the 1964 elections saw Greenville Negroes emerge as something more than a cipher in electoral politics, their position remains very weak, and there is little chance that it can be significantly strengthened in the short run.

Organization. Negro leaders in both Winston and Greenville are acutely aware of the role of organization in achieving maximum effectiveness in electoral politics. The extent, structure, and purposes of organization, however, are quite different in the two cities.

The primary objective of organization in Winston is *manipulation* of an existing vote. Greenville Negroes remain in the process of *establishing* a vote to manipulate. Registration activity, of course, is still being conducted in Winston-Salem. The local NAACP chapter, Democratic precinct officials, and the Urban League of Winston-Salem are periodically active. But with over 60 per cent of the eligible voters already registered, gains from such activity are marginal. Negro leaders concentrate on (1) getting registered voters to vote, (2) securing concessions from candidates in return for votes, and (3) promoting maximum cohesion in the Negro vote. Nine precincts, accounting for over 90 per cent of the Negro inhabitants of Winston, are organized by Negro Democrats. Republicans have paper organizations in several of these Negro precincts. Most of the Negro precinct chairmen and committees limit their activities to such things as making cars available on election day. In several precincts, however, Democratic chairmen have begun to apply some of the more rigorous techniques of precinct electoral activity. Systematic attempts are made to canvass all Democratic voters in the precinct, urging them to vote for particular candidates and arranging to provide transportation to the polls. The county Democratic Party in Winston, like its counterparts in a number of rim-South areas, has begun to see in the growing Negro vote one of its largest and most dependable sources of political strength. Money is being provided no longer to buy votes but to support the organizational activity of Negro Democrats. A leading Democratic politician in Winston said:

Republicans make a lot of talk about our buying votes in East Winston [where most of the city's Negroes live]. This is nonsense but I will say this. If we got as much in return in white precincts as we do for the money we spend in Negro precincts, we would do very well indeed.

James Wilson observed that strong party organization, considered not long ago to be *passe*, has been revived because of the movement of Negroes in large numbers into northern cities.[22] The socioeconomic position of Negroes and the discrimination to which they have been subjected have given them an interest in government jobs, services, and favors quite beyond that of most whites. Winston-Salem Negroes do not have what could be called strong party organization; but in Winston as in many other rim-South cities such as Richmond, Raleigh, and Durham, both the rewards of organization and the need for it are such that Negroes have done much more than their white counterparts.

Unlike Negroes in a number of other southern cities, Winston-Salem Negroes have no peak organization to give central direction to their activity in electoral politics. Durham's Committee on Negro Affairs is one of the more successful of the peak organizations. Theoretically a peak organization like CONA should augment the effectiveness of Negro activity in electoral politics. Competing white candidates can be called to present their views on racial issues at a central meeting. Endorsements made by the organization should carry added authority because these are ratified by all major race-advancement groups in the subcommunity. The peak organization, in short, should provide a central and recognized vehicle for scrutinizing and endorsing candidates and for working for their election. In Winston the process has been much more loosely structured. A number of groups are engaged. Most are personal vehicles for active, energetic, and influential leaders. In two precincts the key persons are

[22] James Wilson, "How The Northern Negro Uses His Vote," *The Reporter*, March 31, 1960, pp. 20—22.

a Democratic precinct chairman and his wife, who on their own decide whom the precinct (their) organization will support. They have succeeded in building a core of workers who generally can be counted on to work for the candidate(s) whom they endorse. In another large precinct an organization called the West Winston Civic League Auxiliary, also under husband and wife direction, scrutinizes the pronouncements of candidates, invites them to present their views before the Auxiliary, and makes endorsements. A Negro labor leader and a few close associates have for some time been actively engaged in promoting the cause of candidates considered favorable to Negro interests. They have recently attempted to broaden their base by forming a political club called the Democratic Voters Club. Individual Negro leaders, including the incumbent Negro alderman and his predecessor, are men whose support is sought. Of late, halting steps have been taken by Democratic Party leaders to augment the importance of the Negro Democratic precinct committees, and of the Negro precinct chairmen as a group. Some Negro Democrats have sought over the last decade to organize the nine Negro precincts as a suborganization within the county Democratic Party. No formal action has been taken. Now white Democratic leaders are more actively and consistently seeking to enlist the support of the Negro precinct committees for organization-backed candidates in the primaries and for the party candidates in the general elections. In so doing they increasingly treat the nine Negro precinct units as a *de facto* suborganization.

The center of gravity in the Forsyth County Democratic Party, throughout the postwar era, has rested with economic dominants who are generally "moderate" on racial matters. Negro leaders entered into an informal alliance with the county organization and this alliance is evident in the endorsements made by the Negro precinct committees. In the 1961 mayoralty primary the precinct committee in a large Negro precinct initially decided to support candidate X. His views on race relations seemed "better" to the precinct leaders. The precinct chairman, however, subsequently was asked by the county chairman to support candidate Y. The precinct committee reconsidered and gave formal though unenthusiastic support to the latter candidate. More was to be gained, the precinct chairman said, by remaining loyal to the organization. Negro support not infrequently is as essential in Winston as, for example, in Atlanta to the election of the organization's choice of candidates. Both parties to this alliance have found it to their liking.

In summary, the function of securing concessions from candidates in exchange for electoral support is not being performed by a Negro peak organization, either all-purpose like Durham's CONA or electoral only like Atlanta's Negro Voters League. Winston-Salem Negroes lack a single strong, community-wide organization to perform this function. In the absence of such it has fallen to a number of individuals and groups who at times act after consultation, at times quite independently. With few exceptions, however, they have been united when confronted with competing white candidates. The widely shared criteria for selection, the generally clear differences between the candidates, and a common alliance with the moderate faction of the white Democratic leadership has assured this. Negro leaders recognize, however, that the fragmentation of organization is potentially dangerous.

Greenville Negro leaders confront a different problem. They cannot be primarily concerned with manipulating an existing electorate because they are still involved in building one large enough to count in local politics. Certainly the successful registration activity of 1964—which produced a doubling of the Negro electorate in the city—will lead to a gradual transformation of Greenville voting organizations as their leaders for the first time possess significant electoral sanctions. But Greenville Negro politicians remain much more oriented toward registration than their Winston counterparts.

Over the last decade, five organizations (only two of which are still active in Greenville) have worked to register Negroes. The first was the Greenville chapter of the Progressive Democrats, an organization formed in South Carolina in the early 1940's when Negroes were barred from participation in the regular Democratic party activity. The Progressive Democrats supported the national Democratic party but opposed state Democrats. In 1948 the Progressive Democrats sent delegates to the Democratic national convention, unsuccessfully challenging the regular state Democratic slate. They attempted the same thing in 1956 and again failed.[23] The Greenville chapter limited its activities to attempts to register Negroes. In July 1957 a chapter of the Palmetto State Voters Association was formed.[24] Working with limited resources it made little progress. Then in 1958 the Greenville Committee on Social and Political Action was established, again with the main objective of expanding the number of Negro voters. With these organizations no longer functioning, the Greenville Non-Partisan Voter Registration Committee appeared on the scene in 1962 to "conduct an intensive campaign to register every eligible Negro in the county." It tried without success to get funds from the Southern Regional Council administered Voter Education Project; and as it lost momentum in late 1963, still another voting organization was formed. The Greenville City and County Voters Crusade, while locally led, was established as part of a South-wide NAACP registration drive. The Crusade's campaign was better coordinated and more extensive than that of its predecessors, and it did have rather dramatic success.

[23] Howard Quint, *Profile in Black and White* (Washington, D.C., 1958), pp. 6–7.

[24] The Palmetto State Voters Association was organized in 1954 to promote Negro activity in electoral politics. It has had little success. (See Quint, *ibid.*, pp. 80–81.)

Three basic problems have frustrated much of the activity of these voting organizations. (1) The lack of sufficient leadership talent is painfully obvious: the same nucleus of leaders staffed most of the protest and voting organizations. During the last decade a very small group (with several dropping out and several being added) conducted all of the voter registration activity. These people simply changed hats. The chairman of one organization became vice-chairman of the next. (2) The extremely low socioeconomic position of the Negro population in Greenville compounds the work of the voting organizations. (3) The absence of the structured competition meaningful to most potential Negro voters has discouraged many from registering and voting—a feeling of "What difference does it make?" is prevalent. Organized activity to register more Negroes still goes on and early in 1964 these efforts began achieving fairly significant advances.

Electoral activity designed to deliver the Negro vote in exchange for concessions necessarily has been limited in Greenville. White candidates in local elections have never really sought Negro support. Potential gains are too small and potential losses too large. Negro leaders stated that overtures by white candidates in local elections have been limited to occasional telephone calls to a few prominent Negroes. The candidate would say that if elected he would work hard to represent the interests of all Greenvillians, and that he would be fair in dealings with Negroes. Some effort apparently has been made behind the scenes by representatives of certain candidates in state-wide races. Johnston supporters approached several Negro leaders in Greenville in 1962 and asked them if they could help the Senator; but there has been very little of this and Negro voters have had little incentive to work for the election of a particular candidate. The Republican and Democratic party organizations in the county are "lily white." The only exceptions to the rule of Negro exclusion are the one or two Negroes serving as Democratic party workers in voting boxes near Negro residential areas.

Both the Progressive Democrats and the Palmetto State Voters Association did endorse candidates and urge Negro voters to support the recommended candidates. Immediately before important elections over the last eight years, meetings have been held in a Negro church, sponsored by an informally organized group of Negro leaders. Negroes attending these meetings have been presented with a slate of recommended candidates. Attendance generally has been light, fewer than 150 persons. The sponsors have attempted to get interested persons from all major Negro residential areas in the county to attend, on the assumption that these persons would then go back to their home areas and spread the word. The procedure is so informal that its effectiveness cannot easily be determined.

Greenville ranks next to lowest of all southern cities over 50,000 population in the index of potential political participation. And the city ranks low indeed in terms of the structure and level of organization for electoral politics. Negroes in other deep-South cities such as Mobile, Savannah, and Birmingham are more active and better organized than are their Greenville counterparts.

EFFECTIVENESS OF PARTICIPATION
IN ELECTORAL POLITICS

Differences in the degree of acceptance given Negro participation in electoral politics, demographic differences among Negro populations, resulting differences in the size of the Negro electorate, and the level and structure of organization designed to secure and then to effectively utilize the franchise, mean varying levels of effectiveness in Negro electoral activity. Winston-Salem Negroes first elected one of their number to the city Board of Aldermen in 1947. After this election the city Democratic leadership drew new ward lines, limiting Negroes (who constitute nearly 40 per cent of the city's population) to a majority status in only one of eight wards; but, significantly, white leaders did not resort to at-large elections of aldermen, as many other southern cities did when confronted with a growing Negro vote. The alderman from the all-Negro South Third Ward thus has been free from white electoral sanctions. An important point often neglected in discussing the effectiveness of Negro representatives in southern municipal governments is the extent of their dependence upon whites for appointment or election. Winston's Negro alderman, with only Negro constituents, has been a free agent. The incumbent has not been required to compromise his position in exchange for white electoral support, and this has strengthened his position among Negroes. The Winston-Salem Board of Aldermen has had Negro representation continuously since 1947. Population movement and political pressure finally succeeded in 1965 in opening a second aldermanic position to Winston Negroes.

The size of the Negro vote has compelled white candidates to recognize Negro claims. According to the popular model of voting and democratic government, politicians constantly seek to build up majority coalitions by granting recognition to the political demands of different groups of voters. This model is a good one. And in the urban-South, where any overtures to Negroes by white candidates or elected officials will necessarily alienate at least some white voters, most candidates and officials must be convinced that gains from Negro voters will override the inevitable losses before they will show themselves to be receptive to Negro interests. In the short run things are not always this rational, but in the long run as Mr. Dooley might have said, ideology "follows th' iliction returns." The Negro vote in Winston has on occasion been decisive in contests between whites for aldermanic posts, for the state senate and house of representatives, for county commissioner, and for other municipal and county positions.[25]

The Negro vote has had its greatest impact in city-wide mayoralty elections. As shown in Table 11, Winston-Salem is in the unusual if not unique position of being a southern city which between 1957 and 1963 had mayors who received only a minority of the white vote.

TABLE 11

DIVISION OF WHITE AND NEGRO VOTE FOR REPUBLICAN AND DEMOCRATIC CANDIDATES, MAYORALTY ELECTIONS, WINSTON-SALEM, 1957–1961

	Percentage of white vote	Percentage of Negro vote	Winner's margin	Margin from the Negro vote
1957				
Kurfees	42	96	534	2,150
Morrow	58	4		
1959				
Kurfees	47	92	1,882	2,390
Morrow	53	8		
1961				
Surratt	42	83	622	2,727
Darr	58	17		

Even in the 1963 mayoralty election, when the margin between the Republican loser and the Democratic winner was greater than in the three previous elections, the defeated Republican candidate would have won had he polled 55 per cent of the Negro vote instead of the 7.2 per cent he actually received (see Table 12). A shift by 2,295 Negro voters, 47.8 per cent of the total, would have altered the results.

[25] Only 10 per cent of the Forsyth county Negro population lives outside the eight wards of Winston-Salem. Outside the city the county is only 6 per cent Negro. Negro strength in county-wide races then is considerably below what it is in city elections. Negroes are only 18.5 per cent of the county's registered voters.

TABLE 12

DIVISION OF WHITE AND NEGRO VOTE FOR REPUBLICAN AND DEMOCRATIC
CANDIDATES, MAYORALTY ELECTION, WINSTON-SALEM, 1963

	Percentage of white vote	Percentage of Negro vote	Winner's margin	Margin from the Negro vote
Benton	52.0	92.8	4,589	4,090
Booker	48.0	7.2		

The Winston-Salem white population over the last decade has accommodated itself to the reality of the important Negro vote. A white candidate can appear at Negro meetings, can make appeals for Negro electoral support, and can, within carefully defined limits, publicly support Negro demands in such touchy areas as school integration and the integration of swimming pools—he can do these things and still win majority support from white electors. This happened in the 1963 mayoralty election. Negroes, of course, are not just another political interest group in Winston-Salem, and even cautious overtures to Negro voters will result in the loss of some white support. But the level of Negro participation in electoral politics and the white reaction to that participation have permitted Negroes to enter the pluralistic balance that prevails in Winston-Salem politics.

One white politician played an especially important role in the entrance of Negroes into electoral politics in Winston-Salem, and in the development of their position. His story should be told here. Marshall Kurfees was, from 1949 to 1961, Winston-Salem's mayor. Of lower-class origins and with little formal education, Kurfees had tried frequently before 1949 to gain election to public office, and had failed consistently. As a young man Kurfees had served a prison sentence for a minor crime, and he maintained a reputation for something less than sobriety. It is not surprising, then, that when he entered the Democratic mayoralty primary in 1949, the city's economic leaders looked on him with disfavor. Not only did he lack "dignity" but he did not seem "safe." For he appeared to have been more than slightly touched by southern populism. The city's Negro voters were even less enthusiastic about Kurfees' candidacy—for lower-class southerners generally are not the Negro's strongest allies. Kurfees' victory in the 1949 primary represented a revolt of the little (white) man. Once in office, however, he followed a course which alienated the people who elected him and attracted the city's business elite and Negroes. He secured the support of the former by being "safe"—for example, solidly anti-union. Kurfees' attitude toward Negroes closely paralleled that of the late Earl Long. Kurfees says, "I've always thought of niggers as just people." His approach to Negroes represents a curious blend of paternalism and genuine respect. He promised that if elected his door would always be open to Negroes as well as whites, and it always was. Moreover, any event in East Winston from a state Masons' convention to a dog show could count on the Mayor's presence. He frequently visited Negro leaders at their homes. And Kurfees did not stop with gestures. With his blessing, and partly through his activity, Negroes were added to the city's fire department; recreational facilities in Negro neighborhoods were greatly improved; and, most significantly, the participation of Winston-Salem in the Federal urban renewal program (in Winston-Salem principally a renewal of Negro neighborhoods) was achieved. In all this Kurfees had the support of the city's business elite who were anxious to avoid the serious racial tension that could curtail the city's growth and prosperity. It earned for Kurfees the epithet "nigger's mayor" in poor white sections—and the overwhelming support of Winston Negroes. With the same kind of coalition that kept Hartsfield mayor of Atlanta, Kurfees managed to get re-elected five times, although there were two occasions when defeat seemed certain.

Kurfees appointed Negroes to all city boards and commissions (housing, urban renewal, recreation, the school board, the city-county planning board, etc.). Winston became the only North Carolina city with "across the board" Negro representation. Militant Negroes complained (rightly) that Kurfees' initial appointees were conservative leaders and that, with only one Negro to a board, representation remained token.

Kurfees decided not to seek re-election in 1961. The city's Democratic leadership (including Kurfees himself) concluded that the mayor's close identification with the Negro vote had brought the party to the brink of defeat. There was no desire to change policies—only faces. Kurfees had presided over a major transition in the relations of Negroes and whites in Winston-Salem, and in the process he had been badly scarred. But his legacy in terms of the structure of Negro participation in electoral politics remained. He did yeoman's service in getting whites to accept a fairly high level of Negro political activity.

In 1963 three Negroes were appointed to the twelve-man city-county school board, and a second Negro was appointed to the seven-man recreation commission. These appointments represented the first steps by this southern city toward giving Negroes more than token representation on municipal government bodies.

Negro politicians in Winston-Salem in 1964, then, held a position of considerable strength. Behind them was a large electorate with a fairly high level of political consciousness, a decade of representation on all major city government bodies, and acceptance as a major bloc in the city's Democratic coalition.

Greenville Negroes have had much less success. No Negro holds elective office in the city, and the only Negro to seek office in 1964—the first in other words who could have benefited from the expanded Negro electorate—met overwhelming defeat. Greenville Negroes still are not a significant electoral force. The Democratic and Republican party organizations exclude them, and city and county government bodies are all white.

It appears that Greenville Negroes are simply confronted by too many obstacles to effectively participate in politics. The higher birth rate and lower life expectancy of Negroes in the city has meant that they make up considerably less than 30 per cent of the voting-age population, although they do constitute 30 per cent of the total population. Their low socioeconomic position in fact drops their share of the potential electorate still further. Operating in a political climate strongly hostile to any Negro participation beyond voting, and lacking a large reservoir of leadership talent (which is even more vital to success in electoral politics, with its continuous, often unspectacular activity, than to success in direct action), Greenville Negroes remain a weak element in election politics. They simply do not have sanctions adequate to force recognition of their interests.

PROTEST ACTIVITY

Like the voting organizations, the protest groups in Winston and Greenville reflect the major differences in the structure of race relations in these two cities. NAACP branches function in both cities, but the Winston branch is far stronger. At one time in the mid-1950's it ranked among the top (in membership) for cities of comparable size. The branch reached a membership high of over 1,000 but has since declined. Membership fluctuated between 450 and 750 in the 1960-1963 period. The Greenville NAACP branch has never had more than 309 members; in 1963 its membership stood at 232. The risks attendant membership in Winston are not so great, of course, as in Greenville. While many schoolteachers and other vulnerables in Winston remain reluctant to join, or if they join to have their membership made public, the wife of the man who was for most whites racial protest incarnate taught and continues to teach in the city's public schools.[26] NAACP membership is notoriously low among the lowest socioeconomic groups and these constitute a much larger proportion of the Negro population in Greenville than in Winston-Salem. Monthly branch meetings in both cities are poorly attended, and more than twenty-five persons at any one of these meetings constitutes a crowd. The executive committees of the branches carry out whatever work is done.

A unit of the NAACP Commandoes, a youth organization, was established in Winston in 1963. Greenville has none. There is a college NAACP branch at Winston-Salem State College and these students provided much of the manpower for the 1960 sit-ins in that city and for the 1963 demonstrations. The nearest Negro college is 100 miles from Greenville, and the city's Negroes are thus cut off from this source of "inspiration and perspiration." It is no coincidence that such cities as Greensboro and Durham, North Carolina, with their Negro colleges, pioneered in large-scale direct action demonstrations.

Greenville had a chapter of the Congress of Racial Equality in 1959 and 1960. This chapter was dissolved because its leadership was simply the leadership of the local NAACP wearing new hats. The same people staffed both. A CORE chapter was first organized in Winston-Salem in June 1963, by Negroes who felt that the local NAACP branch was not doing enough.

In general, the protest organizations in Winston-Salem have been able to draw upon a large reservoir of leadership talent. Although protest activity has not been as extensive in Winston as in some other southern cities, the resources are

[26] The Florida state NAACP president in 1964 was a public-school teacher.

there. Protest organizations in Greenville have been and remain weak, poorly financed, and largely inactive.

I have referred in this chapter to "the setting for race leadership." This concept of a "leadership setting" is based on a number of assumptions. Central among them is the assumption that major situational variables shape a given leadership structure and hence must be understood if the leadership is to be understood. The setting for Negro political leadership in the urban South includes the demographic characteristics of the Negro populations of the various cities, white attitudes toward Negroes and the place of Negroes in society, patterns of segregation in the various public institutions, and the level and the structure of Negro participation in race-advancement activity. Other facets of the biracial structure could have been introduced but the above are central.

It would be foolish indeed to begin a comparative study in Negro political leadership in the urban South without recognizing the rich complexity in variables determining the structure of leadership in each city. Specifically, there are major differences in the leadership structure in Winston-Salem and Greenville which extend beyond the capacity of Negro leadership to change. Negro leaders in Winston operate in a vastly more permissive race relations situation than do their Greenville counterparts. They bring far greater resources to the struggle and can maneuver much more freely. Negro leaders in Winston have achieved community recognition of their right to political action within a broad area; Negro leaders in Greenville have yet to achieve this and inevitably must be more preoccupied with "means-goals" such as registering voters, building an electorate. In brief, because racial conditions in Greenville are different from those in Winston-Salem, Negro leaders in the two cities pursue different goals by different means, with quite different patterns of interaction with white leaders and the white community.

Part II

THE STRUCTURE OF
RACE LEADERSHIP

CHAPTER III

Selection of Race Leadership

THERE has been more than a little ambiguity about the concept of leadership. Agreement that the political leader is a decision maker, affecting the structure of political activity and policy choice in the area in which he operates, does not end this ambiguity. The difficulty follows from the fact that all leadership—political, economic, and so on—is conditioned by a given setting. In the highly institutionalized and routinized areas of decision making to be found in such large bureaucratic structures as modern corporations, the leader (i.e., decision maker) is an individual selected by co-optation, occupying part of the "commanding heights" of the organization's hierarchy. People below him follow his directives not because they necessarily think them correct or because they are attached to him but because they will lose their jobs if they do not. In marked contrast, in the highly unstructured activity of the street mob, the leader may simply be one who by the force of his personality or forensic skills wins the acclaim of the crowd which then catapults him into leadership. His period of leadership may last only a few minutes, coming to a sudden end when he loses contact with the wishes of the crowd. A school board chairman appointed by the mayor of the city is a political leader when making politically relevant decisions (for example, those affecting the level of integration). But in the mechanism of selection and in his relationship to those affected by his decisions, he occupies a position quite different from that of the mayor who appointed him or the head of a white citizens council who opposes his decision to desegregate a school. All three differ from the economic leader whose views on school integration carry weight because the corporation he directs dominates the economy of the city, and because the nature of his position and his wealth (as well as his economic power) give him social prominence. In brief, political leaders share the function of making politically relevant decisions, but differ in a number of important respects, some of the more significant of which follow from differences in the processes by which the leaders are *selected*. Selection includes (1) the formal mechanism by which the leader is chosen; (2) the skills, socioeconomic and institutional positions, and so on, necessary for leadership; and (3) the leader's relationship to those affected by his decisions. The third factor encompasses not only the extent to which "followers" determine who their leaders shall be and the content of this leadership, but also the source of the leader's authority.[1] To ask questions about the selection of Negro political leadership is to ask some very basic questions about the nature of that leadership and about the larger subject of Negro politics.

RACE AS THE ISSUE

Ethnic group leadership is, by definition, concerned with promoting the interests of the ethnic group. It exists because

[1] See in this regard Weber's classic statement in "Politics As a Vocation," in H. Gerth and C. Wright Mills, eds. *From Max Weber: Essays in Sociology* (New York, 1958), pp. 78–79. Weber refers to "three inner justifications, hence basic legitimizations of domination." These are "traditional domination exercised by the patriarch"; "the authority of the extraordinary and personal *gift of grace* (charisma), the absolutely personal devotion and personal confidence in revelation, heroism, or other qualities of individual leadership"; and "domination by virtue of 'legality,' by virtue of the belief in the validity of legal statute and functional competence based on rationally created *rules*. In this case, obedience is expected in discharging statutory obligations."

the ethnic group is conscious of itself as competing for certain scarce values with other ethnic groups. The sharper the competition and the greater the estrangement, rejection, and isolation of the ethnic group in the political system, the more firmly will such leadership be identified with the interests of the ethnic group *as* ethnic group. The experience in the United States has been that as ethnic groups are accepted, they have increasingly fewer interests ethnically defined, and their leaders become differentiated by nonethnic considerations: they become Republican and Democratic leaders; upper-class, middle-class, and lower-class leaders; business, social welfare, labor, and intellectual leaders. The extent of this differentiation is a reliable index of the ethnic group's acceptance. Frazier has noted that with the transition of Negro Americans from "a mass of inarticulate, illiterate, rural folk" to a group which "has acquired education and developed diverse economic and cultural interests," a functional leadership has developed. But Frazier recognized that his functional leaders still are judged by their "stands on the integration of the Negro into particular spheres of American life." [2] The fact remains that Negroes, one of the first ethnic groups to arrive in the United States, have been the least accepted. Negroes who are political leaders are *Negro* political leaders. Negro leadership in the United States has been and remains issue leadership, and the one issue that matters is race advancement.

FROM OUT-GROUP TO IN-GROUP SELECTION

The dominant form of Negro political leadership in the South from the end of Reconstruction to World War II has been variously described as "Uncle Tom-ism," as "conservative" or "accommodating" leadership. The "Uncle Tom" was a leader (i.e., a decision maker) because the white community, with its dominant political, economic, and social power, desig-

[2] E. Franklin Frazier, *The Negro in the United States* (New York, 1957).

nated him a leader and supported his decisions, and because his own subcommunity was unable to support an alternative form of leadership and hence deferred to the authority of the white community. This, then, was political leadership based on the support and sanctions of a dominant out-group. To become a leader in such circumstances required, of course, a certain measure of prominence and the possession of certain necessary skills; the main criterion for selection, however, was the acceptability of the leader-candidate's definition of the position that Negroes should occupy in society. But acceptable to whom? Acceptability was defined by whites. Events of the last two decades, however, have enabled southern Negroes to sustain their own political leadership, particularly in the urban areas of the South. The basic criterion for selection remains the same, but the definition must now be acceptable to Negroes.

The transition is not as complete as the above might indicate. The dominant position occupied by whites in the power structure of every southern city still enables them to "make" leaders to a certain (though diminishing) extent. For example, Negroes appointed to the various commissions and boards of Winston-Salem's city government in the early and mid-1950's with few exceptions were selected because their views on race relations were quite acceptable to whites. They made binding commitments or decisions for Winston-Salem Negroes in that the authority of the city government was imparted to their decisions. Though Militants complained bitterly about the lack of representation, and argued that the appointeees were "all cut from one cloth" and did not truly represent Winston-Salem Negroes; Negroes by and large did accept them. They were, after all, the first Negroes ever appointed to these positions, and representation in itself seemed of primary importance. The whites selected accommodating Negroes to siphon off discontent (how could Negroes disagree with decisions made by their own representatives?);

and at the same time to achieve acquiescence to the major dimensions of the racial *status quo*. It soon became obvious, however, that Negroes accepting the racial *status quo* found themselves rejected by their own community, and hence of little or no use to whites. With this came a noticeable shift in the kinds of Negroes appointed to city boards and commissions in Winston-Salem. Recent appointments have gone to Negroes considerably less pliable, and who much more actively seek changes in the structure of race relations. This phenomenon can be seen in the composition of the biracial committee in Winston-Salem. The city's current biracial committee, called the Good Will committee, is the fourth to have been appointed. The first was set up in 1960 to meet problems arising from the sit-ins which began in nearby Greensboro and quickly spread to Winston-Salem. The second was established in February 1962, after Winston Negroes tried to integrate the city's skating rink. The third was created in the summer of 1962, after the successful attempt to integrate the city's swimming pools and certain other park facilities. The mayor appointed the current committee shortly after his election in 1963 as fulfillment of a campaign promise. Unlike the first three, this committee was not formed as a merely reflex reaction to a specific racial conflict.

The representation of conservative Negro leaders declined with each committee while the number of more militant leaders greatly increased. Of the ten Negroes on the first committee six represented the most conservative Negro leadership in the city. None of the Negroes on this committee were Militants. Three committee members were on the executive board of the Winston NAACP branch but none of these were actively involved in the protest activities of the branch. None of the ten Negroes on the committee were leaders or participants in the sit-in demonstrations which brought the committee into being. The white leadership, in short, had reached the point where it would enter into formal communication with Negroes, with equal representation for both racial groups. It continued to insist, however, that only reasonably amenable Negroes be brought into the institution for communication. It still assumed that the "good" Negro leaders would be able to carry Negro public opinion with them, if necessary over the opposition of the sit-in leadership, to a compromise solution. Because the biracial committee was a new instrument (the idea, after all, that Negro leaders be given equal representation with white leaders on an important quasi-governmental body was a sharp departure from previous practice), this biracial committee enjoyed some success. But it had become painfully obvious to a number of white leaders by the time the committee's work ended that the only persons in any position to modify protest activity are the leaders of it. In the context of the Winston-Salem biracial structure in the 1960's, any attempt to use conservative Negro leaders to control protest activity is bound to be an exercise in futility.

Consequently, as Table 13 indicates, the representation of Militants has increased and that of Conservatives declined with

TABLE 13

NEGRO REPRESENTATION ON FOUR BIRACIAL COMMITTEES, WINSTON-SALEM, BY STYLE OF LEADERSHIP OF NEGRO REPRESENTATIVES

Style	First committee	Second committee	Third committee	Fourth committee
Conservative	6	1	2	1
Moderates	4	2	3	2
Militant	0	1	5	6

each subsequent committee. The meaning is clear: Even where whites play a formal role in selecting Negroes for governmental boards and biracial commissions, the judgment by Negroes of the acceptability of the leader-candidate's racial views is decisive.

Developments in leadership selection have followed the same general progression in Greenville, but there are important differences. The breakdown of the two-standards system began much later there and has not progressed nearly as far. Historically, the system has been much more rigidly enforced in Greenville than in Winston-Salem. With the *Brown vs. Board of Education* decision in 1954, Greenville, along with almost all other deep-South cities, was hurled into the "great silence," as previously accepted patterns of communication and interaction between white and Negro leaders were rejected.

It had been possible in 1948 to bring together under the auspices of the Greenville Community Council white and Negro political leaders on twelve fact-finding committees. Each committee was concerned with a specific area such as education, welfare, health, transportation, and housing. These committees were established to study in a comprehensive manner conditions affecting the city's Negro citizens. Whites and Negroes on the committees agreed at the outset that "Greenville's biggest problems were not just the business of white people or colored people . . . but everybody's business." [3] More than two hundred white and Negro Greenvillians participated in these studies. The committees reported frankly that in many areas the conditions under which the city's Negroes were living were deplorable and needed immediate improvement. And certain concrete improvements did result from the committees' recommendations: a park for Negroes was opened; lights were installed at school crossings in Negro neighborhoods; additions were made to two Negro schools; the city's newspapers began capitalizing the word Negro and began using courtesy titles before the names of Negro women; plans were made to appoint Negro policemen. And a white member of the project could say:

[3] *Greenville's Big Idea*, a report of the Community Council of Greenville County (May 25, 1950), p. 1.

The best thing about the survey was that it got people together. We didn't know each other well enough. Now we do. Meeting and working together, not as people of two races, but as citizens with a common purpose, has been a release and a relief.[4]

The members of the recreation committee found working together so rewarding that they decided not to disband. The white participants in this project were not, it should be noted, eccentric millionaires, but rather the "pillars of the community." Many were in the public employ. Yet they saw fit to sign their names to a document which declared that race is not a biological reality but rather a social fact; and which strongly condemned and doggedly exposed the inequities of the situation in which Negro Greenvillians found themselves. None of the Negroes involved in the project were publicly associated with protest organizations. There were no NAACP leaders, no Progressive Democrats. The Negroes selected were "safe." They did not demand rights, but instead requested improvements within the framework of "separate but equal" and thanked their white benefactors for small favors. They did get some results. Since whites approved this type of race leadership, Negroes in extremely sensitive positions, such as schoolteachers, could participate.

As long as the two-standards system seemed secure, white leaders could and did support certain welfare improvements for Negroes. After the *Brown* decision, however, any Negro request for improved conditions, no matter how carefully phrased, was suspect as part of an assault on the "southern way of life." When the system was attacked and its existence put in jeopardy, few whites came forward to accept the risks involved in being associated with even the most innocuous (from the standpoint of jeopardizing the system) improvements for Negroes. At once the whole basis of the system of accommodating leadership was swept away. An

[4] *Ibid.*, p. 31.

increase in Negro expectations—to be sure not as sharp in Greenville as elsewhere—coincided with this.

Winston-Salem and the other rim-South cities also experienced a version of the "great silence," but it was not the same. Patterns of race relations in Winston have historically been more permissive, and *Brown* was not seen as nearly so great a threat there. As part of this greater permissiveness, whites had recognized the legitimacy of leadership roles other than those prescribed by the pattern of accommodation before 1954. As a result, *Brown* affected the Negro leadership structure in Winston only in a marginal way: alternate leadership roles had already been accepted, and certain accommodating patterns continued. But the *Brown* decision fell upon a deep South that had no intention of modifying the old biracial system. No alternative leadership roles had been recognized. Changes in Negro expectations throughout the United States had made accommodating leadership of the old order—that is, leadership based on Negro acceptance of the two-standards system—impossible. But the reaction of Greenville whites precluded even such modified forms of accommodating leadership as that provided in Winston-Salem by the Urban League and by the first Negro appointees to city government boards and biracial committees. Virtually every form of Negro leadership was labeled protest leadership by the white community. Direct action was the only weapon that could succeed in this situation, but Greenville Negroes lacked the resources necessary to maintain a large-scale protest movement. It is easier to find men to provide leadership in socially accepted directions than to find those willing and able (in terms, for example, of economic security) to invite the considerable sanctions of the white majority.

A decade after the *Brown* decision there are indications of a major change in the position of Greenville whites in Negro leadership selection. There is now partial recognition of the legitimacy of what we have called "modified" accommodating leadership. This change resulted in part from the gradual erosion of white opposition to certain forms of desegregation. The principal and immediate cause, however, was the wave of direct action demonstrations which swept the South. Fearing that "Greenville will be next," some city leaders turned to negotiations with Negro leaders in the interest of avoiding racial clashes. In May 1963 a biracial committee was formed in Greenville with twenty Negro members and an equal number of whites. This committee was instrumental in achieving the desegregation of eleven lunch counters in the city. Then, in July 1963, the Greater Greenville Chamber of Commerce announced the creation of a permanent biracial committee to "preserve the good reputation of Greenville and the peace and harmony which has prevailed among its citizens." Selection of the Negro representatives was made only after consultation with Negro leaders, and the committee is broadly representative. Greenville still lags far behind Winston-Salem and other outer-South cities in opening the way for new leadership roles recognized as legitimate by both Negroes and whites.

We have noted a shift, at varying rates and with varying degrees of completeness, from "out-group" selected to "in-group" selected leadership. The acceptability of race leadership roles is increasingly being determined by the Negro community rather than by the white. The success of the old style of leadership, that of the "Uncle Tom," was predicated on acceptance of the system of racial segregation. The success of today's Negro leadership in Winston-Salem and Greenville is predicated on the opposition of that leadership to segregation and discrimination in all its forms.

AVAILABILITY

The availability of an individual for a particular leadership role depends upon his possessing certain attributes deemed necessary—both by himself and by those selecting the leader

—to the successful performance of the leadership functions. Not all "available" candidates assume leadership, but only those meeting the demands of the "availability" standard can be considered. At present a woman, because of her sex, is not "available" for the presidency of the United States; nor is a Jew "available" for the presidency of General Motors. Similarly, certain Negroes are not "available" for positions of race leadership.

THE CHANGING STANDARD FOR AVAILABILITY

A major change in the determination of availability has occurred with the shift from out-group to in-group selection. When whites dominated leadership selection, only "respectable" Negroes were considered eligible. That is, the leader-candidate had to be old enough to possess proper maturity, his personal life had to be characterized by the strict observance of the standards of middle-class respectability, and he had to be a long-time resident of the community. He had either to hold a white collar position—preferably in the ministry, but perhaps in small business or in teaching—or else possess a long record of deferential service in a lower position. For example, of the fifteen Negroes appointed to the steering committee of the "Greenville's Big Idea" project in 1949, four were teachers in the city schools, two were doctors, two businessmen, one a minister, and one a social worker. Of the remaining five, two were unemployed women with records of church and philanthropic activity, and three were custodians, each an old and trusted employee with an impeccable personal life. What has happened under the new pattern of in-group selection is that the standards for determining availability have been relaxed or broadened. The central goal now—removal of patterns of discriminatory treatment—is considered of such overriding importance that virtually any Negro possessing sufficient personal ability and offering an acceptable definition of the role of race leader must be considered available. This is not to say that all Negroes acceptable as race spokesmen

123

are available for all leadership positions. College education is necessary, to cite one example, for a Negro to be considered for appointment to the board of education in Winston-Salem. But with in-group selection has come a proliferation of possible leadership roles. A Negro college student would never have been able to attain a leadership position under the old system. Yet in 1960 Carl Matthews, a Winston-Salem State College student, gained considerable prominence and short-term power through his leadership of sit-ins in Winston-Salem. In 1963 Robert Moorman, another college student, became president of the Winston-Salem unit of the NAACP Commandoes—a youth action group—and as such a power whom city officials had to consider.

THE WITHDRAWAL OF THE VULNERABLES
AND THEIR RE-EMERGENCE

Traditional accommodating leadership operated with white approval. It was open, then, to Negroes whose position, principally their economic position, made them particularly vulnerable to sanctions from whites. In both Winston-Salem and Greenville, in fact, Negro leadership was drawn heavily from such vulnerables.[5] The post-World War II "revolution" changed this in both cities, although in somewhat different

[5] We know from other studies that this pattern was the general one. See, for example, Hylan Lewis, *Blackways of Kent* (Chapel Hill, N.C., 1955), p. 245; Gunnar Myrdal, *An American Dilemma* (New York, 1944), p. 769; and Lewis M. Killian and Charles Smith, "Negro Protest Leaders in a Southern Community," *Social Forces*, XXXVIII (March 1960), 253–257. Hylan Lewis discusses the important position occupied by "white men's cooks" in "Kent." Killian and Smith refer to the significant numbers of public employees and other vulnerables among the old leadership of Tallahassee. Myrdal observed that the race relations structure in the South in the 1930's was such that there were few Negro leaders who were not vulnerable to certain kinds of sanctions. We found that public employees were prominent among the old leadership in both Winston-Salem and Greenville.

ways. The initial effect of the revolt in both cities was to drive vulnerables from the leadership ranks.

The structure of Negro political leadership in Winston-Salem was dramatically altered with the unionization activity at the Reynolds plants during and shortly after World War II.[6] New race leadership working through electoral politics, the trade unions and protest organizations largely displaced the old accommodating leadership. This new race leadership was rejected as illegitimate by Winston-Salem whites. The net effect of these developments—the rejection by Negroes of the old accommodating leadership and the rejection by whites of the newer leadership dedicated to the eradication of the old biracial system—was to remove vulnerables from the ranks of race leadership. As an example, the president of Winston-Salem State Teachers College was a key leader before the revolt. His position prevented him, however, from assuming a leadership role strongly rejected by whites.[7]

Beginning in the mid-1950's for reasons which have been discussed above, whites in Winston-Salem began to recognize the legitimacy of certain of the new race leadership roles, and this in turn made possible a re-emergence of the vulnerables. Perhaps the greatest opening has come in the area of electoral politics. In 1947 when the Reverend Kenneth Williams became the first Negro to be elected to a city council in North Carolina since Reconstruction, whites interpreted any participation by Negroes in electoral politics as a serious threat to the traditional white control of the city's politics. Fifteen years later a Negro high-school teacher could announce his candidacy for the Board of Aldermen without fear. It is still true that the Negro leader who draws his income solely

[6] This was discussed in Chapter II.

[7] It is also true in this case and others that the old leaders, their styles shaped by the demands of the old biracial structure, were temperamentally unable to make the transition from the old leadership pattern to the new, quite apart from the question of their vulnerability.

from the Negro community feels a greater freedom than does the vulnerable. He is not confronted with the choice of jeopardizing his economic position on the one hand or inviting the label "Uncle Tom" on the other. But vulnerables are now available for leadership roles from which, a decade ago, their positions in fact excluded them.

We could put this another way and say that Negroes are not now subject to victimization in Winston-Salem to anything approaching the extent that they once were. The concept of vulnerability still has meaning. But the vulnerables are no longer nearly as "vulnerable" as they once were, and they are free from threat of sanctions in a much wider area. In Myrdal's South of the 1930's most Negroes, regardless of their occupational position, were vulnerable because if everything else failed brute force would be used to enforce the will of the white majority. Today in relatively progressive rim-South cities like Winston-Salem vulnerability must be defined largely in economic terms and even here it is no longer as restricting as it was a short time ago.

The large majority of Negroes recognized as top leaders by the members of their subcommunity are dependent upon Negroes rather than whites for their income. No Negro leader prominently associated with protest organization activity in Winston-Salem is an economic vulnerable. Two top Negro leaders, however, are vulnerables, teachers at the state Negro college in Winston-Salem. Significantly both are politicians. One is the first Negro to be elected to a city council in North Carolina in this century; the other, the first Negro to be elected to county-wide office in Forsyth County.[8]

Negro participation through the channels of electoral

[8] It should be noted that white political leaders are drawn for the most part from the self-employed—lawyers, small-business owners, etc. Few white schoolteachers are active in politics. In short, although the absence of vulnerables from positions of race leadership is significant it is not quite as dramatic as it might appear at first.

politics is assuming in Winston-Salem and a number of other rim-South cities an importance and position quite similar to that of electoral participation for the newer immigrant groups in northern cities at the turn of the century. Large segments of the old majority are plainly unhappy about the development, and oppose the challengers because of their ethnic identity alone; but the challenging ethnic group—largely because of the weight of its vote—is able to win allies and realize some of its political objectives. Negro voters in the major North Carolina cities have free access to the ballot box and are important elements in the Democratic coalition in these cities. Despite the effectiveness of Negro participation in electoral politics, this participation has not evoked nearly so strong a hostile reaction as has participation in direct action demonstrations. Electoral politics involves formal constitutional procedures and whites find it harder to deny Negroes the right to use this channel for race advancement. Moreover, electoral politics is much more antiseptic; the physical confrontation present with direct action demonstrations is not there. Electoral politics, then, provides an arena in rim-South cities like Winston-Salem in which Negroes who are dependent on whites for their livelihood can play a leadership role recognized as significant and valid by their own constituents without incurring a serious threat of sanctions.

The withdrawal of the vulnerables came later in Greenville than in Winston-Salem, occurring only with the school desegregation decision of 1954. In the first six to eight years after the *Brown* decision, virtually all race-advancement activity in Greenville was suspect. In Winston and other rim-South cities vulnerables were pushed from leadership positions largely because of their inability to assume new leadership roles which enjoyed widespread Negro support. In contrast, they were removed from leadership in deep-South cities like Greenville less by Negro insistence on the newer, more aggressive forms of race leadership (although this factor was present) than by the withdrawal (by whites) of recognition of legitimacy from all forms of Negro political participation.

The so-called great silence began to break in Greenville around 1960. Throughout the South, Negro demands rose from a murmur to a crescendo and forced a redefinition by the Greenville whites. Whereas in the 1950's almost any criticism of the old biracial system seemed extreme, by 1963 demands for modification of the system could be considered "moderate" if limited in scope and properly presented. We found in our interviews that this change in evaluation of race goals extended as well to the Negro leaders advancing them. White and Negro leaders agreed that a Negro physician in Greenville was generally considered a "real militant" by the city's white population in 1958. In 1963, however, many whites looked upon the doctor with some favor, considering him "moderate." The doctor's position had not changed, but the perspectives of Greenville whites had. In brief, in the decade after *Brown* Greenville whites had come to recognize that the old biracial system would indeed be modified in certain respects; hence they categorized Negro leaders in terms of the rapidity and extensiveness of the change which they saw these leaders proposing.

In 1963 electoral politics in Greenville remained closed to vulnerables; it was still considered "radical" activity. Negroes were, however, able to present certain demands for modification of the biracial system through channels recognized as legitimate. In particular, the establishment of a community relations committee made it possible for vulnerables to assume an effective role in race leadership. Five Negroes whose economic position made them especially vulnerable to sanctions from whites were appointed to this biracial committee—established to consider Negro demands for integration of certain public facilities—and all five felt able to accept.

Economic independence remains an important determinant of the availability of Negroes for most leadership positions in Greenville—and indeed throughout the deep-South. No vulnerable ranks among the top leaders in Greenville. Respondents in a survey of the Negro population of Greenville were asked to name the Negroes whom they considered to be their outstanding local leaders. No vulnerable was named. To be effective in a deep-South city like Greenville, a Negro leader must at times antagonize local whites. Greenville Negroes are seeking extensive modification of the existing race relations structure, and whites are intransigent in their opposition to many of these changes. Racial conflict in a quite intense form cannot be avoided. The vulnerable in Greenville cannot stand such conflict.

Still, a gradual re-emergence of the vulnerables can be seen throughout the American South. The availability of vulnerables for leadership roles, greatly diminished by the collapse of the old structure of accommodating leadership, has been re-established in much of the urban South. The re-establishment is principally due to two interdependent factors: (1) the increase in Negro political power—which means that Negroes can reply in kind if whites impose sanctions; and (2) a general liberalization of white attitudes toward various race goals—which means that there are fewer activities for which whites want to impose sanctions. Both the increase in power and the liberalization in attitudes have occurred unevenly in the South, and the meaning of vulnerability for the selection process varies accordingly. But even in the cities of the deep South, vulnerables are beginning to re-enter positions of race leadership. In 1961 the city government of Albany, Georgia, flatly refused to negotiate grievances with the city's Negroes. Yet two years later Albany whites established a biracial committee. The same thing happened in Greenville, in Columbus, Georgia, and in a number of other deep-South cities. By acceding to the idea of a biracial committee established to secure limited desegregation of public facilities, white leaders in Greenville and these other cities were reopening a channel for effective leadership by vulnerables.

THE ABSENCE OF TRANSFERABILITY

A militant Negro leader, asked to comment on what if any leadership was being provided by a certain prominent physician, dismissed the good doctor summarily: "Why him? He's not doing anything. He doesn't even know what's going on!" The doctor was, in fact, a leading member of several Negro social organizations, was active in church work, and contributed generously of his time and money to philanthropic work in the Negro subcommunity. Were he white his record would have made him particularly attractive for candidacy for local political office, for leadership in a committee working for the fluoridation of the city's water system, for political activity in general. Negroes in today's urban South, however, are unable to transfer reputations acquired in other areas to the political realm. Reputation as a civic leader generally enhances the availability of a white man for local political leadership; it does not do so for a Negro in the urban South. A national Negro celebrity such as Jackie Robinson, of course, can transfer prominence gained in another arena to the political. Negro-Americans, like their fellow citizens, hold their sports and entertainment celebrities in extremely—one is tempted to say ridiculously—high esteem. Moreover, because of the pervasive system of discrimination to which they have been subjected, Negro-Americans have produced relatively few celebrities or folk heroes. Identification with those who succeed brilliantly in the white man's world is understandably strong. But at the local level, significantly, modest success in the arenas of economic and civic activity cannot be transferred to the political arena. In the explanation of this absence of transferability we find an important difference in the nature of Negro-American and white-American political leadership.

Political activity for most white Americans is a relatively casual involvement. There simply are not any issues on the local level in which white Americans find their most vital interests continuously involved.[9] When white Americans select leaders, then, it is often enough that the leader-candidates have shown themselves to be "good" and "trustworthy" and of "proved ability." Moreover, a leader-candidate is frequently forced in issueless politics to turn to other areas— such as civic work—to establish a reputation and to make himself sufficiently well known.

The Negro-American, in contrast, finds the stakes in political activity on the local level extremely high. His most vital interests are continuously involved. Access to public facilities, good jobs at fair pay, security from legal and extra-legal violence, claim to acceptance as a full and equal participant in the American democracy—all these are at issue in the political struggle. The past record, then, of a leader-candidate in the United Fund or the Queen Street Baptist Church is of only the most marginal interest and importance to Negroes when compared to the overriding importance of that leader-candidate's definition of the role of race leadership. The opinion of John Smith, a white college student, on the location of a new school generally will not count for much against that of J. Albert Goodwill, respected white civic leader. Status carries the day because few people care that much where the school is built. The issue falls on the periphery of white interests, and the psychological stake is minimal. To be sure, a few are deeply involved—like Mrs. Tate who hates children and can't bear the thought of a school playground next door. But even Mrs. Tate can move. The Negro-American cannot "move"—cannot, that is, change his color. The implications of patterns of discriminatory treatment confront him in all phases of his life. We should not be surprised, then, that he

[9] Things such as property taxes are undeniably important for many white Americans. But it would be hard to say that significant numbers find their most vital interests involved here. Moreover, involvement is rarely continuous. Taxes may be a concern for three days and then forgotten for six months.

says to leader-candidates: I really do not care what you have been, or even what you will become; my only concern is what you will do to promote better treatment for me and for my children.

We have been using very rough models in comparing transferability as a factor in the availability of Negro and white leaders. There are many Negroes for whom activities outside the political realm are important in evaluating the capacities of a leader-candidate. Frazier argues, for example, that the new "black bourgeoisie" tries to set itself apart from the Negro masses in a kind of compensation for the indignities which it suffers from whites whose values it has adopted; and that in so doing it places extraordinary emphasis on achievements in the social, educational, and economic spheres.[10] The "black bourgeoisie" of Winston-Salem and Greenville is more insistent that its leaders conform to the success standards of the white middle class. But the generalization still seems valid: a feature distinguishing the selection of Negro-American leaders from that of white leaders is the relative absence of transferability for the former. Success in civic work, in social, economic, or educational activity, contributes little to the availability of a candidate for race leadership.[11]

[10] E. Franklin Frazier, *Black Bourgeoisie* (New York, 1962), pp. 124–128.

[11] This conclusion contradicts the findings of M. Elaine Burgess (*Negro Leadership In A Southern City* [Chapel Hill, N.C., 1953]) and Floyd Hunter (*Community Power Structure* [Chapel Hill, 1959]). For example, Burgess found (pp. 80–81) that all but two of the seven top power nominees represented the principal Negro financial firms of Durham. The cities involved in these two studies, Atlanta and Durham, are, of course, centers for Negro business. Few Negro subcommunities have leaders with such formidable economic bases, then, as those in these two cities. The methodology utilized by Hunter and his disciple, Burgess, seems, however, to have committed them in advance to the conclusion that economic dominants play the preponderant role.

RELATIONSHIP OF LEADERS TO FOLLOWERS

Different types of leadership are distinguished by different relationships between those who make decisions and those for whom these decisions are made. This relationship has a number of different facets, one of which is particularly relevant to this analysis of the selection process for Negro political leaders. We will refer to this as the *fluidity potential* of leadership. A leader-follower relationship so structured that the incumbent leaders are generally able to maintain their position against challengers over extended periods with little difficulty may be said to be characterized by a low fluidity potential. Certain forms of bureaucratic leadership have very low fluidity potentials, as does military leadership. (This is the basis for the quip that the army is always preparing to fight the last war.) Issue leadership, in contrast, generally has an extremely high fluidity potential. We include as issue leadership those types whose basis of support is in the agreement of followers with the way that leadership seeks the realization of objectives highly valued by the followers. This leadership type is rarely found in its "pure" form. Attempts are always made to create institutional structures around issue positions. Once created the institutional structure tends to perpetuate itself. Mass involvement is often minimal in even the most pressing issues, and organizations are able to turn this apathy to their advantage. However, as long as the leadership position remains based on a particular definition of the proper posture on a burning issue, the potential remains high that a new group of leaders may successfully challenge that definition and hence supplant the incumbent leaders. The fluidity potential is especially high in periods of rapid social change, when followers and leaders alike are groping their way toward successive revisions of the definition of the proper position to take on the issue. Negro political leadership in the urban South is issue leadership. The issue—race advancement—is caught up in cyclonic social change, and the fluidity potential of that leadership is extraordinarily high.

Killian examined the effects of a major racial confrontation—the bus boycott of 1958—on Negro leaders in Tallahassee.[12] He found that the boycott resulted in the displacement of virtually all the old leaders of Tallahassee's Negro subcommunity. New leader-candidates challenged the old leaders over the proper means for advancing the race. Specifically they argued that boycotts, lawsuits, and related types of activity were necessary. The majority of Tallahassee Negroes agreed. During the boycott some of the old leaders openly challenged the influence of the new ones, but they were rebuffed and quickly came to accept the fact that they had been displaced.[13] Killian concluded that the new leaders supplanted the old, not because of organizational skills or personal attractiveness, but because they adhered rigorously to a form of leadership which was gaining widespread Negro acceptance. There has been at least one major displacement of race leaders in virtually every southern city in the last decade. Killian's conclusion that the new leadership is "becoming permanent" cannot be accepted, however.[14] Instead, we can expect that each successive racial confrontation will produce important changes in the personnel of Negro leadership.

Developments in Winston-Salem support the hypothesis that there will be a continuing high fluidity in Negro leadership structures. In January 1963, the leaders of the Winston-Salem Negro subcommunity, having established themselves in a series of racial crises since 1957, appeared to be in an extremely secure position. Essentially the same people had occupied the top leadership positions over a three-year period.

[12] See a report of this in Lewis Killian and Charles Grigg, *Racial Crisis in America* (Englewood Cliffs, N.J., 1964), pp. 81–90.

[13] *Ibid.*, pp. 85–89.

[14] *Ibid.*, p. 88.

The position of this group of leaders was reinforced by the fact that a large number of highly emotive issues, such as integration of swimming pools and lunch counters, had been resolved. But in the spring of 1963 protest demonstrations swept the South. The most militant leadership in Winston-Salem was appointed to a mayor's goodwill committee and through extended negotiations the committee achieved fairly significant results—results comparable to what Negro leaders in other North Carolina cities such as Durham and Raleigh achieved only through large-scale demonstrations. But the goodwill committee did not meet all outstanding grievances and came under attack for "moving too slowly." The critics, who had not been prominently associated with race-advancement activity previously, stressed the need for more aggressive protest activity to "push" reluctant businesses.

The leaders identified in January 1963 as the most militant, then, found themselves in the position of "ins," and hence open to criticism for failures to quickly realize race objectives. The attractiveness of access to the city's power structure was clearly irresistible for some who hence became willing to compromise in the interest of maintaining their new positions. For others it was merely "guilt by association"; that is, they were now prominently associated with solving problems through negotiation rather than direct action.[15] The dissatisfaction led to the creation of two new protest organizations: a youth group, the NAACP Commandoes, and a chapter of the Congress of Racial Equality. A few of the old Militants participated in the organization of the CORE chapter and are now leading members of it, and the NAACP is still functioning with its old leadership, with some, although diminished, prestige. The point is that with racial conflict sweeping the South many Winston-Salem Negroes came to

[15] The entire Winston-Salem NAACP was implicated here because the branch had gone on record as having "full confidence in the mayor's goodwill committee."

feel that the existing protest leadership was not adequate to the task. Their dissatisfaction indicates less the failure of the old leadership than the nature of the situation in which that leadership found itself. Negro grievances were so real and so great that inevitably the existing leadership would be accused of not doing enough. New men saw and seized the opportunity which this conflict provided to argue that new approaches were needed, and thereby come to power and prominence. This partial displacement of the old protest leadership in Winston-Salem illustrates the high fluidity potential of Negro political leadership in today's urban South.

In periods of relatively low Negro-white tension the stability of the leadership structure is considerably greater. Negro leadership more closely approximates white leadership in such periods because domination by the central overriding issue is less intense and complete. When that issue, race advancement, is brought to full public consciousness and its capacity to involve the Negro community is realized, as in major racial confrontations, the conflict of competing definitions becomes intense and inevitably some must lose community support.

The Negro revolution is still moving "always to the left"; it has yet to reach Thermidor. Negro leaders in Winston and indeed in most southern cities must run very hard indeed to escape being outflanked. Nationally, the displacement of the NAACP from its once preeminent and predominant position appears less the product of its failure, as Lomax and others have charged, to adequately assess the temper of the Negro community, than of its position as an established organization working with an issue which involves the most vital interests of the constituents. There was no position from which it could have successfully defended itself.

The race leadership model introduced here, then, posits a type of leadership particularly vulnerable to challenges from rival leader-candidates because of three characteristics of this type of leadership. (1) Most local race leaders operate from weak institutional and status positions. Negro political leaders in most southern cities work either from race-advancement groups that are poorly organized, have few members and get little financial support; or from relatively insignificant positions in government. At the same time they are, as indeed are most Negro-Americans, persons of relatively low status. Excluded by a long history of race discrimination from leading positions in the various economic and social enterprises, few Negro leaders bring to race leadership a strength comparable to that which their white counterparts derive from positions of economic dominance and high social status. (2) Race leaders possess few sanctions with which to secure the compliance of their followers. They cannot get jobs for their followers or provide security. They cannot provide the kinds of services, like supplying distressed families with food and fuel, which sustained machine politicians in the great northern cities. Since there is little which they can do, there is little which they can threaten not to do.[16] (3) Negro political leadership is concerned with one broad issue, the cause of race advancement. It is true, as Frazier has observed, that with the occupational and educational differentiation of Negro-Americans, once largely a mass of "inarticulate, illiterate rural folk," and with the concomitant development of "diverse interests" among Negroes, the old "accommodation-protest" or "gradualist-revolutionary" typologies of Negro leadership styles have become inadequate.[17] There are now religious leaders, politicians, labor leaders, and so on. A functional typology, then, taking into account the increasing differentiation particularly in the North and the urban South, is

[16] The race leader, of course, can apply certain sanctions. For example, a precinct leader in Winston-Salem can be instrumental in electing or defeating a Negro candidate for a city office in certain elections, depending upon whether he gives or withholds support.

[17] Frazier, *The Negro in the United States*, pp. 547–.

necessary for certain analytical purposes along with the old "race leader" typology. It is also true, however, that in the urban South at present there are few Negroes who are political leaders who are not Negro political leaders. Negro and white attitudes are such that political leaders who are Negroes have been judged and selected on the basis of their prescriptions for and activities in behalf of advancing the race.[18] The deepest and most vital political interests of Negroes are involved in the issue of race.[19]

The weak institutional and status positions of race leaders, the fact that sanctions to enforce compliance are not available, and the presence of an issue of transcending importance to the group require Negro leaders to bid for support on their effectiveness in meeting the demands of their group within the issue-area. And the already high fluidity potential is made still higher by the unparalleled rate of transition from one definition of the proper role of race leadership to another and yet another. While a particular group of community leaders may well succeed in maintaining their position through an extended period and while individual leaders have and certainly will continue to maintain their positions, the fluidity

[18] Burgess noted in her study of Negro leadership in Durham that even those who have chosen to subordinate their role as race leader to their role as functional leader "are nevertheless classified by their peers as race leaders, and because they have chosen to be vocal in areas other than Negro protest they are considered moderate (race) leaders" (Burgess, *op. cit.*, p. 182).

[19] The literature on the central importance of race in the lives of Negro-Americans is so extensive and well known that it needs little discussion here. See, for example, as representative statements from different intellectual perspectives: Abram Kardiner and Lionel Ovesey, *The Mark of Oppression* (New York, 1951); John H. Rohrer *et al.*, *The Eighth Generation* (New York, 1960); Gunnar Myrdal, *An American Dilemma* (New York, 1944); Lewis E. Lomax, *The Negro Revolt* (New York, 1962); James Baldwin, *Nobody Knows My Name* (New York, 1961); Ralph Ellison, *Invisible Man* (New York, 1952).

potential of Negro political leadership is and will remain very high in comparison to that of other types of leadership.

Thus far we have been discussing in quite general terms those factors contributing to the exceedingly high fluidity potential of Negro leadership. There are, however, varying levels of fluidity in the leadership structures of Negro sub-communities. Three principle factors operate to raise or lower the stability of the leadership structure in a given city within the framework outlined in the above analysis.

(1) The fluidity of Negro leadership is affected by the number of leader-candidates not included within the established leadership. The level of political talent varies greatly among the Negro populations of the various southern cities. In some cities it is so low that finding sufficient people to staff existing leadership positions is a major problem. This is the situation in Greenville. There really is relatively little competition among leader-candidates because there are more positions than there are leader-candidates. In one sense, of course, this is an over-simplification. Few can be presidents of race-advancement organizations, and there is competition for these positions. Complete satisfaction within the leadership structure can never be attained. But the scarcity of manpower is such that virtually everyone with time, inclination, and talent has found a position within the leadership structure. In other cities, however, large numbers of potential leaders or leader-candidates are waiting in the wings. This is the situation in Winston-Salem. It partially accounts for a higher level of fluidity in that city.

(2) Fluidity is affected by the strength of the organizations devoted to race-advancement activity in a Negro sub-community. Leaders of a well-organized and reasonably well-financed group have a little bailiwick of power which the leaders of weakly organized, more or less ephemeral organizations lack. This variable, in contrast to the first, is translated into somewhat greater stability for Winston than

for Greenville. Winston-Salem race-advancement groups are better organized and better financed. The structure of race advancement organization in Greenville is weak and rapidly evolving. But the second variable thus far has had less impact than the first. Even though the structure of race-advancement organization has changed rapidly in Greenville, the same group of leaders has reappeared in each of the new organizations. The abundance of leader-candidates in Winston-Salem has permitted the formation of new race-advancement organizations to outflank the old even when the existing leadership has been able to maintain its position in the established organizations.

(3) The frequency and extent of Negro-white confrontations influence the fluidity of Negro leadership; and, related to this, the response of the existing leadership to those confrontations affects fluidity. If the first part of this statement is not carefully delimited it runs the risk of becoming merely tautological. The point is that major racial confrontations (like sit-ins, boycotts, etc.), regardless of their origins, provide opportunities for rival leader-candidates to dramatize their positions—opportunities otherwise absent. Involvement of Negroes in these conflicts is more intensive and extensive. The subcommunity becomes more self-conscious. Its frustrations are sharpened. In short, it is not enough for rival leader-candidates to criticize the established leaders; in the absence of the heightened focus of a major racial confrontation, their challenge probably cannot achieve sufficient momentum. In Greenville overt racial conflict, even if initiated by the established leadership, would provide new opportunities for potential leader-candidates. Most Winston-Salem Negroes were no more dissatisfied with their leaders in the spring of 1963 than they were in the spring of 1962 or 1961. Yet the leadership structure was significantly altered in 1963, although it had remained intact the two preceding years. The direct action demonstrations which began on an extremely modest

note in Winston-Salem in 1963 made the city's Negroes more aware of their difficulties and generally more self-conscious. Thus the way was opened for rival leader-candidates.

Overt Negro-white conflict is one thing; the response to this by the existing leadership is another. Three quite different postures toward racial confrontations can be assumed by the established leadership, and each contributes to a different level of fluidity.

(1) The old top leadership may fail to identify with and take direction of the new protest. The major cause of this failure has been the occurrence of the racial conflict in the midst of the transition from out-group selection to in-group selection. The established leadership has been composed largely of old-style accommodating leaders. These have found themselves confronted by the demands of a new pattern of race relations and the demands have been intensified by the suddenness of racial conflict. Since the *forte* of this old leadership has been "getting along" with white leaders, not defying them, it has been helpless in the new situation. Generally it has attempted to perform its old role of mediation. Failing to resolve the racial conflict in a way satisfactory either to whites or Negroes, it has been badly discredited. This happened in Winston-Salem in 1947 during the great Reynolds strike. The old accommodating leadership tried to mediate, tried to bring the strike and the violence that accompanied it to an end. The attempt failed and the accommodating leadership disappeared as an effective force. Similarly, during the Tallahassee bus boycott the pre-boycott leaders sought to preserve their position by complying with the request of the Tallahassee city government to get Negroes to call off the boycott. Their attempt ended in ignominious failure and they disappeared from the scene.[20]

(2) When racial conflict demands a wholly unprece-

[20] Killian and Grigg, *op. cit.,* p. 86.

dented involvement of the Negro subcommunity, new leadership organizations are required. Some of the old leaders may be able to adapt to the new leadership demands and hence maintain their positions. Others will fail to make the transition and will decline in influence. But above all this, new men will find themselves thrown into positions of importance and thus presented with an unparalleled opportunity. The old leadership here does not align itself against the new form of race-advancement activity. But its response from both an organizational and conceptual standpoint is inadequate. It is still fighting the last war. Developments in the Negro leadership structure in Montgomery, Alabama, during the 1956 boycott followed this second pattern.

(3) The old leadership may initiate, or at least identify itself with, the new protest. There has been sufficient differentiation within the leadership structure so that welfare organization leaders and politicians can remain aloof; and sufficient organizational development to enable protest organization leaders to effectively channel the protest. Even here, however, new men generally are promoted through community recognition to top leadership positions. The pressures, tensions, frustrations, and triumphs of major racial confrontations, with the greater mobilization of the Negro subcommunity, allow new men to dramatize their positions even in the absence of serious community dissatisfaction with the established leaders. The old leadership, then, is not really displaced, but significant additions are made and the *style* of leadership is altered. There is less fluidity here than in the first two responses but it is by no means eliminated. In the 1963 demonstrations Greensboro, Durham, and Raleigh experienced this kind of development.

The Negro leadership structure has been relatively stable in Greenville over the last decade. Although race-advancement organizations are weak and ephemeral, fluidity has been limited because of the shortage of potential political participants and the absence of the major racial clashes which serve to galvanize an alternative elite. The old leadership structure has remained intact to a large extent simply because an alternate set of leader-candidates has not arisen to offer a challenge. When asked how the local NAACP leadership maintained itself in light of the obviously low repute of certain branch leaders, a Greenville leader replied: "Well, we are all very busy and there really isn't anyone else who wants it [leadership] bad enough." The pool of potential political participants and leader-candidates is much larger in Winston-Salem. While race relations there are good when compared to Negro-white relations in many other southern cities—good in the sense that there has been less direct confrontation and overt conflict—there has been much more race-advancement activity in Winston than in, for example, Greenville or Columbus, Georgia. While race-advancement organizations in Winston have been much stronger than their counterparts in Greenville, Winston Negroes have not succeeded in establishing organizations with the strength, prestige, and stability of, for example, Durham's Committee on Negro Affairs. As a result, there has been considerable fluidity. Pressures operate to drive the "left wing" or militant section of Winston's Negro leadership to the center, with new militants supplanting the old on the "left."

Two factors are of central importance in understanding the process of selection for Negro leadership. First, Negro leadership is single-issue leadership and that issue—race advancement—involves the most vital political interests of all Negroes. Negro expectations relating to race advancement are changing in such a kaleidoscopic fashion that extraordinary demands are made on the existing leadership. Second, the reduction of white influence in the selection of Negro leaders has been so great quantitatively as to represent a qualitative change. We have referred to this as a shift from out-group selection to in-group selection. This has brought major changes throughout the South in the personnel of race leadership; and, more broadly, it has brought about changes in the factors determining the availability of leader-candidates for positions of race leadership.

Today, Negro political leadership in the urban South is a leadership pressured, indeed squeezed, by three forces set in play by developments in the process of selection: (1) the desire for personal and economic security, and for respectability, felt by the leaders themselves; (2) the demands of Negro followers, particularly strong because the issue of race advancement is of such importance; and (3) the resistance of many southern whites to changes in the structure of race relations in the region. The styles of race leadership evident today in the cities of the South represent attempts by Negro leaders to reconcile these conflicting pressures. To these styles of race leadership we can now turn.

CHAPTER IV

Styles of Race Leadership

THE ways in which Negro political leaders work at their trade has been and remains a subject of intense discussion. Most Negro leaders do seem to share certain general ideas about what they should work for—what James Wilson has labeled "race values." There is general agreement about the desirability of full integration into American society and "equal right for all, regardless of color." [1] There are, however, many roads leading to Rome and many stopping places along the way. Disagreements arise, as inevitably they must in a large and differentiated community, over how the central objective should be pursued. These disagreements are not minor; they involve the most fundamental elements of strategy. [2]

We refer here to the style of race leadership. A Negro political leader's style is a composite of (1) the race goals

[1] The Black Muslim movement, of course, rejects the basic race value, integration. Muslims insist that Negroes can solve the problem of identity through segregation rather than through integration, by becoming fully proud of their blackness. The Muslims' most telling criticism is that the basic race values of the integration movement cannot be realized.

[2] Negro leaders frequently say with reference to fellow race leaders: "We are all after the same thing. We simply use different strategies." Strategy here, of course, is in one sense everything.

which he chooses to emphasize; (2) the means which he uses in seeking to realize these goals; and (3) his rhetoric—that is, the language and manner in which he discusses his race goals and in which he assesses the motives and actions of the Negroes and whites with whom he interacts. Goals, means, and rhetoric so defined are the constituent elements of leadership style as the term is used here.

Style, then, is of central importance in a study of race leadership. For the style of a leader tells us where he wants to lead his race and how he proposes to get there. When in a given community at a given time we are able to describe the continuum of race leadership styles, we are able to determine areas of consensus, where Negro leaders operate with a high level of internal agreement, and areas of conflict, where differences over how to advance the race are sharpest. And, of course, to describe the continuum of race leadership styles is to describe the content of Negro political participation.

THE CONTINUUM OF RACE LEADERSHIP STYLES

Before the content of the leadership continuum can be discussed, four questions central to the concept must be raised and answered. (1) What variables define the content of a style of leadership? We have given a brief and preliminary answer to this question by saying that goals, means, and rhetoric will be understood to constitute style. This will be discussed further below. (2) What factors determine the relationship of the various styles to one another and the positions of each on the leadership continuum? (3) Is the content of each style on the continuum fixed, or are the categories some kind of relational constructs? This question can be clarified by posing it in another way: Must a Militant leader in Chicago, Illinois, have the same goals-means-rhetoric orientation as a Militant in Biloxi, Mississippi? (4) How many distinct styles are evident on the continuum and what variables determine the number of categories into which the continuum is divided? Typologies of leadership styles are found in all major studies of Negro political leadership, and the questions raised above are generally treated either explicitly or implicitly. Some of these other race-leader typologies will be referred to as the questions are answered.

Table 14 brings together data on race leader typologies as they are structured in five major studies of race leadership. Categories have been treated in all but one of these studies as self-contained units, each completely distinct from the others.[3] Like billiard balls they bang together and fly apart. We do not wish to quarrel with the construction for certain analytical purposes of what James Wilson has called "artificially polarized ideal types." But it is necessary to make quite clear that we in fact are dealing with a *continuum* of leadership styles. Categories are formed by drawing lines through the continuum. The location of these lines is determined by what appears to be significant differences in approach to the cause of race advancement.

Different variables are used in categorizing leaders in each typology. But central to each is "behavior and actions in the field of race relations." Both Thompson and Wilson have added a second: attitudes toward race and race relations. Thompson categorized leaders on the basis of (1) "[their] conception of the Negro race and race relations" and (2) "[their] attitudes toward race and race relations." [4] Wilson's "militant" closely resembles Eric Hoffer's "true believer," while his "moderate" sees the world "as it is." [5] The distinction between behavior and underlying attitudes cannot be too finely drawn, of course. Any discussion of the former necessarily involves the latter. But there is a danger in free speculation on the attitudes toward race and race relations of various

[3] The exception is James Q. Wilson's *Negro Politics: The Search for Leadership* (Glencoe, Ill., 1960).

[4] Thompson, *op. cit.*, p. 59.

[5] Wilson, *op. cit.*, pp. 215–217, 233.

TABLE 14

Race leadership typologies in five leadership studies*

	Myrdal	Johnson	Wilson	Burgess	Thompson
No. of types	2	2	2	4	3
Types	Accommodationist Protest	Gradualist Revolutionary	Moderate Militant	Conservative Moderate Liberal Radical	Uncle Tom Race Diplomat Race Man
Race relations situation	United States, 1930's	United States, 1930's	North (Chicago), 1959	South (Durham), 1960	South (New Orleans), 1963
Variables used in categorizing leaders	Acceptance or rejection of old biracial system	Acceptance or rejection of the old biracial system	Type of race-advancement activity; attitudes on race relations	Type of race-advancement activity	Type of race-advancement activity; attitudes on race relations
Definition of the relationship of the types			Position in a number of polar divisions; e.g., status vs. welfare goals, direct action vs. bargaining	Aggressiveness in opposing all forms of discrimination	Degree of opposition to discrimination

* Sources: Gunnar Myrdal, *An American Dilemma* (New York, 1944), p. 720 ff.; Guy B. Johnson, "Negro Racial Movements and Leadership in the United States," *The American Journal of Sociology*, XLIII (July 1937), 56–72; Wilson, *op. cit.*, pp. 214–254; M. Elaine Burgess, *Negro Leadership in a Southern City* (Chapel Hill, N.C., 1962), pp. 176–186; Daniel C. Thompson, *The Negro Leadership Class* (Englewood Cliffs, N.J., 1963), pp. 58–79.

types of race leaders. Data from interviews of Negro leaders conducted in the course of this study indicate a rich complexity of motivation for each style of race leadership. A Negro politician in Winston-Salem generally considered a Moderate revealed himself in lengthy intimate discussions to be utopian in his thinking, bitterly resentful of racial discrimination and impatient with the slowness with which improvements come. But he held a job which made him highly vulnerable to retaliation, and apparently for this reason he put on a mask of moderation. Some Conservatives may, as Thompson claims for his "Uncle Tom," accept segregation as right and necessary.[6] Other Conservatives, however, accept it simply for reasons of expediency. In this study, then, leaders will be placed on the continuum solely on the basis of the goals they choose to emphasize and the means and rhetoric with which they pursue these goals. This does not mean that all discussion of attitudes and values must be omitted. But after 400 interviews with Negro leaders we have become very skeptical about the possibility of extrapolating reliable information on personality traits and basic attitudes from the public behavior of aggregate groups of race leaders. About the best we can offer in this area are correlations between a style of race leadership and personal biographical data, some of which are suggestive of motivation.

Surprisingly, none of the studies referred to in Table 14 give any explicit indication of whether the content of the various leadership styles are fixed or vary with the pattern of race relations. Yet we know that the goals-means-rhetoric orientation of Negro leaders is determined to a very significant extent by the larger pattern of race relations in which they operate. The content of the leadership continuum in Harlem in 1963 must be quite different from what existed in Birmingham in 1900. It seems necessary to make very clear that the

[6] Thompson, *op. cit.*, p. 62.

content of a style is related to the pattern of race relations existing at a given time and place.

Moreover, it is not enough simply to make explicit that the goals of Wilson's "militant" are the goals of a Chicago 1958 Militant. We need a continuum construct that will enable us to readily compare the content of different styles in different times and places. The continuum must have a constancy of meaning, and this cannot be found in the content of leadership styles. The goals of a 1963 Winston-Salem Militant are not the same as those of a 1963 Chicago Militant, nor indeed the same as the goals of a 1947 Winston-Salem Militant. Constancy must be found, if it is to be found, in some kind of functional equivalency. This appears to exist in the kind of threat to the existing race relations structure which whites find contained in a given style. There is a constant relationship among the various categories of the continuum even though the content varies. The definition of this relationship which satisfies both the way the categories are understood by whites and Negroes is how offensive or acceptable the style is to the dominant segment of the white community.

The typology used here contains three categories which have been labeled Conservatives, Moderates, and Militants. We are saying that militant leaders in each race relations situation are, in their rhetoric, goals, and means, less acceptable to the dominant group of whites than are Moderates, who in turn are less acceptable than Conservatives. Southern whites certainly use these descriptive categories to indicate the extent to which they accept the styles of leadership. And Negroes do so as well. The Militant, for example, is one who is "far out" from the white consensus, who treads in areas in which maximum white opposition can be expected. Negroes clearly do not ascribe the same value to the different styles of race leadership as do whites. White and Negro reactions in approval-disapproval terms differ extensively. But for both whites and Negroes, the factor which determines the location of a particular style on the leadership continuum is the degree of acceptability of that style to whites.[7]

In all the studies referred to in Table 14 there is some discussion of the relationship of the various styles to each other. The relationship is defined, however, as the degree of opposition to segregation and related patterns of discriminatory treatment. Thompson, for example, argues that his "race man" is more strongly opposed to segregation than his "Uncle Tom." [8] This definition of the relationship is by no means generally accepted or supported. Thompson's "Uncle Toms" and "race diplomats" certainly do not concur. And there is strong evidence which will be discussed at length below that many rank-and-file Negroes do not see the relationship simply in terms of the degree of opposition to segregation.

For our part, then, we insist that there is nothing inherently militant (moderate, conservative, etc.) about a given leadership style. Instead the limits and content of the continuum of race leadership styles are determined by the prevailing pattern of race relations which varies with time and geography. Because of this the composite of goals, means, and rhetoric that in one period would be called conservative or accommodating leadership might not even be on the continuum in a later period. Negro expectations have increased and the margin of freedom for Negro protests has broadened significantly. Myrdal explained the existence of a particular

[7] Something roughly analogous to the "always to the left" posture of the French working class is assumed by significant numbers of Negro-Americans. The leadership style which "bothers" whites the most is applauded because it does bother the most. This is not surprising, since Negro-Americans have experienced a long history of discriminatory treatment. There is some reason for Negroes to be afraid that their leaders will "sell out" to whites, and hence for Negroes to be acutely sensitive to how whites treat race leaders. In this kind of situation you tell how good a job your leaders are doing in representing your interests by how hostile the "enemy" is to them.

[8] Thompson, *op. cit.*, pp. 75–76.

pattern of accommodating leadership in the South in the 1930's:

The southerner keeps watching all the time for germs of unrest and dissatisfaction in the Negro community. He preserves the machinery of caste controls in a state of perpetual preparedness and applies it occasionally as an exercise or a demonstration. In this system, the Negroes *have* to accommodate individually or as a group. This is the situation in the South.[9]

There is in today's South the functional equivalent of Myrdal's accommodating leadership, but its goals, means, and rhetoric are quite different. In the South of the *Dilemma* the pattern of race relations was such that the main division on the continuum of race leadership styles was between those working within the two-standards system and those insisting that substantial modifications of the system must be effected. In today's urban South, in contrast, virtually all leaders agree that the biracial system must be removed, not merely modified. Divisions arise over such questions as how fast and in what ways. The categories into which the continuum is divided are relational constructs indicating the degree of white opposition elicited by the various patterns of goals, means, and rhetoric which claim significant Negro support.

A final element is necessary in a continuum construct permitting comparison of the content of continuums and their styles at different times and places. This is a precise determination of what factors establish the number of categories into which the continuum is divided. Here these relate to the permissiveness of the pattern of race relations, to the extent to which patterns of segregation and other forms of discriminatory treatment are enforced, and to the degree of integration of Negroes into the main political institutions. Under the old biracial system a two-category typology was the only one that made sense. Either one worked within the system or he was a "radical" working to modify it in some way. Neither

[9] Myrdal, *op. cit.*, p. 768.

whites nor Negroes recognized any other differences. As the system has broken down, other types of leadership have become possible. And both whites and Negroes have come to recognize differences in approach that either did not exist previously or were considered unimportant.[10]

For certain purposes it would be desirable to divide the continuum into more than three categories; and in still other cases a two-unit typology would be more useful, focusing attention on a central division. But if the purpose of the typology is to describe the continuum as Negroes and whites on the scene see it, a three-unit typology is generally adequate for the urban South today. In the present race relations situation most whites and Negroes seem to recognize three main approaches to race advancement. We will refer, then, to the conservative style, the moderate style, and the militant style of race leadership. These encompass the entire spectrum of Negro political leadership.

THE CONSERVATIVE STYLE

The transition from the old pattern of out-group selected leadership to in-group selected leadership has progressed far enough in the major cities of the South that there are few Negro political leaders whose style of race leadership is not acceptable to significant segments of the Negro population. Despite this development the image of the conservative leader as a "white man's Negro" persists. The "Uncle Tom," one who bows and scrapes, begs for favors and preserves "a biracial system which perpetuates white paternalistic men of power in their status of hosts and Negroes as parasites" is no longer a race leader.[11] Whites may chuckle over the actions

---

[10] Wilson's two-category typology is purely an instrument of analytical convenience. It does not represent nor does it pretend to represent the actual divisions Negroes and whites see in the leadership continuum (Wilson, *op. cit.*, pp. 214–254).

[11] The quotation is from Thompson, *op. cit.*, p. 63; and represents part of his evaluation of the "Uncle Tom" in New Orleans.

of this type of Negro and make much of him; but neither they nor Negroes consider him a political leader. In Greenville in the summer of 1963, while Negroes were actively seeking to integrate certain public facilities in the city, a Negro welfare worker wrote a letter to the *Greenville Piedmont* in which he proposed that instead of freedom rallies Greenville Negroes should launch "a few moral, educational and recreational rallies. Civic responsibility rallies would not be out of order and an I.Q. rally would be just the thing." He went on to attack "our self-appointed leaders" who seem oblivious to evils existing in the Negro community: teenagers "guzzling" alcohol, young men "shooting craps," and illicit sex "practiced right under our noses on every ill-lighted stairway." What should Negro leaders do? Work for integration? No, they should "form or work with neighborhood boys' clubs or Scout troops." He concluded: "Let me remind our caucus ridden, factionalized, self-appointed leaders that 'people get closer shoulder to shoulder than they do face to face.' " [12]

Even in the relatively inactive deep-South Negro subcommunity of Greenville such a definition of the proper role of race leadership found little support. This was recognized even by white segregationists, who wish that all Negroes felt this way. Any Negro who fails to declare himself firmly for integration cannot hope to attain a position of race leadership.

Conservative leadership is the functional equivalent in one sense of the accommodating leadership which Myrdal describes in that its effectiveness depends upon its access and acceptability to white leaders.[13] Conservatives try to alter the prevailing pattern of race relations by working within it and its demands. They seek the maximum benefits possible through channels considered legitimate by whites. Still, the pattern of race relations which produced the old accommodating leader-

[12] *Greenville Piedmont,* July 7, 1963.
[13] See Myrdal, *op. cit.,* pp. 720–735.

ship no longer exists in the urban South, and today's conservative leadership differs sharply from its counterpart of two and a half decades ago.

GOALS

Wilson has pointed out that since virtually any goal which has been firmly established as a race goal will get at least the verbal support of all Negro leaders, the distinction as to what goals are sought by various types of leaders cannot always be drawn too fine. Still, if normally there is commitment to the whole range of race goals, all leaders must in practice choose among competing race goals as they determine where to expend their energies. And on occasion Negro political leaders are confronted with mutually exclusive objectives. Distinctions can be made, then, between the goals emphasized by Conservatives, Moderates, and Militants.

The specific content of the conservative style (and the others) varies with the pattern of race relations. Race relations are essentially the same in certain important respects throughout the urban South today. And there are certain basic similarities in the kinds of goals sought by conservative leaders throughout the urban South. The goals that are shared by Conservatives throughout the urban South will be discussed first. Then differences in the goals sought by Conservatives in Winston-Salem and in Greenville will be noted.

Status goals versus *welfare goals*. Conservative leaders throughout the South tend to be preoccupied with welfare goals and to shun status goals. This distinction between welfare and status goals which Wilson makes at some length in *Negro Politics* is an extremely important one. Welfare goals involve "gut" needs: more money, a warmer house, better medical care, safe travel for children to and from school, greater influence in determining how the city tax dollar is spent, and the like. These are compelling for Americans in general but particularly so for an underprivileged group like

Negro Americans. Status goals, in contrast, involve the individual's image of himself. The demand for integration of recreational facilities, hospitals, housing, and the like is essentially the attempt of a group which has been branded inferior in quite literally a thousand ways by white America to gain recognition as a fully equal partner in the American democracy. The compartments are not watertight. Better jobs, for instance, have a status-conferral function and the integration of swimming pools is certainly one means of improving the quality of recreational facilities open to Negroes. But the general distinction is a useful and valid one. The Negro leader who consistently emphasizes welfare goals to the exclusion of status goals has for certain reasons committed himself to their primacy. He has publicly declared that the most pressing need of the race is for "bread." The converse is true for Negro leaders emphasizing status goals.

Welfare goals—higher pay, better schools, better hospital facilities, fair treatment in the courts—generally arouse less white antagonism than do status goals, which involve putting Negroes and whites together in swimming pools, lunch counters, and neighborhoods. The goals sought by conservative leaders are seen by southern whites as presenting a lesser threat to the "southern way of life." Conservatives, of course, disagree with this judgment, a judgment which is used against them by Militants. In rebuttal the Conservative will frequently emphasize the primacy of economics in determining a man's position in American society. Typical is the statement of a Winston-Salem Conservative:

In America money talks. The only color that really matters is green. If you have enough money you can do anything you want. I think that once Negroes achieve a really strong economic position everything else will fall into place.

A case in Winston-Salem in which Negro leaders were forced to choose between welfare and status goals brings the position of the conserative leader into sharper focus.

Most of Winston-Salem's top leaders had agreed by 1959 that a new hospital was urgently needed in the area. An expanding population was already making demands that the existing hospitals could meet only with serious overcrowding. To construct a new hospital would, however, require a substantial increase in the city's bonded indebtedness. The question of the issuance of bonds would have to be submitted to the county's voters in a referendum and it was not at all certain that the voters would approve the measure. For this reason the pro-hospital leaders initiated a major campaign to win voter approval. In this campaign the substantial Negro vote was not forgotten. There would have been little difficulty in securing Negro support if the pro-hospital leaders had been willing to state that the new plant would be open to all. But the leaders would not give that assurance. Some simply did not want Negroes in the new hospital. Most felt that any suggestion of integration would lose too many white votes. Instead a plan was devised to offer Winston-Salem Negroes the old white city hospital, City Memorial, in exchange for Negro support for the new (white) county hospital. The choice presented to Negroes in Winston was not an easy one. On the one hand they were being asked to give their support to a plan which explicitly provided that Negroes would take a "hand-me-down." Whites were saying: "We won't need City Memorial Hospital now that we're getting a nice new one, so you can have it if you will help us get our new one." The pro-hospital leadership was seeking Negro support for a plan which would provide for continued segregation of the city hospital facilities. Negro leaders were being asked to endorse their exclusion from the new county hospital. On the other hand, City Memorial as it stood was clearly superior to the Kate Bitting Reynolds Memorial Hospital, Winston's Negro facility. The "Katie B" was built as a Negro hospital, which means it was not built well. There was an appalling shortage of facilities; for example, each floor had only one bathroom. With substantial renovation City Memorial would be incomparably better. In short, it would give Negroes an adequate facility in place of the clearly inadequate one they had. More importantly perhaps, voting for the hospital plan would in no way prevent Negroes from contesting to gain admittance to the hospital later. The outcome of legal action by Negroes was not in question, since the new hospital was to be a public rather than a private facility.[14]

The hospital controversy represents the conflict of mutually exclusive goals. Support of the hospital plan required the sacrifice of a Negro status goal: recognition as full and equal participants in the American democracy. But to insist on the status goal and urge Negroes to vote against the hospital plan might well be to deprive Negroes of much needed hospital facilities. Conservative leaders generally considered the choice an easy one. They supported the hospital plan. The need for better facilities was too pressing. Their position was summed up by a leader who said:

I didn't like the idea of "your people" trying to put a deal over like this, but we were in desperate need of more and better hospital facilities. Anyway, we knew that so much public money was going into the new one that Negroes would be in it when it opened.

clear, but what was clear was the necessity of Negro opposi-
Conservatives, then, thought that they could have their cake and eat it as well. Militants generally saw the choice as equally tion to the hospital plan. As one Militant put it: "I will never vote segregation on myself." For Militants, the fact that Negroes later could contest to gain admittance to the hospital was immaterial. It was necessary for them to repudiate the

[14] In the spring of 1963, nearly a year before the new hospital was to open, white leaders in Winston-Salem were stating publicly that the hospital would be operated on an integrated basis. Winston-Salem's Mayor, M. C. Benton, for example, stated in May of 1963 that there was "no question" about integration of the hospital. "There is no way we can have segregated facilities."

very suggestion that segregation can provide a legitimate or tenable position.

Not all Negro leaders, to be sure, arrived at their positions solely by weighing competing status and welfare goals. One leader, an NAACP board member, publicly supported his branch's stand against the hospital plan. Privately he conceded that he believed the plan should have the support of Negroes. When asked to explain the conflict between his public position and his private preference he said:

Look, I'm an NAACP leader here. The NAACP can't go around supporting segregation whatever the case. We are an organization that protests against all forms of discrimination and can't compromise our position. So I had to denounce the plan.

Following the demands of a role against a preferred position is not uncommon.

In the hospital controversy in Winston-Salem, as in race-advancement activity throughout the South, Conservatives gave priority to welfare goals over status goals and showed themselves ready to sacrifice the latter in favor of the former whenever the two were in conflict.[15]

Emptying the race problem of its dynamic content. Conservative leaders tend to emphasize race goals the merits of which are generally conceded by both whites and Negroes.

[15] In June, 1963, the Winston-Salem Hospital Commission presented the city's Board of Aldermen with a proposal to construct a new $6 million hospital in East Winston, that is, in the Negro section of the city. The Board of Aldermen gave preliminary approval to this proposal. Conservative leaders warmly endorsed the idea of a new Negro facility, contending that even with integration of the existing hospitals a need for first-class facilities in the Negro area would remain. Interestingly enough the Winston-Salem NAACP branch came out against a new East Winston hospital, calling instead for an enlargement of the new county hospital sufficient to enable it to accommodate all citizens. The conflict between welfare and status goals thus is an ever-present part of the hospital controversy in Winston-Salem.

Whereas Militants champion race goals which attract strong Negro support while drawing the determined opposition of whites—goals which are in the sensitive areas of interracial activity and hence those which maximize the dynamic content of race—Conservatives favor race objectives which in their high degree of community acceptance serve to minimize racial tensions. Conservatives still work for race goals (better schools *for Negroes*, for example) rather than general community goals (better schools), but the goals are of a kind which reduce racial protest rather than mobilize the subcommunity for action. For example, conservative Negro leaders in Winston-Salem were prominently associated with the city's urban renewal project. The project is producing reconstruction of a large portion of the Negro residential area in Winston-Salem, and unquestionably involves race objectives of the greatest importance. But it is the kind of project that influential whites can support. Conservatives thus were able to work with white leaders for a goal which took on a community flavor. In the same way conservative leaders are participating actively in electoral politics in Winston-Salem, and in other rim-South cities in which such activity has the stamp of legitimacy. The objectives—more Negro voters, more Negro representation on city boards and commissions, a fairer distribution of city services, etc.—do not exploit latent tensions in race.

In the same way, Conservative leaders are more frequently associated with projects in which Negro political objectives are *not* involved than are either Moderates or Militants. Burgess noted that some Durham leaders "have chosen to subordinate their role as race leader to their role as functional leader." [16] They have sought to be known as prominent educators, businessmen, civic leaders, and so on, rather than as race leaders. Conservatives frequently play leading roles in Negro businessmen's groupings, in parent-teachers associations, in

[16] *Op. cit.*, p. 182.

United Fund drives, and the like. Militant leaders, in contrast, devote little time to leadership outside the area of race advancement. Conservatives (and to a lesser extent Moderates) are multipurpose leaders. Militants tend to be unipurpose leaders.

Conservative leadership in Winston and Greenville: Differences in race goals. Along with these basic similarities in the goals-orientation of conservative leaders throughout the urban South there are certain important differences. The principal difference between the goals-orientation of Conservatives in Winston-Salem and that of Greenville Conservatives follows from the fact that the scope of "legitimate" race-advancement activity is much broader in the North Carolina city. Extensive participation by Negroes in electoral politics, for example, is recognized as "legitimate" by large numbers of Winston-Salem whites but not by their Greenville counterparts. With the acceptance of the legitimacy of Negro participation, electoral politics in Winston-Salem has become to a significant extent the sphere for what we have called welfare goals: for example, securing more representation on various city commissions in order to assure a fair distribution of city goods and services. But since Greenville whites continue to reject Negro participation in electoral politics as "something Negroes aren't ready for," participation remains primarily a status objective, part of the broader claim by Negroes for recognition as full and equal partners in the American democracy. Electoral politics has been the sphere of Conservatives and Moderates in Winston-Salem, but of Militants in Greenville.[17]

Because of massive white resistance to any communication with Negro leaders after the *Brown* decision—a resistance

[17] There were signs in 1963 and early 1964 in Greenville of white recognition of the legitimacy of limited participation by Negroes in electoral politics, and interestingly, Moderates were beginning to appear where previously only Militants had tread.

which is only now beginning to break—Greenville Conservatives have had a far narrower range of choice in race goals than their Winston-Salem counterparts. Committed to cooperating with white leaders who for the most part have refused to cooperate in anything other than the enforcement of the two-standards system, Greenville Conservatives have worked for only the most innocuous and limited of welfare objectives.

MEANS

The central and identifying element of the means-orientation of conservative leaders is their avoidance—in fact their rejection—of direct action. Boycotts, protest marches, sit-ins, mass protest meetings, picketing, and the like receive at most the token support of Conservatives. Because of their stand against direct action, Conservatives receive heavy criticism from militant leaders. But Conservatives insist on the effectiveness of other means in advancing the cause of the race.

Although conservative leaders never participate in and rarely publicly advocate direct action, their private responses to direct action demonstrations initiated by others differ sharply. Two main types of responses can be identified. One group of Conservatives categorically rejects direct action as an instrument for race advancement. On the other side are those Conservatives who argue that various approaches to race advancement are needed. The latter insist that their style of race leadership is a necessary complement to the leadership provided by Moderates and Militants. A prominent Conservative in Winston-Salem observed:

I will admit that demonstrations help soften things up for us, but they [Militants] should recognize that we are doing an important job too. We need all approaches: demonstrations, negotiations, everything. I don't mind them disagreeing with the way I handle things, but calling me an "Uncle Tom" is going too far. They know there are things I can't do because of the position I'm in.

When those Conservatives who most strongly oppose the use of direct action are asked to explain their opposition the following arguments generally are used. (1) "Demonstrations can get out of hand." What begins as a peaceful protest can easily turn into a very nasty racial clash. Tempers once aroused are not easily quieted. Moreover, demonstrations invite counter-demonstrations by white racists and there may be degeneration into an ever-increasing pattern of violence. The editors of the *Birmingham World*, a Negro newspaper, had this in mind when they warned at the beginning of the 1963 demonstrations in Birmingham:

But it should also be realized that the opposition has scouted, appraised and studied the new techniques being used by the younger civil rights organizations. The opposition has caught on and made counter-plans. The opposition is better organized, more shrewd and has more tricks than in the early days of non-violence.[18]

(2) "Direct action demonstrations harden the lines." Flexibility is lost as white and Negro leaders are forced by public opinion within their own communities to "hold the line." Direct action demonstrations raise the "community blood pressure." As involvement increases around a sensitive issue, extremists are called from both camps. The rule of "gangster elements" is substituted for the rule of the best.

(3) "Militants needlessly antagonize whites by direct action demonstrations." One Winston-Salem Conservative put it this way:

Marches on City Hall and that kind of thing make whites mad. When people are mad you can't talk with them, can you? If you wanted to get me to do something for you, you wouldn't walk into my office and insult me.

A Greenville Conservative felt that demonstrations in that city would jeopardize progress made:

[18] *Birmingham World*, April 10, 1963.

Look, for the first time we have some genuine communication. If there are some big demonstrations now, they'll just get them [influential white leaders] mad and we'll be right back where we started.

Big demonstrations frighten and antagonize whites. You can't, these Conservatives argue, lead a march on City Hall and then have a relaxed and productive discussion with city officials.

(4) "Access is the key." These Conservatives insist that their access to white leaders and the confidence whites have in them as responsible citizens offer the best opportunities for advancing the race. It should be noted that in this emphasis on negotiations with the "power structure" as the most effective means for race advancement, these Conservatives are brought to a position where they must argue for the possibility of persuading whites on the legitimacy of their appeals.

Bargaining. Militants insist that white leaders are by definition opposed to Negro interests and hence must be prodded into action by what James Wilson has called "negative inducements": boycotts, threats of demonstrations, demonstrations, and so on. Conservatives, on the other hand, insist that there are influential whites in each community who can be persuaded to act in behalf of Negro interests. When he talks about persuading white leaders, the Conservative is usually not so naïve as to believe that all whites are open to persuasion. But he will usually insist that there are some who are.

It is important to realize that the model which guides Conservatives here is one lifted from other areas in which competition for scarce values goes on. How, after all, does a young man rise in the structure of a large American corporation? He does it, according to the model, by persuading his superiors that he merits respect and confidence. How, according to the democratic creed, do Americans realize their political objectives? They do so (1) by educating their fellow citizens and elected officials on the wisdom and legitimacy of the desired action; (2) by persuading their fellows and elected officials that the desired action will be advantageous to all segments of the community; (3) by threatening their elected officials, if the first two methods prove inadequate, with the withdrawal of support unless the desired action is taken; and (4) then if all else fails by trying to "throw the rascals out" and replace them with new officials who agree on the wisdom of the desired action. A petition calling for the redress of grievances, yes; the use of the sanction of the ballot box, yes. But the model of white middle-class politics in twentieth-century America does not include mass demonstrations, boycotts, or defiance of laws one does not like. Conservatives seem to be profoundly attracted by the model of white middle-class politics. It is not surprising that when asked why he thought he was able to make headway in his discussions with white leaders, a leading Winston-Salem Conservative replied:

Because they respect me. I don't bow and scrape. I am firm but I always try to be fair. My positions are sound. They are carefully thought out and they are recognized as such. I try to be mature, calm and sensible.

And if this is not enough, he would say (although he did not do so in this conversation), there are positive inducements available to achieve compliance.

The position of Conservatives today in the cities of the outer South and to a significant although lesser extent in the urban deep South with respect to means for realizing race objectives is far different from that of the old accommodating leadership. According to one white man's description the "Uncle Tom" came

hat in hand, stood at my desk, waiting for an invitation to be seated as was his custom . . . as a humble but great supplicant for the friendship of the white man for his race.[19]

[19] Quoted by Thompson, *op. cit.*, p. 62.

Contemporary conservative leaders do emphasize negotiations rather than "going to the barricades." But their power position is much stronger and they know this. They are not representatives of a totally powerless group as were their counterparts three decades ago. However much Conservatives may criticize direct action, many clearly recognize that one of the strongest arguments they can advance is the need for programs to redress Negro grievances in order to spare the community serious racial conflict. Although many Conservatives shun "negative inducements," they find no objection to "positive inducements" made possible by the existence of the "negative inducements."

Conservatives are able to offer inducements which involve the concrete economic and political interests of whites. For example, the Urban League of Winston-Salem has recently had some success in promoting plant integration and in opening up new jobs to Negroes in the city's factories and stores. On the surface the appeal seems to be the old one to the standard of racial justice and to the need to maintain the city's "good reputation" in race relations. But in fact the League's director offers this choice to the business establishment of Winston-Salem: either do it peacefully through the League or do it under the glare of public harassment from protest organizations.

Conservatives are active in electoral politics in Winston-Salem, where Negro participation has been firmly established. Here the Conservative-as-bargainer attempts to trade political support for concessions. Conservatives will rarely publicly threaten white politicians with the loss of Negro support unless certain actions are taken, but in behind-the-scenes discussions they will trade on their ability to influence the Negro vote.

"With all deliberate speed." Conservatives insist that they are as anxious as any of their fellow leaders to see every vestige of racial discrimination removed. But they claim a

greater appreciation of the difficulties involved in changing patterns of race relations. They insist, moreover, that precipitous action by Negroes not only is doomed to failure but often sets back the cause of race advancement. Conservatives frequently accuse more militant leaders of "jumping into things" without familiarity with the subject. An example of this is a Conservative's criticism of the way a Moderate handled a case of alleged police brutality in Winston-Salem. He argued that the Moderate, the Negro alderman, had "popped off" without getting the facts.

He looked pretty foolish, shouting about police brutality. I know that there is a problem of police treatment, but by his rash action he handled the wrong case in the wrong way. He wanted publicity, mass support, but he didn't succeed. People knew that she [the woman accusing the police of brutal treatment] has a real bad record. . . . It looks now as though the police acted with a great deal of circumspection.

Asked how he would have handled the matter, the Conservative replied:

I would have looked into all the facts before blasting away. I would have made sure of my case before going down to City Hall and making accusations.

In defense of the alderman, more militant leaders stressed that it was immaterial whether or not the police were guilty of brutality in this particular case.

They [the police] are always pushing Negroes around and he did right in letting them know we don't like it and aren't going to stand for any of it. This keeps them aware of how we feel. They will be more careful.

Illustrative of the Conservatives' emphasis on "all deliberate speed" is an editorial which appeared in the *Birmingham World* at the height of the protest demonstrations in Birmingham in April 1963.[20] With the city in a virtual state of siege the *World* asked, "What should we do?" Its answer was that first, there was the need to "deal factually with the Birmingham situation." After a careful examination of the various facets of the problem, goals should be set, a "basic Birmingham program" formulated, methods selected, and targets painted. Then and only then Birmingham Negroes could and should "move with dedication." [21]

More militant leaders in Winston and Greenville reject the Conservatives' charge that they are prone to rash and precipitous action. They argue that their race-advancement activity is in fact carefully planned and that the accusations of Conservatives are but a smoke screen concealing the latter's reluctance to do anything. It is true that Conservatives frequently charge "rash, unplanned action" when their real target is *direct* action. But the Conservatives' emphasis on careful planning cannot be dismissed as a mere mask for inactivity. In their emphasis here as in their general reliance on means which are recognized as legitimate by the community as a whole, Conservatives are choosing means which they see being used by "respectable" white political leaders.

Conservative leadership in Winston and Greenville: differences in means. We noted above that Negro participation in electoral politics in Winston-Salem is far advanced for the South. Negroes are occupying positions of the middle range in city government and in the Democratic party organization. Conservatives are active in this area. In Greenville, in contrast, Negro participation in electoral politics, until very recently at least, has been considered "radical" activity, off limits for Conservatives. The importance of the participation at any rate has been minimal.

[20] The *World's* editorial views at the time clearly reflected the opinion of the city's conservative leadership.

[21] *Birmingham World*, April 10, 1963.

In general, Greenville Conservatives find themselves much more restricted in the means available for race advancement than their Winston-Salem counterparts. White opposition to desegregation is much stronger in this deep-South city, and there are few kinds of race-advancement activity that are not subject to sanctions. Through the Urban League, Winston-Salem Conservatives work side by side with leading white industrialists for better job opportunities for Negroes. They contribute to the desegregation of public facilities through the city's effective biracial committee. Through their positions on municipal government boards and commissions they can initiate and support programs considered beneficial to Negroes. In general, through free access to white leaders, Conservatives are able to promote Negro interests in a fairly effective way. Greenville has no Urban League, and its only comparable organization, the Phillis Wheatley Association, has had to limit its activity to relatively modest service projects in Greenville's Negro subcommunity. No Negroes occupy policy-making positions in the city government or in the party organizations. Conservatives—like other leaders—have been unable in the recent past to enter into any regular, effective give-and-take discussions with influential whites, because the latter either have not wanted to participate or have felt unable to so legitimize race-advancement activity. Although there are indications of significant changes in this situation with the activity of the two biracial units which were created in 1963 (one replacing the other), the basic point remains unchanged: Greenville Conservatives seeking to advance the race by means bearing the stamp of legitimacy (if not approval) have thus far not been successful.

RHETORIC

Rhetoric as used here includes the language, tone, and manner with which leaders publicly refer to matters involving race and race relations. As such, rhetoric is a major element of style. A leader may support goals and means which by themselves would put him in the "militant" category in a given community, and yet be regarded as a Moderate because of his rhetoric. Unusual but not unique is the case of a Greensboro, North Carolina, minister whose program for race advancement was indistinguishable from that of the most militant leadership in the city. But, in the long years which he spent in the South Carolina low country before moving to urban North Carolina, he had acquired a manner of addressing whites, a way of putting things that quite disarmed them. His speech was filled with homey anecdotes and parables, and with frequent allusions to Biblical personages and events. He spoke slowly, never raising his voice in conversation. He never used words like "demand" or "insist." He never denounced whites for discriminating against Negroes—or, more precisely, his words were rarely if ever *taken* by whites as denunciations. As a result, although those who knew him well recognized that he had consistently supported direct action and had worked energetically for the most sensitive status goals, he was not universally regarded as one of the city's more militant leaders. He blended the rhetoric of a Conservative with the means and goals of a Militant. *He is, of course, an exception.* The component parts of a leadership style generally form a consistent whole because they are but different facets of a unidimensional phenomenon. Each represents a *similar response to the pattern of race relations*. But exceptions to this general consistency of leadership styles do occur, for a variety of reasons, many of them apparently idiosyncratic. This case does illustrate well the point that rhetoric can at times be even more important than goals and means in determining how whites and Negroes classify a leader.

Amelioration versus *confrontation*. The Conservative typically seeks to ameliorate racial conflict through his rhetoric, rather than to strip discrimination of all the rationalizations in which whites clothe it. Race objectives are presented in such a manner as to reduce white opposition to a minimum. "They can talk to me"; "They find me calm and reasonable"; "I don't go around pointing my finger and making accusations"—these are the reasons Conservatives frequently offer in explanation of their greater access to white leaders. They are strongly critical of the more militant leaders, who, they argue, gratuitously insult the whites with whom they have contact:

They go out of their way to insult them [white leaders]. Now I don't "Uncle Tom it" when I talk to whites, but I don't try to find ways to make them mad either. That doesn't make any sense. Look, if you came in here and started making accusations you wouldn't get far with me, would you? Instead, you spoke to me civilly and we got along all right. Well, it's the same thing. When you are talking to them it just doesn't make sense to try to be rude and insulting.

Whites of course concur with this. A Greenville white whose racial views are relatively liberal gave the following evaluation of the effectiveness of a militant Negro leader:

Well I don't think he is very effective at all. Whenever we get together in a meeting he makes a long-winded speech giving us all hell. "We are not going to take this any longer from you people!", and things like that. So most people just won't have anything to do with him. I think his stock has dropped a lot as whites have seen more and more of him on the [biracial] committee. He seems to go out of his way to make people mad.

Conservative leaders do not accuse whites of bad faith. They do not point fingers. They do not sound bitter. They do not choose the most emotive words. They do not attempt to dramatize racial conflict. Instead, Conservatives frequently make reference to common interests, common problems and the importance of preserving good race relations. They choose neutral, conciliatory words even when pushing hard for certain race goals. Attempts by Conservatives at conciliation extend beyond words to gestures and facial expressions. A white speaker at a biracial meeting in Winston-Salem made certain remarks clearly offensive to the Negroes present. Conservatives managed generally to look calm and contemplative while these remarks were being made; but a Militant laughed derisively and made his extreme displeasure obvious. This is a small incident and the data is wholly impressionistic. Still, attendance at many such meetings and frequent discussions with Negro and white leaders has given us reasonably good indication that such actions are part of the stuff of leadership styles. They are important to both Negroes and whites in classifying leaders.

In his rhetoric, then, as in race goals and means, the conservative leader imitates white political leaders. His approach is essentially one which he sees whites using successfully. His model is white middle-class politics. The golden words of this type of politics are *moderation, consensus, respectability, persuasion*, and *access*. If conservative leadership is not the most effective style of race leadership in the urban South today, it is because the nature of politics and the political struggle is so significantly different for Negroes than for whites that a style of leadership well suited to the latter is inadequate for the former.

EFFECTIVENESS

We must proceed cautiously in this assessment of the effectiveness of the conservative style of race leadership because different approaches to the cause of race advancement seem more frequently to complement than to conflict with each other. Still, certain general conclusions can be advanced, first as to what conditions minimize and maximize the effectiveness of the conservative style, and second as to the effectiveness of the conservative style in relation to that of the other styles on the leadership continuum.

The conservative style has its greatest effectiveness-potential in those southern cities with the most permissive patterns of race relations. Conservatives have greater success in Winston-Salem than in Greenville. This is the case (1) because the broader spectrum of race-advancement activity considered "legitimate" in the North Carolina city gives Conservatives there a broader scope for activity; and (2) because Conservatives in Winston have a far larger arsenal of "positive inducements" to use in race-advancement activity.

Second, conservative leadership enjoys a greater effectiveness-potential in those southern cities which have recently experienced large-scale direct action demonstrations or which have a high potential for such demonstrations. This is only superficially paradoxical. White leaders can better appreciate the value of the conservative approach when they have been confronted with a more militant approach. Southern whites cannot be expected to "give" any more than they consider it in their interests to give. In Greenville, where direct action demonstrations have been few and of the "corner store variety"—sit-ins in the summer of 1960, "read-ins" at the library in 1961, "skate-ins" at the roller skating rink in 1962, and "serve-ins" at the tennis courts in 1963—white leaders have felt little pressure to respond to the overtures of Conservatives. Only a handful of people were involved in each of these demonstrations, and with the exception of the sit-ins in 1960, none of the demonstrations were sustained. The wave of direct action demonstrations which swept the South in 1963 did strengthen the hand of Greenville Conservatives somewhat because of the fear that "Greenville may be next." One conservative leader freely admitted that he thought the biracial committee on which he and a number of other conservative leaders were serving had been able to negotiate the desegregation of some lunch counters in Greenville in June 1963 because "the power structure was afraid that Greenville would be another Birmingham or Greensboro, and they couldn't afford that. . . . They are trying hard to bring new business in and racial conflict is bad for that sort of thing." Direct action demonstrations have been more extensive in Winston-Salem and the potential for them there far greater. Pressure applied by Militants in such demonstrations resulted directly in the opening of channels—such as the biracial committees —for Conservatives.

Three important qualifications must be inserted at this point with respect to the generalization that direct action or the potential for direct action increases the effectiveness-potential of conservative leadership. First, the generalization is valid only for a particular period. The first response of most southern cities to the postwar assault on patterns of discrimination was a *closing* of doors once open to the old type of conservative leadership. A great slience ensued and in this period all forms of communication and cooperation were suspect. Greenville entered the great silence after the *Brown* decision; Winston-Salem, seven years earlier. As southern cities have emerged from the great silence, however, direct action demonstrations have strengthened the hand of the new Conservatives. Second, this generalization should not be interpreted to mean that the more direct action demonstrations there are in a city, the more effective is the conservative leadership there. Rather, we mean only that in cities like Greenville which have been largely untouched by the demonstrations which have swept wide areas of the South, the "peaceful solution" pleas of Conservatives have less force. Finally, we do not mean that the position of Conservatives is strengthened with respect to that of the other leadership styles by a history of effective direct action; but simply that the position is *absolutely* stronger.

While Conservatives perform certain important functions in race advancement in both Winston-Salem and Greenville, they serve primarily to supplement the leadership of Moderates and Militants rather than to initiate changes in the patterns of race relations. They are not a driving force in race advancement. Just as Conservatives are unable to set the direction of race-advancement activity, so they are unable to challenge Moderates and Militants in areas where the latter are active. Both Negroes and whites recognize this. The Conservative's great strength is in his access to white leaders. The weaknesses of his position result from his lack of mass support and his reluctance to use sanctions to force whites to recognize Negro interests. When there is general agreement among whites and Negroes on the need for action, Conservatives are usually able to produce more impressive results than are the protest organizations. (For example, when both whites and Negroes in Winston-Salem agreed that job opportunities for Negroes should be improved, the Conservatives' strategy of approaching key white employers through the Urban League was more effective than the boycotts of the protest organizations.) But in those issue-areas where Negroes and whites are at opposite poles, Conservatives have not been effective. They achieve their greatest successes, then, consolidating positions achieved through the activity of Moderates and Militants. Conservatives are not innovators. They do not bring sharp departures from the prevailing pattern of race relations.

Surveys which we conducted in Winston and Greenville revealed that most Negroes have little knowledge of the activities of conservatives leaders. No Conservative was identified as among the top leaders in either city. But this is not to say that the leadership activity of Conservatives is rejected by the rank and file. Rather, the nature of their leadership is such that little attention is focused upon it. In the few instances in recent years in Winston-Salem and Greenville in which Conservatives have attempted to challenge Moderates and Militants over the means of achieving a particular race goal, they have found without exception their position subjected to sharp criticism from other Negroes. Recognition of this by all parties has reduced the effectiveness of conservative leadership in such areas. But when there is general agreement among white and Negro leaders on the necessary and/or desirable solution, and when different means are not mutually exclusive, Conservatives have operated with the general approval of those Negroes who are cognizant of their activity. There is, for example, a general agreement among white and Negro leaders in Winston that Negroes must be given better job opportunities. The means used by the Urban League do not conflict with those of the NAACP. The League here has enjoyed some success and its role, where understood, is generally applauded.

THE MILITANT STYLE

Militants occupy the opposite end of the continuum of race leadership styles. They offer the style of race leadership which of the various competing styles in a particular area is most strongly opposed by whites. The goals which they pursue include those around which interracial tensions are greatest; the means which they select to advance the race generate the greatest anxieties among whites; and their rhetoric tends to sharpen rather than ameliorate racial conflict.

The literature on race leadership styles has been characterized by a very large measure of highly partisan analysis. There is a tendency, for example, for many white and Negro scholars with liberal convictions to see the Militant as a knight in shining armor. Thompson argues that while the "Uncle Tom" apparently is satisfied with second-class citizenship and the "racial diplomat" works well within the framework of the separate but equal doctrine,

the race man [the equivalent of our Militant] . . . *has been a perennial enemy of the bi-racial system.* . . . The race man is *not a racist*. He is *not chauvinistic*. Instead he sees himself as the Negro symbol of mankind's struggle for dignity. He does not apologize for his Negro-ness and yet he continues to insist that he is an American and feels that being Negro should not in any way limit the rights, duties and opportunities inherent to American citizenship.[22]

This kind of partisanship accounts for some of the most notable errors in the analyses of race leadership styles.

Thompson correctly observes that "there has been no period in the history of Negroes in American society when there was not recognized militant Negro leadership."[23] The goals, means, and rhetoric of militant leaders have, however, varied considerably with time and place. The activities of the NAACP in the South in the 1930's—now viewed as quite modest indeed—were at the time labeled by Negroes and whites as "radical" or "militant." Today, emphasis on the same race goals—for example an end to lynching—and the same means—court action—would hardly categorize a leader as a Militant. But if there has always been some form of race leadership considered militant, it is still true in one sense that the militant style is "just emerging."[24] The "Uncle Tom" was numerically predominant throughout the South in the 1930's. Militants had few sanctions to apply to secure their objectives. Behind them was a Negro population which had come to accept the old biracial system as a more or less permanent evil. And these Militants were subjected to very serious sanctions for their race-advancement activities. Today, in contrast, militant leaders in many southern cities have rather impressive means for securing white acquiescence to their objectives, have the firm support of large numbers of Negroes who now see destruction of the biracial system as immediately possible, and despite certain exceptions such as the vicious murder of Medgar Evers, generally face milder sanctions less consistently and severely applied. Indeed, in outer-South cities like Winston-Salem militant leaders have reasonable assurance of

[22] Thompson, *op. cit.*, pp. 75–76, 78.
[23] *Ibid.*, p. 75.
[24] See Burgess, *op. cit.*, p. 185.

personal security. The impressive increase in the number of Negro professional men dependent only on Negroes for their livelihoods has enlarged the pool of potential militant leadership.

GOALS

Militant leaders in both Winston-Salem and Greenville devote their energies to the realization of status goals as distinct from welfare goals. Their position in the hospital controversy in Winston-Salem was noted in the preceding section. Still another controversy in Winston-Salem, over the integration of the city's swimming pools, further illustrates how welfare and status goals are at times mutually exclusive, and when this is the case, the consistent preference of Militants for status goals.

Welfare versus *status goals: wade-ins at Reynolds Park.* Negro college students returning home in June 1962, together with a few local NAACP leaders, went to the city's then all-white swimming pool at Reynolds Park and sought admission. Winston-Salem Mayor John Surratt and other city leaders took the position that the city could not violate the law; that is, the pools as public facilities could not be operated with enforced segregation. Negroes were admitted. Another pool was integrated a few days later. Negroes continued to use these pools regularly and whites for the most part stopped using them. Strong pressures were generated to close all the city's pools as nearby Greensboro and many other southern cities had done. Winston-Salem at the time was operating two pools used exclusively by Negroes and a third "Negro" pool at Winston Lake Park was about to be opened. The integration of the swimming pools, unlike the hospital controversy, evoked little open debate in the Negro community. No Negro leader could, after all, come out against integration of the swimming pools. But where most conservative leaders either sat on their hands or worked on a biracial committee established to try to find some way to resolve the dispute, militant leaders tended to give vociferous support to the integration activity.

The questions which Negro leaders had to answer were these: Should Negroes continue to use the "white" pools regularly and run the risk of having all the pools closed? The poor in general and hence the Negro subcommunity in particular would suffer most from closing the public pools.[25] Or should Negroes, having formally established their right to use the pools, restrict their exercise of that right for the present time?

Some of the more conservative leaders said privately that "getting together in a big bathtub" was too touchy an issue and should be left alone. They admitted that they had had in the first place little interest in integrating the pools. It was "too much trouble for so small a benefit." But the issue having been raised, the best solution was for Negroes to use the pools for a period of time on an occasional basis. They were ready in effect to apply tokenism to pool integration. Moderate leaders would make no concession to the fears of whites. They bitterly resented the charge that they would be undesirable poolmates. But they believed that keeping the pools open was so important that compromise would be justified. Negroes might well submit to restricted access for the present "until things cool off." Most militant leaders in

[25] The director of the city's recreation program told the author in November 1962 that as a result of the integration activity it had become impossible to get funds to build new public pools even though these were badly needed. In addition, two new private—i.e., white—community pools had already been built and more were planned. He maintained that once large numbers of whites had access to private community pools there would be much greater pressure to close the public pools. In such a development the poor in general, and hence Negroes in particular, would suffer. The Winston-Salem experience is not atypical: there has been virtually no construction of public swimming pools in the South in the last decade.

Winston-Salem, in contrast, agreed with the position of an NAACP leader:

Close them up. Close them all up if neccesary. I will never agree to any compromise where we in effect stop using the pools. If they are closed, the whites suffer too. If they are left open but segregated, only we suffer. If they are closed, the whites will soon get unhappy and will want them opened even if it is on an integrated basis.

To these leaders, agreement to use the "white" pools only occasionally and then in small groups would be a concession to the charge that Negroes are too dirty or sexually dangerous to be acceptable poolmates.[26]

[26] Pressure to close all city swimming pools was very strong in the summer of 1962. On July 16 of that year one of the aldermanic representatives on the city's recreation commission proposed that all pools be closed. After intense discussion his motion was voted down 5–3. Against this background a biracial committee was appointed to attempt to resolve the issue. One of the four Negro members of a subcommittee of that biracial committee proposed that the integrated pools be used on an alternate-day basis by Negroes and whites: one day for whites, one day for Negroes, the third day, anyone. This proposal was accepted by the subcommittee with only one Negro objecting. The Negro who voiced opposition to this proposal was one of the leaders of the pool integration activity; of the three Negroes on the subcommittee who supported the proposal, one was a Moderate and two were Conservatives. Only two of the ten Negro members of the biracial committee were adamantly opposed to the proposal. Those two members, however, were the two principal leaders of the integration activity. Given their opposition, any attempt to put the proposal into operation would have been an exercise in futility. This was quickly recognized and the proposal was dropped. In later months, after it had become obvious that the pools would remain open even without Negro compromise on access, those who had initially supported this compromise proposal conceded privately that they had been in error. But at the time, with the threat of closing all pools hanging over them, Conservatives and Moderates gave support to the proposal. Only Militants strongly objected. The biracial committee was unable to take any effective action toward resolving

Goals which maximize the dynamic content of race. Whether in a fully rational political world white Americans would be more strongly opposed to Negro attempts to integrate a lunch counter or a swimming pool than to Negro attempts to get better jobs or tax dollars for urban renewal is not at all certain. But in the American South in the mid-1960's whites *are* more strongly opposed to the former than to the latter. Whether in a fully rational political world Negro Americans would demonstrate greater involvement and interest in integration attempts like sit-ins than in efforts to achieve better jobs and better pay is also questionable. But they in fact do in the American South today. Sit-ins, to continue with the example, have a greater immediacy and reality.

---

the dispute and the pools remained open throughout the summer of 1962 with white attendance drastically reduced. In the fall of 1962 there was some support among whites for not opening the pools in 1963. In the 1963 mayoralty campaign held in the spring of 1963 the Republican candidate in effect endorsed closing the pools. His argument was that the 1962 attendance was too low to justify the expenditure. The Democratic candidate, however, made it clear that he favored continued city operation of the pools. The Republican candidate gained nearly half the white vote but was buried under an avalanche of Negro votes; and the pools reopened in May 1963 with no announcement and no comment on the situation. In 1963 one of the two integrated pools became in essence an all-Negro pool. Attendance at both pools was somewhat higher than in 1962, but still lower than the preintegration level. It was really not made clear until the fall of 1963 that the city would indeed continue to operate swimming pools. Then in March 1964, in a very dramatic gesture, the city of Winston-Salem announced plans to spend at least $570,000 in the next two years for the construction of two or more swimming pools. One of the two pools scheduled to be built will be in a Negro neighborhood, the other in a white neighborhood. It was a bold statement that the desegregation issue had not eliminated swimming pools from public recreation in Winston-Salem. The decision to build new public pools is almost without parallel in the post-*Brown* South where cities have been considered "enlightened" if they were merely keeping their existing pools open.

Militants throughout the American South have placed greater emphasis on status goals, the most sensitive race goals. Given the generally greater hostility of southern whites to status goals and the greater identification of southern Negroes with them, these goals tend to become focal points for Negro-white antagonism. Biracial cooperation around these goals is impossible. Through these goals, then, the capacity of race to move and shape Negro and white is enhanced. The dynamic content of race is maximized.

Militants generally do not emphasize goals on which a significant level of Negro-white consensus exists. There are, of course, very few race goals on which Negroes and whites in the American South today find themselves in full agreement, and the opposite situation of optimum confrontation— all Negroes strongly disagreeing with all whites—is also reached only rarely. But the gradations between optimum confrontation and complete consensus are important, indeed crucial, and the race goals emphasized by the Militants are all located near the conflict pole.

The Newsweek-Harris survey tried to determine precisely how white America is reacting to various kinds of race-advancement activity and race objectives. When southern whites were asked, "Should the law guarantee Negroes equal rights to white people in . . . ?" the responses were as follows:[27]

	Percentage answering yes
Job opportunities?	62
Voting?	92
Getting good housing?	81

But when the same questions were directed to other kinds of activity the percentage of favorable responses among southern whites dropped sharply:

[27] "How Whites Feel About Negroes: A Painful American Dilemma," *Newsweek*, October 21, 1963, p. 45.

Percentage answering yes

Using restaurants and
lunch counters?   49

Giving their children
integrated schooling?   43

When the question was "Would you favor a federal law for-bidding discrimination in housing against Negroes?" 80 per cent of southern whites answering said no. Finally, when asked if Negroes were justified in conducting sit-ins at lunch counters, 84 per cent of southern whites answering replied in the negative.

Myrdal found the same kind of responses in his investigations two and a half decades before. White southerners were asked in the Myrdal study to rank in order of importance various types of discrimination. The following rank order was determined:

Rank I. . . . the bar against intermarriage and sexual intercourse involving white women.

Rank II. . . . the several etiquettes in discriminations, which specifically concerned behavior in inter-personal relations. (These are the barriers against dancing, bathing, eating and drinking together and social intercourse generally. . . .)

Rank III. . . . the segregations and discriminations in the use of public facilities such as schools, churches, and means of conveyance.

Rank IV. . . . political disenfranchisement.

Rank V. . . . discriminations in law courts, by the police and by other public servants.

Rank VI. . . . the discrimination in securing land, credit, jobs and other means of earning a living. . . .[28]

In short, white opposition has been and remains significantly greater to goals which fall in the general category of status goals, precisely the objectives to the realization of which Militants devote their energies and talents. It has proved pos-

[28] Myrdal, *op. cit.*, pp. 60–61.

sible for white moderates and Negro leaders to come together to promote better job opportunities for Negroes. There is here, first of all, consensus at some level on the existence of a serious problem, and second, on certain steps to be taken to remedy the problem. Given this agreement, race is not always present in discussion. But when the integration of housing, swimming pools, and schools is at issue, the line of cleavage between Negro and white is sharply drawn. Cooperation becomes virtually impossible, and the dynamic capacity of race is enhanced.

The second point noted is that status goals carry a far greater attractive power for Negroes than welfare goals; or more precisely, that Negro Americans show a greater personal involvement in those goals involving their claim to consideration as full and equal partners in the American democracy than to those goals in which greater welfare benefits are at issue. Integration activity throughout the South over the last decade stands as irrefutable testimony to this. We should not be surprised at this in light of the very extensive and persuasive literature on the effects of racial discrimination on the Negro American's self-image. The attractive power of goals which offer emancipation from the damning, pervasive sense of inferiority which has been the legacy of segregation is necessarily great.

Although conservative leaders frequently demonstrate a desire to subordinate their position as race leaders to a position as functional leaders, Militants rarely do so. Militant race leaders rarely become known for activity such as heading up a Red Cross drive, a businessman's organization, or the Negro Masons. The "typical" Militant is a unipurpose leader, and he shows little interest in recognition for work outside of the area of race advancement.

The militant leader, then, by (1) emphasizing race goals which evoke strongest white opposition and hostility, by (2) championing goals in which Negro involvement is greatest, and by (3) shunning recognition as a functional leader and devoting time and effort primarily to the cause of race advancement, works to maximize the dynamic content of race.

Militant leadership in Winston and Greenville: differences in race goals. Differences in the goals-orientation of Militants in Winston-Salem and Greenville all flow from the greater permissiveness in patterns of race relations in the North Carolina city. To be specific here, the idea of Negro representation on various city boards and commissions is widely accepted in Winston-Salem. Representation somewhere between tokenism and parity is now part of the *status quo* in race relations. Working to get another Negro on the school board, then, is not going to arouse particular hostility among whites. In the same way, it is not going to be regarded as a bold new assertion of equality by Negroes. This kind of means-goal, then, is regularly pursued by Conservatives and Moderates in Winston-Salem, and only occasionally by Militants. On the other hand, such representation is considered by Greenville whites to involve a quite radical departure. It is only slightly less objectionable than integration of lunch counters, motels, theaters, swimming pools, and the like. Negroes in Greenville rightly see representation in policy making positions in city government as involving an important assertion of status. In much the same way, token school integration achieved in Winston-Salem in 1957 has now become pretty much accepted there. Moderate extension of school integration, then, is not a goal associated with militant leaders (although proposals for "immediate and total" integration do come from Militants).[29] But in Greenville, where public

[29] For example, in March 1964 a leading Winston-Salem Militant announced the formation of the Citizens Committee for Equal Education, later called the Citizens Committee for Equal Rights. The committee was established, in his words, to promote "a plan for complete desegregation of local schools." This leader was not satisfied with the moderate extensions which were being achieved.

schools remained segregated until the academic year 1964–1965, school integration is an objective associated only with the city's most militant leadership.[30]

MEANS

The central, identifying element in the approach of Militants to race advancement is their emphasis on direct action. Militant leaders in both Winston-Salem and Greenville, of course, make use of other means in attempting to realize race goals. But Militants stress that they consider direct action an integral part of their program to realize the most vital political objectives of Negro Americans. Boycotts, protest marches, sit-ins, mass protest meetings, picketing, and the like have

[30] Perhaps it is necessary to summarize again here exactly how a goal such as school integration can be considered "militant" in Greenville while "moderate" in Winston-Salem. The answer in the first instance is that this is in fact how Negroes and whites in Winston-Salem and Greenville so consider it. The same race objective is classified differently by the inhabitants of the two cities because its position with respect to the existing pattern of race relations is quite different. School integration represents an important departure from the existing pattern of race relations in Greenville; it is now part of the race relations pattern in Winston-Salem. School integration thus represents a claim by Negroes for new recognition in Greenville; the claim has already been partially recognized in Winston-Salem. The response of Negroes and whites in a given city to particular race goals both reflects *and determines* the significance and meaning of those goals for all participants. It is, then, not only how Negroes and whites classify a particular race objective, but what it is about that objective in the existing pattern of race relations that leads them to so classify it which is crucial. The Negro leader who works for school integration in Greenville must expect to encounter strong opposition from whites; the opposition is much less intense in Winston-Salem. The white citizenry of Winston-Salem and Greenville may have different definitions of what constitutes militant goals but their response to goals which they consider militant is essentially similar. It involves rejection, hostility, and quite possibly the application of sanctions.

become the stock-in-trade of the militant style of Negro leadership. Militants have had to pay a rather heavy price for their emphasis on direct action. They have been the target for white hostility and sanctions. And they have been attacked frequently within their own community as publicity seekers. Moderates and Conservatives regularly accuse Militants of unnecessarily provoking white hostility through an insistence on direct action when negotiations and bargaining would be adequate. But it is also true that direct action demonstrations have a capacity for securing mass Negro support and involvement to an extent not equalled by any other means of race advancement.

The Negro Militant and the concept of self-interest. The following analysis by a militant Winston-Salem leader is unusual only in its self-consciousness and its perceptiveness.

Look, whites around here aren't going to do anything more than what they have to do. It's silly as hell to think that out of the goodness of their hearts they're going to give us anything. We should have been convinced by what has happened, or rather what has not happened, over the last two hundred years that this simply will not be. You can sit around the table and talk for the next five years and it won't do any good. The man on top wants to stay there and he'll do anything he can to do so. This is why we demonstrate. Whites don't like demonstrations. Demonstrations are bad for business. They frighten people. So we put it to them this way. "Either you meet the legitimate objectives of our people or we'll demonstrate. It's as simple as that."

Militant leaders often soften this argument, referring to the capacity of direct action demonstrations to "prick the consciences" of white citizens, and to vividly dramatize the extent of the Negro malaise. But however the argument is put, militant leaders display little confidence that whites would in fact accede to their demands in the absence of strong pressure on them to do so. And they insist that direct action through boycotts, marches, and sit-ins in many cases is literally

187

the only weapon Negroes have to quickly establish reasons for whites to meet certain legitimate Negro interests.

Most militant leaders quickly dismiss the charge that direct action often "unnecessarily" antagonizes whites. They believe that whites, in the absence of any action by Negroes, are antagonistic to Negro interests, and indeed to Negroes themselves. While many militant leaders in Winston-Salem and Greenville would agree that an excessive reliance on direct action could produce a rigidity in Negro-white relations, they really are not concerned with this problem.

It's not a question of whether they like us or dislike us. The white man has been saying how much he likes good darkies for a couple of hundred years and look how much it's gotten us.

Militants, then, consider the white man committed to maintaining hegemony over nonwhites. Direct action is necessary to force him to do something which he does not want to do— give recognition to the interests of Negro Americans.

Community involvement. We have noted that the means used by conservative Negro leaders generally do not call for the involvement of large numbers of Negroes. The Conservative typically works quietly behind the scenes. When he does want mass involvement, as, for example, in the area of electoral politics, the involvement sought is of a very limited and antiseptic kind. The Negro is asked to vote for particular candidates. Militants want a different kind of involvement. They want warm bodies. They affirm the value of immediate physical involvement through mass meetings, picketing, and sit-ins. Militant leaders argue that even if this kind of involvement does not succeed in realizing its immediate objective, it may well have long-term utility. It increases the political consciousness of the people, and serves to mobilize them, to bring them into the battle for equal rights. Militants insist that the kind of racial confrontation produced by direct action demonstrations almost without exception is able to secure a higher level of mass commitment than any other means utilized by Negro leaders.

Many militant leaders support direct action because it provides a vehicle for contact and involvement with the masses of Negro citizens. Mass involvement, then, is supported not only because it is seen as efficacious in advancing the race, but also because the Militant finds continuous physical involvement with the Negro masses in their political struggle desirable. There is here, it seems, a direct parallel between conservatism and militancy in race advancement and conservatism-liberalism in American ideology generally. Most Conservatives, whether Negro race leaders or white political leaders, are "haves," and as such they feel separated from the "have nots." As a "have," the Conservative at the least is hesitant about altering the system in which he is a "have." Before altering it he wishes to make quite certain that the change will not destroy the bases of authority and/or the general position which he has been able to attain under the system. As a "have" he wants to keep the *hoi polloi* at arms' length. The Militant, in contrast, feels no threat from the "have nots" because he considers himself one. He has no doubts that he will gain from a drastic alteration of the existing system. Association with the Negro masses becomes a vehicle for economic and status advancement.[31]

Freedom now. Militant leaders constantly profess impatience with the rate of change. On the other hand, more than either Conservatives or Moderates, Militants seem to

[31] It is somewhat strange to talk of Conservatives and Militants as "haves" and "have nots" respectively, because, of course, virtually all Negroes in the larger context of American society are "have nots." Conservatism means, in many respects, things quite different for Negro and white political leaders. The Negro Conservative certainly does want change, extensive change. But many feel that the use of means different from those previously followed in advancing the race or sudden departures from the prevailing pattern of race relations pose, in some sense, threats to their position.

expect that great breakthroughs will occur in the very near future. The Militant is both amused and dismayed by the Conservative's charge that he "jumps into things without adequate preparation." His reply is that Negroes have been trying for two or three centuries to gain recognition and treatment as equals and hence that nothing done now can be termed "jumping into things."

The means for race advancement selected by Militants reflect their public profession of impatience with the rate of change. Boycotts, protest marches, mass demonstrations of whatever form, carry with them the illusion if not the substance of sudden and dramatic action. It may or may not be true, as Conservatives frequently insist, that the seemingly slower wheels of negotiations in fact produce more real improvements than does direct action. But the kind of racial confrontation involved in direct action demonstrations gives the appearance to friend and foe alike that the participants are actually, immediately, directly moving to correct long-standing wrongs.

Militant leadership in Winston and Greenville: differences in means. Today Militants in both Winston-Salem and Greenville are committed to the principle of direct action as a major means for realizing race goals. In fact, however, while direct action is a major instrument in the arsenal of Winston-Salem's Militants, it has been used in only the most modest way in Greenville. Indeed, the 1960 sit-ins in that city mark the only significant use of direct action, and even these were modest when compared to sit-ins in other southern cities. In Greenville, Militants have relied on litigation, on the presentation of formal demands to city government officials, on threats of mass demonstrations, on voter registration activity, and the like. They are sufficiently a part of the larger South-wide pattern of Negro militancy that they have an intellectual commitment to direct action. But the realities of the Greenville situation are such that in practice they have relied upon means which in Winston-Salem and many rim-South cities are recognized as part of the arsenal of Moderates and even Conservatives.

Until late 1963 all voter registration activity in Greenville had been conducted by militant leaders. In fact, Greenville Militants devoted more time to voter registration than to any other single race-advancement project. In Winston-Salem, in contrast, voter registration activity has for a decade and a half been a means used regularly, and in the last decade primarily, by Moderates and Conservatives.

Differences in the means-orientation of Militants in Greenville and Winston-Salem result in large part from the fact that Greenville did not begin until the early 1960's to emerge from the "great silence" which followed the *Brown* decision, a period in which any attack on the old biracial system, however made, was considered radical. Pressures presently operating in Greenville to increase race-advancement activity and to alter its content should over the next decade bring the definitions of militant means of race advancement closer together for the two cities.

RHETORIC

Militants are frequently described as more "outspoken." This is true only in one sense, and it is necessary to be quite precise. Militants are not, for example, less "polite" than Conservatives or Moderates. There are "polite" Militants and "impolite" Conservatives. Militants are as a group younger than either Conservatives or Moderates and there is a certain brashness in youth. But outspokenness does not here mean rudeness. It would also be incorrect to interpret the statement that Militants are more outspoken as meaning that they *speak out* more on racial problems. Conservatives do avoid reference to racial disputes to a greater degree than Militants, but Moderates generally speak out as freely and as fully. Militants are more outspoken in the sense that their rhetoric poses racial controversy firmly, clearly, unavoidably. Their rhetoric frequently serves to dramatize existing racial injustices, to heighten the tension present in racial controversies. The Militant avoids neutral or conciliatory words. He will accuse white leaders of bad faith if he feels this criticism justified. Typical of the use of high emotive words by Militants is a speech by a South Carolina NAACP leader at a 1963 Emancipation Day service:

You seek jobs and it doesn't matter how bright you are. You can't get the jobs because you're black. You seek service in a restaurant and it doesn't matter how well you're dressed or how much money you've got in your pocket. You won't get it because you're black. You take your little boy to their nice high school and no matter how bright he is, he can't get in because he's black. It doesn't matter what you do or who you are or what you say, you won't get a fair deal because you're black. . . . How much longer will the proud American boast of freedom and equality for all men mean for all men except Negroes?

On the national scene, many of the speeches of Martin Luther King, Jr., are choice illustrations of the Militant's ability and desire to pose racial injustices in highly emotive terms. In a speech made Monday, December 5, 1955, a speech which catapulted him into leadership of the Montgomery boycott and national prominence, King said: [32]

But there comes a time that people get tired. We are here this evening to say to those who have mistreated us so long that we are tired—tired of being segregated and humiliated; tired of being kicked about by the brutal feet of oppression. We had no alternative but to protest. For many years, we have shown amazing patience. We have sometimes given our white brothers the feeling that we liked the way we were being treated. But we come here tonight to be saved from that patience that makes us patient with anything less than freedom and justice.

[32] Martin Luther King, Jr., *Stride Toward Freedom* (New York, 1960), p. 50.

The reaction to "Uncle Tom." Militant leaders in their rhetoric seem to be quite consciously reacting against the image of the "Uncle Tom." The extremely deferential "yes, massa" behavior of the "Uncle Tom" is so much an object of scorn and ridicule, of course, that all Negro leaders are on guard to avoid any action that might be interpreted as resembling it. But the burden appears to be a particularly heavy one for the Militant and he frequently seems to go out of his way to prove that he can boldy and courageously present his views. The strong reaction of Militants to the rhetoric of the "Uncle Tom" is both a personal response to the pattern of race relations which required the "Uncle Tom" to scrape and beg, and a recognition by Militants that their constituents, more than the constituents of Conservatives and Moderates, expect a polar alternative.

Militant leaders were asked about the Conservative charge that they antagonize potential white allies with their rhetoric. The response of a Winston-Salem minister, a leader in the local NAACP branch, is typical:

I found that they've always respected me for talking straight and being willing to speak out. I try to be fair but to speak fearlessly and boldly. It's been my experience that whites really respect a man for doing this. When you bow and scrape and pussyfoot around you can be sure that they [the whites] won't think much of you. Everybody looks down on anyone who acts like that.

The rhetoric of the Militant reveals dramatically a measure of the acute humiliation experienced by many Negroes over the pattern of behavior—generally called "Tom-ing it"—that was forced upon them by whites.

The protest model. We noted above that in his rhetoric as in the means selected for promoting racial interests, the Conservative follows the model of white middle-class politics. Militants reject this model. Consciously or unconsciously they find it unsuited to the demands of a "have not" ethnic group seeking equality in the American democracy. They follow instead the model of mass-oriented protest movements. This model has never posited "moderation" as a desirable element of leadership style. Mass-oriented protest movements of whatever type—for example, Marxist, agrarian socialist, racial, or religious—have placed a low value on consensus. They have sought to sharpen conflict. Leaders have pictured the struggle as one between the forces of light and the forces of darkness. Their task has been to make clear "who are our friends and who are our enemies." Direct confrontation of the injustices, then—in this case racial injustices—is seen as salutary because it dramatizes the evils, forces the uncommitted to choose sides, and hopefully thereby contributes to a favorable resolution. The Militant believes that the function of rhetoric is to dramatize the essential evil of racial discrimination. The rhetoric of Conservatives is seen as retarding the breakdown of patterns of discriminatory treatment by making it possible for whites to readily convince themselves that things are really not too bad and that the slow evolutionary approach is satisfactory.

EFFECTIVENESS

All forms of race leadership are generally stronger, of course, in those southern cities in which the pattern of race relations is more permissive. This is so because greater permissiveness translates itself into greater opportunities for Negroes, which in turn means more available leadership talent. Also, the greater permissiveness usually is *a result* of the greater effectiveness of race leaders. It is also true, however, that certain forms of leadership suffer more from a rigidly enforced pattern of segregation and general discriminatory treatment than do others. We noted that in many deep-South cities in the post-*Brown* period, with lines of communication between Negroes and whites cut off, there has been literally no vehicle for conservative leaders to use in promoting race goals. Conservatives depend upon the possibility of interracial negotiations and discussion. Yet whites have refused to permit these. Of the three main styles of race leadership the militant style has found its effectiveness reduced much less in cities with rigidly enforced segregation. The position of Militants in relation to Conservatives and Moderates has generally been stronger in the cities of the deep South than in those of the rim South. In part, of course, this is a definitional problem. We have said that Militants are those who are operating outside the pale of what the white community recognizes as a legitimate activity. Hence, in communities where the boundaries of legitimate activity are narrowly drawn, a broader segment of the total race leadership is labeled "Militant." But it is more than a definitional problem. In the cities of the deep South (and in certain rim-South cities) in the first decade after the *Brown* decision, direct action was literally the only means available for effectively promoting Negro interests.

Militant leadership has enjoyed a greater effectiveness-potential in those southern cities in which large numbers of the "foot soldiers" of direct action are present. The "foot soldiers" of direct action are, of course, the Negro college students. The presence of a Negro college in or near a city increases significantly the effectiveness-potential of militant leadership in the area. Those cities noted for their large and effective protest movements have with few exceptions been those with large Negro colleges: Durham with North Carolina College; Greensboro with North Carolina A. & T.; Tallahassee with Florida A. & M.; Orangeburg with South Carolina College and Claflin, and so on. Winston-Salem State College furnished many of the demonstrators in the 1960 and 1963 protests in Winston-Salem. The protest movement in Greenville has suffered enormously from the fact that there is no Negro college within one hundred miles of the city. It is possible, of course, to recruit other people for direct action demonstrations. High school students participate. So do some adults. And Greenville is the home of a good number of Negro college students who return to the city during the summer. But high school students are too young and too unsophisticated politically. Most adults generally are not willing or able to give time to a series of protest demonstrations. They are open to economic sanctions, and for economic reasons if for no other, they are not able to spend several days in jail. And then it seems something of the excitement and color of direct action demonstrations vanishes as people grow older. College students, free from economic pressures and with surplus energy to expend, are the logical foot soldiers for direct action. Protest movements in the South suffer from their absence.

Militant leaders in Winston-Salem have probably been less effective over the last decade in promoting race goals than have Moderates. This in part is due simply to the personalities of the leaders involved. Also, Moderates have had unusually good vehicles for race-advancement promotion. In addition, Winston-Salem whites have, it seems, moved fast enough for the most part to funnel off discontent that might well have strengthened the hand of militant leaders. Militants have played an important role in race leadership in Winston-Salem. They have served as a prod. There is always difficulty in assessing the effectiveness of militant leadership because many of the things which are done in southern cities are done out of fear of what Militants might do if these things are not done.

In Greenville, whatever of significance has been accomplished in the area of race advancement in the last decade has been accomplished as a result of the activity of militant leaders. There are signs that this is changing, that the position of Moderates is being strengthened. But so far achievements have been the result of court action and modest direct action demonstrations. It should be noted, however, that race leadership in Greenville has on the whole been ineffective and that to say that militant leadership there has been relatively more effective is really to say very little.

Negroes in Winston-Salem and Greenville were asked to evaluate their leaders.[33] Of the four leaders in Greenville receiving the most nominations as "the outstanding Negro leaders in this community" the first three are Militants and the fourth a Moderate.[34] The two "top leaders," who together received 38 per cent of all nominations, were at the time generally recognized as the two most militant Negro leaders in the city.

None of the four Negro leaders receiving the most nominations in Winston-Salem were Militants.[35] Other questions referring to the work of protest organizations on the one hand, and voting organizations on the other, drew the same evaluation. Winston-Salem Negroes did not credit Militants with providing the most effective race leadership.

[33] The construction and execution of these surveys is discussed in some detail in the Appendix.

[34] The question asked in the survey was "Who would you say are the five most outstanding Negro leaders in this community— that is, people who are the best spokesmen for Negro interests?" The four leaders receiving the most nominations received 52 per cent of the total number of nominations made.

[35] It should be noted that this survey was conducted in December 1962. At that time no direct action demonstrations were being conducted in Winston-Salem. Had the survey been conducted in the spring of 1963, when demonstrations were going on, militant leaders would have received greater recognition than they did in our survey. It is difficult to tell just how much greater recognition. We would venture the opinion that three of the four nominated as "top leaders" in our survey would also have been named had the survey been conducted in the spring of 1963. The four top leaders received 63 per cent of the total number of nominations made.

THE MODERATE STYLE

Having examined the opposite ends of the continuum of race leadership styles, we can now turn to the center of the continuum, occupied by the Moderates. The moderate style of race leadership as it has appeared in the urban South over the last decade is a style made possible by the development of greater permissiveness in Negro-white relations. As long as the white leadership in a southern city chooses to say, "All those who are not for us are against us," a middle ground is really impossible. One either commits himself to changing the existing biracial system, in which case he is a Militant, or he accommodates himself to the system, in which case he is a Conservative. There are, of course, even under the most rigid patterns of segregation, other responses than all-out opposition and all-out acceptance, but the extreme rigidity of Negro-white relations makes it far more difficult for a middle ground to appear. Negroes and whites alike see the only significant choice as that between working within the system and working to change it. Two decades ago, then, a realistic typology of leadership styles for most southern cities would have had only two categories, Militant (or the equivalent) and Conservative (or the equivalent).[36] With the gradual erosion of the old biracial system, however, has come a greater variety of leadership responses. "Either-or" typologies are no longer adequate. Particularly in the cities of the rim South there has been a dramatic expansion of the means available for realizing race goals. Goals not considered possible a decade ago are now within reach. With the extraordinary changes in the level and content of race-advancement activity, both whites and

[36] Typologies developed for race leadership in the South in the thirties were in fact two-category typologies. Myrdal's, for example, encompassed accommodation and protest (*op. cit.*, p. 720), and Guy B. Johnson described Negro leadership as "gradualist" and "revolutionary" (*op. cit.*, p. 71).

Negroes have come to base their evaluation of Negro leadership on a recognition that important modifications will continue to be effected in the pattern of race relations. The question now is: What kinds of changes will come and how will these be effected? Throughout the urban South today whites and Negroes seem to recognize three main answers to this question.

Differentiation in the continuum of race leadership styles varies, then, directly with the degree of permissiveness in Negro-white relations. In the South, with a caste system firmly entrenched, the continuum of leadership styles was historically dominated by accommodationists, while a small group kept the flag of protest flying. When the old biracial system began collapsing, the position of the second category, the protest style, became more prominent. We have now reached the point in virtually all major cities of the South where three, and on certain occasions four, distinct styles of race leadership are readily discernible.

Race relations are less permissive in Greenville than in Winston-Salem, and as recently as five years ago most informed white and Negro leaders recognized only two basic types of race leadership in that South Carolina city. Developments since 1959, principally the enormous expansion in the amount of protest activity throughout the South which in Greenville culminated in greater white receptivity to certain Negro demands, have made three broad categories of race leadership styles discernible. It is still difficult in certain issue-areas to define an intermediate response: Moderates exist less as a distinct style than as leaders somewhat less militant than the Militants and less conservative than the Conservatives.

In both Winston-Salem and Greenville, as in the urban South in general, the erosion of the old two-standards system is continuing. We can expect, then, further differentiation of the continuum of race leadership styles. While a typology containing three units provides the best representation of the actual differences in approach existing at present, we may expect that a decade hence this three-unit typology would obscure significant differences to the point that it would be inadequate as an analytical tool. Frazier has written that with the differentiation of the Negro population of the United States race-leader typologies in general have become less useful and adequate as descriptions of Negro leadership.[37] The erosion of the old biracial system seems to us to be even more important in explaining the reduced utility of race-leader typologies for the urban North.[38] For the urban South, differentiation thus far has meant not a reduced utility of the typology but the clear emergence of a third leadership style —that of the Moderate.

GOALS

The position of Militants and Conservatives on the welfare goals—status goals distinction has been discussed at some length. Moderates cannot be as readily identified through this distinction because they are not as clearly committed to one in opposition to the other. Moderates can be found supporting both sets of goals under different circumstances, for the moderate style is a kind of middle way. In general we can say that Moderates in both Winston-Salem and Greenville find more merit in welfare goals than do Militants and more value in status goals than do Conservatives. Moderates find the choice in those cases in which these two kinds of race goals are in conflict a very hard one to make. Their position will

[37] Frazier, *The Negro in the United States* (New York, 1957), p. 548.

[38] How much, for example, does a race-leader typology identifying Militants, Moderates, and Conservatives tell us about the struggle within the Negro leadership in New York City over school integration? A race-leader typology still has some analytical utility there, but it is much less than that of a comparable typology for Atlanta, Georgia. The alternatives and options in a northern city are infinitely more varied.

become clearer as we examine three specific controversies, two in Winston-Salem and one in Greenville, which involve the conflict of welfare and status goals.

We noted that in the 1959 hospital controversy in Winston-Salem Militants and Conservatives were aligned against each other. Where then were the Moderates in this controversy? Their position can be described as one of skepticism and detachment. Moderates did not lead the opposition to the hospital plan, but neither were they its most ardent supporters. Most Moderates indicated in interviews that they had finally decided to vote for the hospital plan, but they were clearly not happy with it. One moderate leader, the incumbent Negro alderman, refused to lend his name to the group supporting the hospital plan and failed to appear on a radio program in which a large number of Negro leaders endorsed the proposal. Moderates were torn by their reluctance to support a plan calling for segregation and their recognition of the need for better hospital facilities for Negroes. When confronted with this conflict of a welfare goal and a status goal they chose to say, in effect, "A plague on both your houses!" The following response was typical:

I didn't like the idea at all of them [the white leadership] trying to perpetuate hospital segregation, but of course they're not going to be able to do it. When the new hospital opens we're going to be there. That's all there is to it. So I decided to vote for the hospital plan because we need more facilities so badly, but I couldn't go around endorsing it publicly. I let them know that we weren't happy about it at all.

Most Moderates could not bring themselves to vote against the welfare goal, better hospital facilities.

The position of Moderates in the 1962 controversy over swimming pool integration in Winston-Salem was very much the same. Militants, we noted, initiated the desegregation activity and would not consider any compromises on Negro access; Conservatives wanted to use their newly established right so gingerly as to not jeopardize other race goals, principally good recreation facilities for Negroes. Moderates for their part did not initiate the desegregation activity at the pools. No moderate leader was involved in the planning or execution of the integration. Most Moderates conceded that they had not given pool integration very high priority. They ranked many other race objectives higher. But once the pools had been desegregated Moderates were not as ready as most Conservatives to criticize Militants for hasty and ill-conceived action. They were not as worried as Conservatives professed to be that desegregation of the pools would jeopardize other race goals. Their position was, in brief, that although pool desegregation was not a high priority goal, it was a legitimate goal that should, once achieved, be supported fully. Nothing should be done to imply that the militant leaders who had initiated the integration activity had acted improperly. They agreed with Militants that a basic right, equal access to all public facilities, had been exercised. Moderate leaders on the biracial committee which was established to mediate the pool controversy did not insist with Militants that "we are going to use the pools whenever we want just like other citizens and nothing is going to stop us"; neither did they join Conservatives in seeking a compromise formula, although they did indicate they would accept a proposal for restricted access during a cooling-off period. The position of Moderates was summed up in this statement made at a meeting of the biracial committee:

Two things must be recognized as definite here. First, the pools must remain open. We cannot deny our children the rights to use wholesome recreation in the hot summer months. If you close the pools you are extending an invitation to juvenile delinquency and all kinds of problems. We must keep the pools open. At the same time, we must recognize that Negroes are full citizens of Winston-Salem and have full rights to use all public facilities. This committee cannot do anything to deny Negroes the right to use their tax-supported facilities.

In short, Moderates assigned to the welfare goal and the status goal involved in this controversy approximately equal merit. They were not really satisfied with the course of action proposed either by the Militants or by the Conservatives. For their own part they resolved the conflict (1) by insisting that whatever happened the pools must remain open, that keeping the pools open must be given the very highest priority; (2) by insisting that since pools were public facilities the right of Negroes to use them could not be questioned; but (3) by themselves not actually urging Negroes to use the newly integrated pools and by showing some tolerance for proposals for voluntarily restricted access during a transition period.

The third case of conflict of welfare and status goals, this one in Greenville, is in a sense an artificial one; for it has not yet become a real source of division in the Negro subcommunity but was raised in hypothetical fashion in certain discussions with Negroes in that city. Negro leaders were asked: "Would you be in favor of the establishment of a state-supported Negro college in Greenville?" The question was brought to our attention when Negro leaders in Greenville repeatedly made reference to the fact that there was no Negro college within a hundred miles of the city and that this lack of facilities for higher education in the immediate area was a real burden, making it even harder than usual for Negroes to secure a college education. As a result, the Negro subcommunity in Greenville suffers from a particularly acute shortage of highly educated individuals. We also asked: "Would you be in favor of going before the state legislature and petitioning for a state-supported Negro college for the Greenville area?" We noted for the sake of argument that the state legislature, concerned at the time with the integration of Clemson College, a white state-supported institution only twenty miles from Greenville, might welcome the initiative of Negro

leaders on this point. They might be persuaded that the establishment of a state school for Negroes in the South Carolina
Piedmont would remove certain pressures for the integration
of Clemson.

This poses essentially the same kind of conflict between
status and welfare goals that was noted in the two controversies in Winston-Salem. It seems likely that the positions taken
by Greenville Negroes in answer to our questions would be
the same when and if the matter becomes an active political
controversy. Greenville Militants made it clear in response to
our questions that they strongly opposed the idea of establishing a state Negro college in the area. The educational goal
which for them deserved clear priority was that of integrating
Negroes into the existing system of higher education. They
argued that establishing a Negro college with state funds
would simply retard integration. They granted that there was
a very pressing need for better educational facilities for
Negroes, but they insisted that the way to get better facilities
was through integration rather than through the creation of
more segregated facilities. Some Militants recognize that for
some time there would be a need for Negro colleges in South
Carolina, that integration of the whole state system would
come slowly regardless of how much pressure Negroes
applied, and that even after Negroes had achieved access to all
units of the state educational system there would continue to
be many Negroes who, because of the after-effects of the long
period of segregation, would choose not to apply to integrated
institutions. They argued, nonetheless, that they could hardly
be expected to ask the state to establish segregated facilities.
Conservatives, in contrast, referred to the importance of getting more educational facilities for Greenville-area Negroes.
They maintained that a Negro college in Greenville would
have no effect whatsoever on the integration of the state educational system. It would merely supplement the system, providing greater educational opportunities and a broader choice

for Negroes in the South Carolina Piedmont. They said that they would give unequivocal support to any attempt to secure a branch of the state university in Greenville even if it were formally stated that this would be a unit for Negroes. Moderates again were somewhere in between. They were not as ready as Militants to insist that petitioning by Negroes for a state-supported Negro college in the Piedmont would mean Negro endorsement of segregation. At the same time they could not agree with the Conservatives who maintained that the proposal would deserve the unequivocal support of Negroes. They were torn between the competing goals and were unable to commit themselves wholly to one at the sacrifice of the other. Much more than Conservatives or Militants, Moderates showed appreciation of the tension between welfare and status goals. In the case of facilities for higher education for Greenville Negroes, as in the case of swimming pools and hospitals in Winston-Salem, Moderates insisted on both the legitimacy of the status goal and the necessity of the welfare goal.

Race goals and race consciousness. Goals sought by Moderates typically are not "frontier area" status goals; neither are they welfare objectives lying in the area of maximum Negro-white agreement. To be concrete on this point, moderate leaders in Winston-Salem in 1962 and 1963 were working in the following areas. (1) They sought extension of full city services to Negroes. This meant trying to get streets paved in Negro neighborhoods, trying to improve recreational facilities, and trying to bring expenditures for Negro pupils into line with expenditures for whites. Moderates have also tried to get more Negroes employed in city government jobs. (2) Moderate leaders worked for "means-goals" such as greater representation of Negroes on city boards and commissions. (3) They tried to secure better employment opportunities for Negroes. One moderate leader related how he had finally succeeded in getting a job for a Negro secretary at the Duke Power Company. He emphasized that he had had to engage in considerable verbal "arm twisting" to get the girl the job.

These goals are not the kind that maximize race consciousness. They are not of the variety that can mobilize masses of people. At the same time, they are generally more "visible" than the goals of Conservatives and draw racial lines more sharply.

The capacity of a goal or a set of goals to heighten race consciousness and divide Negroes and whites into opposite camps varies inversely with the extent to which Negroes and whites can agree upon the merits of the goals. When there is a large measure of agreement as on the desirability of renewal of Negro residential areas in Winston-Salem race consciousness is minimized. A common enemy is then present. On the other hand, Negroes and whites are in virtually complete disagreement over the desirability of certain status goals and these heighten racial tensions and the awareness of competing interests racially defined. The goals of Moderates, by definition "in between" those of Conservatives and Militants with respect to the effect on race consciousness, have a very distinct flavor of their own. Essentially they are of the kind which divide Negroes and whites into opposing camps but at the same time do not necessitate a breakdown of access and communication.

MEANS

A case study. Greater representation on city boards and commissions is a major objective of race leaders throughout the urban South. It is seen as valuable in itself (greater recognition of Negroes and their rights) and as a vehicle for the realization of other goals (securing a greater share of money spent for various services such as education and recreation, etc.). Negro representation on boards of education is considered particularly important because improvement of educational opportunities for Negroes is a central objective of the race-advancement movement. In Winston-Salem, Moderates can take the credit for the significant increase in Negro representation on the city-county school board. The means which they used here are those typically associated with the moderate style. Consideration of the successful attempt of Moderates to gain greater representation for Negroes can give us a clearer picture, then, of the means-orientation of the moderate style of race leadership.

A Negro was first appointed to the Winston-Salem school board in 1951. Negro representation on the seven-member board remained at one for the next twelve years. In the fall of 1962, when two positions on the school board became vacant, a major effort was made to increase Negro representation. After a somewhat inept and unsuccessful attempt to persuade the mayor and other aldermen that Negroes needed more representation, the Negro alderman went on the radio to inform his constituents of what he considered to be a serious denial of their rights. Then, at a meeting of board of aldermen, he nominated two Negroes for the positions with the hope, he said privately, of getting one of them appointed. The Negro precinct chairmen, acting on the initiative of two moderate politicians, petitioned the county Democratic chairman, calling on him to use the party's good offices to secure additional Negro representation. Despite this, no Negro was appointed. The Negro alderman then placed before the board of aldermen a motion calling for enlargement of the school board in such a manner as to insure at least two places for Negroes. The alderman's objective here was a traditional one of demonstrating to his constituents that he was working for them and indicating his extreme dissatisfaction with what had transpired. His motion was rejected.

Consolidation of the city and county school systems was approved in January 1963. The 1963 municipal election was held before a new city-county school board was constituted, and Moderates made it clear in the campaign that they expected increased representation on the school board as part of their reward for support of the Democratic mayoralty and aldermanic candidates. The Democratic mayoralty candidate promised Negroes increased representation on the new board. Following the Democratic victory the mayor fulfilled his promise and brought Negro representation on the twelve-member consolidated board to three. Thus Negroes, some 24 per cent of the county's population, were 25 per cent of the board. The Negro members of the consolidated school board are Moderates.

An early indication of the importance of this increased representation came when the board instituted a new school-assignment policy. This policy in essence provided that a Negro child had only to make application to the school nearest his home to be automatically accepted into that school. Previously, children assigned on the basis of race had to make special appeal for transfer—which might or might not be granted by the board. Then in 1964 the board announced that henceforth initial assignments of pupils would be made solely on the basis of geography, rather than race and then geography. All of these changes were made without court order, but the threat of court action clearly was one factor prompting the board to act. The most recent changes must as well be seen, however, as testimony to the effectiveness of the stronger Negro contingent on the new board and, in a more general way, to the increased political power which made possible the increased representation.

Moderates worked in the same way to get Negro law enforcement officers in Forsyth County. They began trying as early as 1952 to get Negro deputies in the county sheriff's department. Appeals were made to the sheriff, to the county delegation, and to the county Democratic executive committee. Finally, shortly before the 1962 Democratic primary—a primary in which the sheriff was seeking renomination—two Negro deputies were appointed. According to a politician who played a leading role, the objective was gained in this way:

We went to see John Gallaher [the county chairman] and told him that we had been good Democrats for a long time and that we needed and deserved Negro deputies and that the sheriff had kept putting us off. We said that a lot of Negroes were upset about our failure to get any. Gallaher said that he would see what he could do. The next day the sheriff called and told us to come down to his office and help him select the Negro applicants. When we got there he would talk of appointing only one. We wouldn't listen to that. They will make it hard enough for the Negro deputies and we wanted two appointed so that they would have someone to talk to. So we left and went back to Gallaher and told him about it. We were plenty sore. The next day the sheriff called again and asked us to come down to help select two Negro deputies.

Several essential characteristics of the means-orientation of moderate leaders are indicated in the above case study and the second example briefly cited.

The need for negative inducements. Moderates have much less faith in quiet negotiation than do Conservatives. A moderate politician in Winston-Salem expressed contempt for Conservatives' criticism of his handling of a case involving alleged police brutality:

When something like this happens I raise hell. Sure I put the police chief on the spot by demanding action on the brutal treatment inflicted on one of my people by one of his men, but that's how we get things done. They will be a little more careful about pulling this kind of thing in the future.

Unfavorable publicity is one of the negative inducements used by moderate leaders. Moderates are not hesitant about publicly embarrassing white leaders who are not responsive to their appeals. Conservatives prefer to handle problems behind closed doors, maintaining that public name-calling only makes it more difficult for the parties to compromise and move toward a mutually acceptable solution; Moderates effectively utilize publicity to achieve race ends.

Similarly, moderate leaders do not hesitate to threaten reprisals if their demands are not met. In seeking more representation on the school board, Negro Democrats told party leaders: "Either give us more representation or we will sit on our hands at election time." [39] Moderates will, in short, make clear demands on white leaders and will utilize certain kinds of negative inducements if their demands are not met.

Avoidance of direct action. At the same time Moderates have not utilized the prime negative inducement of Militants, direct action. Three factors account for this and these are of prime importance to an understanding of the content of the moderate style of race leadership. (1) The goals pursued by Moderates are generally not well suited to direct action. Direct action is often effective in the realization of certain status goals. But goals emphasized by Moderates really do not lend themselves to fulfillment through protest demonstrations. (2) Moderates believe that they have a generally more effective means for promoting race goals and that reliance on direct action would be an ineffective utilization of their power. Moderates in many rim-South cities, for example, have had considerable success in electoral politics. They are inside the major political institutions. The kinds of negative inducements noted in the case study are available to them. (3) Interests and temperament are involved. The same factors that lead Moderates to emphasize certain kinds of race goals similarly contribute to their choice of means. Moderates in both Winston-Salem and Greenville, although interested in securing mass support, demonstrate little interest in mass participation. Indeed, many moderate leaders profess concern with the possible by-products of direct action, a concern closely resembling that of their conservative colleagues. A moderate

[39] There were more than a half dozen contests from 1958 to 1963 in Winston-Salem in which G.O.P. candidates would have won had large numbers of Negroes decided not to support the Democratic candidates.

leader in Durham related how he had at one time called a mass meeting to protest an action of the school board:

I thought it would be a good idea but it got out of hand. There was a lot of name-calling and people were in an ugly mood. I said that I would never do that again and I haven't.

Militants usually can count on the verbal support of Moderates when they initiate direct action demonstrations, but Moderates themselves will rarely utilize direct action as a means of promoting race objectives.

Cooperation versus *protest*. We have noted that the means used by Conservatives are consistent with their belief that interracial cooperation is essential to Negro advancement. Similarly, the means utilized by Militants are well suited to what they consider their role to be: to protest as vigorously and effectively as possible all cases of racial discrimination. Moderates for their part seek to balance cooperation and protest. They are aware that at times cooperation and protest make antagonistic demands. The case study illustrates this. Moderates protested vigorously against the discriminatory treatment reflected in their failure to get more than token representation. But at the same time they were careful not to close channels of communication. They were Negroes first, but they were also Democrats. As Negro Democrats they had a stake in the party. The vigor of their protest was limited by their desire to maintain access to white leaders and the degree of interracial cooperation necessary to their position in the structure of the Democratic party and in city government.

A new role created by new means. The kinds of electoral sanctions available to Moderates in the cities of the rim South, and now to an increasing (though still modest) extent in the urban deep-South, are of recent vintage. The Negro vote in the South, for example, is a post-World War II phenomenon. What did Moderates do before? The moderate role as it now exists is in fact a new one. Under the old biracial system there was a sharp polarization. The type of protest associated with the moderate style of race leadership requires a certain integration of Negroes into regular political institutions, and the style really is not possible until this integration takes place. It still has not taken place in many parts of the South. In those areas which include a large portion of the rural South and some of the urban deep-South, the leadership continuum is very much as Myrdal saw it two and a half decades ago, with the exception that the position of the militant or protest leadership is much stronger.

The moderate style has been defined in both Winston-Salem and Greenville. Negroes have achieved some measure of integration into the regular channels for political decision making in both cities. This integration has gone further in Winston-Salem and the sanctions available to moderate leaders in that upper-South city are much more formidable. But in both cities Moderates rely upon negative inducements effected through the normal, regularized channels for political decision-making.

RHETORIC

The rhetoric of moderate leaders again represents a kind of middle way between the "soft sell" of Conservatives and the strong racial appeals of Militants. Moderates are critical of the rhetoric of both Conservatives and Militants. A moderate politician in Winston-Salem said of his conservative colleagues:

I tell you it almost makes me sick. Those guys [conservative leaders] are afraid to come right out and tell the white man he's wrong. They're always hunting for some "nice way" to make the point. I call a spade a spade and I think I'm respected for it.

But if Conservatives are criticized for lacking courage to state firmly the Negroes' objections to patterns of discriminatory treatment, Militants are found guilty of rudeness, of making wild racial appeals for the sake of publicity, of going out of their way to antagonize opponents. Moderates are regularly accused of "selling out" by Militants, and the resentment is considerable.

Look, I'm as strongly opposed to segregation as any of them [Militants] are, and I think I've done just as much to show it, but whenever I don't do what they want I get accused of "selling out" or "Uncle Tom-ing" it. They're irresponsible in their name calling. For the sake of a little publicity they go around saying anything they want to.

Three cases should make clearer how the rhetoric of Moderates differs from that of Conservatives and Militants. A biracial committee met in Winston-Salem in the summer of 1962 to attempt to resolve a dispute over the integration of the city's swimming pools. The following statements, the first by a Militant, the second by a Conservative, and the third by a Moderate at one meeting of the biracial committee typify the rhetoric of each of these styles of race leadership.

You say that we should compromise on the pools just as you've done in other cases, but all we're asking for are basic rights and these can't be compromised. You say, "Look what we've done for you in the past," but you've never *given* us anything. All we're after is treatment just like anyone else and that's not something *you* can give. We are tired of having to take hand-me-downs and second-rate treatment from you people.

We must be very careful that nothing is done to jeopardize the good race relations which prevail here in Winston-Salem. Negroes should be allowed to use the pools and all other public facilities. But our main job here is to make sure that this doesn't degenerate into name calling which sets us back years.

The pools must remain open. The children of this city depend upon them for recreation. The pools, moreover, are public facilities and as such are open to all citizens. Negroes have every right to use the pools.

The same differences in rhetoric are evident in a verbal battle which took place at a July 1963 meeting of the Winston-Salem biracial committee. Although there had been considerable success in desegregating public facilities, demonstrations had been started in Winston and these culminated in a mass night march on city hall. The Winston-Salem mayor criticized the demonstrators for not realizing the extent of the progress made and for making the task of the biracial committee even more difficult by increasing racial tensions. At a biracial committee meeting a militant member told the mayor that she, too, was disappointed, disappointed that the mayor was disappointed for the wrong reasons. The mayor, she thought, should be concerned with the noncompliance that made the demonstrations necessary. In reference to the argument that parents of the youthful demonstrators "should control their children," she said that she could control her children but that she would not "stifle their drive for freedom." The noncompliance of the store owners, not the actions of the demonstrators, should be forthrightly condemned by the mayor. A steady stream of criticism of this kind from Militants brought tension at the meeting to a high pitch. What were Conservatives saying? One said that she felt the need to "interject something happy." She said that she had learned that a "Caucasian group" had been meeting for some time and that it would soon announce a fairly dramatic breakthrough in the area. She said that she was unable to mention the name of the organization or what it was doing at that time. Moderates for their part said that the recalcitrant merchants and hotel operators should desegregate immediately but they "reaffirmed their faith in the biracial committee" and urged that Negroes indicate confidence in the committee and its work.

The same differences can be seen in a discussion which took place at an integrated ministerial fellowship meeting on "religion and race" in Winston-Salem in 1963. A Negro minister known as a militant leader told his colleagues:

There is no easy remedy for the problems of race relations. There is some discomfort under the cross if you are going to carry it. . . . The desegregation of the communion table is one way to find a remedy . . . Men of Christ, men of God, until we make some statement which affects where we reside we are going to be laughed at.

A Moderate made the same point but in a less emotive way:

It is time everyone realizes exactly what the Negro wants: the same opportunity as any other American citizen. All the rest is secondary. . . . The problem of race relations must be met boldly and with Christian concern.

To summarize, the rhetoric of Moderates represents an attempt to integrate cooperation and protest. The result of the integration is a rhetoric which unhesitatingly and clearly identifies areas of racial injustice but which avoid the highly emotive content of the rhetoric of Militants.

EFFECTIVENESS

Moderates, like Conservatives, are particularly restricted in those southern cities in which patterns of segregation and other discriminatory treatment are rigidly enforced. In those cities Negro leaders really must choose between "begging for crumbs" and instituting direct action protests outside the existing political institutions. When Negroes are voting, when they are sitting on biracial committees, school boards, Urban League boards, and committees of the political parties, the effectiveness-potential of the moderate style is greatly enhanced. In the total absence of this integration the moderate style as we have described it here is impossible. As the integration progresses the effectiveness-potential increases.

More than either the conservative or militant style, the moderate style depends upon a relatively high level of potential political participants. This is because the negative inducements utilized by Moderates require sustained political involvement by a large number of people at a fairly high level of political sophistication. Consideration of two major pieces of race-advancement activity in Winston-Salem in 1963 should make this clearer.

In the spring and summer of 1963, there was a series of direct action demonstrations in Winston. A group of militant leaders working through a chapter of the Congress of Racial Equality organized demonstrations which varied in size from picketing by a half dozen persons at a single store to a march of 500 persons on city hall. The purpose of the demonstrations was to secure integration of certain public accommodations which had resisted the initiative of the city's biracial committee. Two aspects of this participation should be noted. First, fewer than 1,000 persons participated at any time in the demonstrations. Second, the level of political sophistication necessary for participating in the demonstrations was low: the participants were asked to make one or more appearances at a colorful, exciting event; they were asked to march or picket for freedom. This is not to disparage their work or to impugn their motives. It is not to say the demonstrators in fact as a group had a low level of political awareness. We are saying here that it is not difficult to get a good number of Negro youths in an upper-South city like Winston-Salem to picket in front of a cafeteria, and only the most limited political awareness is necessary. Moreover, the involvement does not need to be, and in fact in this case was not, continuous. After one went beyond the leadership group, one found many new faces in each succeeding demonstration.

Also in 1963, Negro voters contributed mightily to the election of a city administration friendly (in the context of the American South) to Negro interests. In contrast to the direct action demonstrations, this electoral feat required a fairly high level of political involvement by a large number of people. A full 62 per cent of all voting-age Negroes in Winston-Salem had been registered. That figure was attained only after a decade and a half of hard work by a large number of people. More than 4,500 Negroes, 30 per cent of the registered Negroes, voted and gave better than 90 per cent of their votes to candidates endorsed by the Negro leadership. Voting organizations worked in each precinct to achieve a big majority for the endorsed candidates.

Moderates played the leading role in this voting drive. Had the level of potential political participants in Winston-Salem been as low as it is in Greenville, however, the moderate leadership would have been unable to achieve effective electoral sanctions, and hence would have been relatively ineffective. The level of political skills and awareness in the Negro subcommunity of Greenville is now sufficient to sustain direct action demonstrations along the order of those conducted in Winston-Salem, but Greenville Moderates will be unable for some time to effect the kind of electoral sanctions which their counterparts in Winston executed in the 1963 city elections.

The race leadership of Moderates in Winston-Salem has, over the last decade, been more effective than that offered by either Conservatives or Militants if effectiveness is defined by the significance of the race goals pursued and the extent to which these goals have been realized. Moderates must be given primary credit for integrating Negroes into the major political institutions of Winston-Salem—the entire machinery of electoral politics, the organs of city government, and so on. Moderates have organized the Negro electorate and from this base have moved into positions of importance in the governmental structure of the city.

Winston-Salem Negroes sustained this evaluation. When asked to nominate the "outstanding Negro leaders" in their city they gave 58 per cent of their nominations to three Moderates who placed first, second, and third. The remaining 42 per cent of the nominations were divided among more than twenty leaders. Five Moderates were among the eight leaders receiving the highest number of nominations. Supported by their own community, with their leadership role recognized as legitimate by whites and with their power based on a firmly established and constantly expanding Negro vote that with increasing frequency holds the balance of power, Moderates should continue over the next decade to play an important role in race advancement in Winston-Salem.

In contrast, the exclusion of Negroes from the major political institutions in Greenville has been too complete, the prevailing pattern of segregation too strongly enforced, for Moderates to have enjoyed much success. Pressures still operate to polarize the leadership continuum. Greenville, South Carolina, is indeed one of the South's many forgotten cities. But much of what has been accomplished in the area of race advancement there has been realized through the initiative of Militants. Greenville Negroes named five Militants among the top seven leaders in the city. The other two leaders were Moderates.

WHO ARE THE CONSERVATIVES, THE MILITANTS, THE MODERATES?

Thus far we have been describing the essential characteristics of the three styles of race leadership as they operate in a rim-South and in a deep-South city. Now we must attempt to identify the practitioners of each of these styles by those biographical characteristics which seem to be of particular importance in explaining why a leader espouses a particular style of race leadership. It is important to make clear that what we are trying to do is to explain, insofar as aggregate biographical data can explain, why different persons use different styles of race leadership. We will not seek to identify Militants, Conservatives, and Moderates *as leaders* in distinction to those Negroes who do not occupy positions of leadership. Race leaders like political leaders in general are better educated, earn more money, have higher status, possess greater political sophistication, and the like than do the rank and file. For example, comparing the leaders in Winston and Greenville with the Negro population as a whole in terms of the percentage having attended college, we have the figures given in Table 15.

TABLE 15

PERCENTAGE OF LEADERS AND GENERAL NEGRO POPULATION WITH SOME COLLEGE, WINSTON-SALEM AND GREENVILLE *

	Winston-Salem †	Greenville ‡
Leaders	90.0	76.0
General Negro population	8.9	5.1

* See pp. 325–328 for a definition of this leadership sample.
† Winston-Salem leaders: N=42
‡ Greenville leaders: N=25

CLASS AND STATUS

Were we to arrange Conservatives, Militants, and Moderates in descending order from those occupying the highest class and status positions to the lowest, Conservatives would be clustered near the top, Moderates in the middle, and Militants at the bottom. There would be numerous exceptions, of course, but the basic clustering would be obvious.[40] Tables 16 and 17 show the class distribution of the three styles of leaders for Winston and Greenville.

TABLE 16

PERCENTAGE OF CONSERVATIVES, MODERATES AND, MILITANTS IN WINSTON-SALEM BY CLASS STANDING

Class	Conservatives (N=16)	Moderates (N=12)	Militants (N=14)
Upper-middle	38	0	0
Middle-middle and lower-middle	62	100	64
Lower	0	0	36

[40] The concept of class as it is used here includes "gradations" and "sources." See C. Wright Mills, "The Social Life of a Modern

A very large portion of the conservative leaders in Winston-Salem are individuals who have "made it" financially. Among Winston Conservatives are two prosperous doctors, two prosperous attorneys, the manager of a successful Negro bus company, and the pastor of a church whose congregation includes a very high percentage of the professional and business people in the subcommunity.[41] In brief, when members of the Negro upper-middle class do participate actively in race advancement in our two cities, they follow the conservative style.

TABLE 17

PERCENTAGE OF CONSERVATIVES, MODERATES, AND MILITANTS
IN GREENVILLE BY CLASS STANDING

Class	Conservatives (N=8)	Moderates (N=8)	Militants (N=9)
Upper middle	25	0	0
Middle-middle and lower-middle	75	75	66
Lower	0	25	33

A smaller percentage of the conservative leadership of Greenville is upper-middle class. This is due first of all to the fact that the upper-middle class in Greenville is infinitely smaller than in Winston, and second, to the fact that most prosperous

---

Community," an essay reprinted in Irving Louis Horowitz (ed.), *Power, Politics and People: The Collected Essays of C. Wright Mills* (New York, 1963), pp. 39–52. That is, we agree with Mills that class is defined by the amount of income and by how one acquires the income. For our purposes here the latter refers primarily to self-employed *versus* wage-earner. Status, on the other hand, involves the prestige, esteem, or honor in which the individual is held.

[41] Burgess found the same pattern in her Durham study, *Negro Leadership in a Southern City*, p. 181.

Negroes in Greenville reacted to the "great silence" by withdrawing completely from politics.

The fact that when members of the Negro upper-middle class in our two cities assume positions of race leadership they do so as Conservatives, indicates a pattern similar to that found among financially successful whites. In numerous interviews, very successful Negroes demonstrated a strong reluctance to participate in direct action demonstrations and other such forms of protest activity. These are men who at last are able to enjoy certain of the amenities of life, often after beginning in great poverty. Violence frightens them. Demonstrations involve risk of arrests and subjection to great personal indignities. In *Black Bourgeoisie*, Frazier noted the efforts of members of this class to isolate themselves from the indignities which the white world heaps upon them and, in their own segregated world, to seek to maintain the life styles and values which they see in their white counterparts.[42] Frazier's analysis is as valid for the "black bourgeoisie" of Winston and Greenville. These more prosperous Conservatives are fully cognizant of and bitter over the indignities to which they are subject. In some cases they give generously to militant protest groups, but they are unwilling to risk the indignities, arrests, and the like that result from the protest activity of Militants. Some indicated a certain distaste for the style of their "hoi polloi" brethren, a style described as somewhat "uncouth" and ill-considered. Many of these economically prosperous Negroes have, moreover, succeeded in establishing a relationship with leading whites that is at least overtly amicable, and they hesitate to jeopardize this. In brief, Conservatives more than either Militants or Moderates have "arrived," and they are most reluctant to endanger their position.

The educational background and occupational position of

[42] Frazier, *Black Bourgeoisie* (Collier Books; New York, 1962), pp. 124 ff.

Moderates is essentially similar to that of Militants. There are, however, these differences. First, most lower-class Negroes who are race leaders follow the militant style. None are Moderates in Winston-Salem, and only two in Greenville are Moderates. It should be noted that relatively few lower-class Negroes in any southern city occupy positions of leadership. Second, Moderates typically have achieved a somewhat firmer and more secure economic position than Militants. The data in Tables 16 and 17 really do not make this clear. About an equal percentage of Militants and Moderates in our two cities are professional people, but typically the militant professional is either just beginning in his profession or for some other reason has not established himself quite as well. There are, it should be noted, sufficient exceptions to this generalization among the Greenville leadership to make it of somewhat doubtful validity in any South-wide analysis.

Conservatives *bring to* race leadership the highest social status. They are the high school principals, the United Fund leaders, the successful physicians, and the like. The major gap in status, however, is not between Conservatives and Moderates but rather between Moderates and Militants. The social prestige brought by Militants to their leadership appears to be, in both cities but particularly in Winston-Salem, much lower than that brought by Moderates. Mills has noted that the reasons for honoring claims to prestige or status include property, birth, occupation, education, income, power, or any other scarce values which "may invidiously distinguish one person from another." [43] The claim of Moderates to higher status than Militants has rested on a somewhat higher socioeconomic position, but more on their greater involvement in the civic life of the community. The status position of Moderates, to approach this in another way, is less dependent upon their race leadership. They bring to their leadership a firmer basis for pro-

[43] C. Wright Mills, "The Sociology of Stratification," in Horowitz, *op. cit.*, p. 310.

moting a claim to prestige. Militants in both cities see race-advancement activity as a readily available means for status advancement.

VULNERABILITY

Only about 20 per cent of the top race leaders in Winston-Salem and Greenville are directly dependent upon whites for their income, and many of the leaders are self-employed. A preponderance of white political leaders as well, of course, come from the ranks of the self-employed. They are often professional men, like lawyers, who are able to take the time necessary for extensive political participation, and whose businesses may actually benefit by it. But the absence of vulnerables from Negro leadership is not simply or even primarily a product of the over-representation of certain professions. The pressures operating on Negro leaders are such that most vulnerables decide it is in their interest to remain aloof. When they do assume leadership positions it is principally as Conservatives and to a lesser but significant extent as Moderates. No militant leaders in either Winston-Salem or Greenville occupy positions of high vulnerability.

Militants, Moderates, and Conservatives in our two cities have been classified by level of vulnerability, economically defined. Three levels are noted. Those highly vulnerable include schoolteachers, other government (local) employees, social workers, and the like. They are persons wholly dependent upon whites for their income. Moreover, they hold "sensitive" positions, positions that are highly visible. Those with marginal vulnerability may gain their income from whites as do, for example, Negro factory workers, but their jobs have a low level of visibility and sensitiveness. This category of marginal vulnerability also includes Negro businessmen who are dependent on whites for supplies and credit. Those in the third category, the Independents, are completely free from potential economic sanctions from whites. They are persons like

Negro lawyers who have only Negro clients. Data on style and degree of vulnerability is summarized in Tables 18 and 19.

TABLE 18

PERCENTAGE OF CONSERVATIVES, MODERATES, AND MILITANTS BY DEGREE OF VULNERABILITY OF OCCUPATION, WINSTON-SALEM

Degree of vulnerability	Conservatives	Moderates	Militants
High vulnerability	44	17	0
Marginal vulnerability	44	33	14
Independence	12	50	86

Of the fourteen top militant leaders in Winston-Salem, five are ministers with all-Negro congregations and four are professional people with Negro clientele. Three are not employed and their source of funds is not open to sanctions from whites. Only two, one a businessman and the other a school teacher whose husband is a professional man, are even marginally vulnerable. On the other hand, four of the conservative leaders are public-school teachers and males whose income is the primary support of the family. Three other Conservatives hold positions of high vulnerability: one is a contractor most of whose clients are white; one is a social worker; the third is a businessman completely dependent upon

TABLE 19

PERCENTAGE OF CONSERVATIVES, MODERATES, AND MILITANTS BY DEGREE OF VULNERABILITY OF OCCUPATION, GREENVILLE

Degree of vulnerability	Conservatives	Moderates	Militants
High vulnerability	63	0	0
Marginal vulnerability	25	37	11
Independence	12	63	89

the good will of whites. Only two conservative leaders in Winston-Salem have occupations which make them virtually independent of white economic sanctions.

The pattern, it can be seen, is the same in Greenville. But there the styles are divided on vulnerability lines even more sharply than in Winston-Salem, reflecting the weaker political position of Negroes and the more rigidly discriminatory structure of race relations. There are highly vulnerable Moderates in Winston-Salem but not in Greenville.

We should not underestimate the importance of economic independence as a factor permitting a Negro to follow the militant style of race leadership. As an example, during the sit-in demonstrations in Greenville in 1960 the president of the local NAACP chapter was criticized severely by some of his colleagues for "dragging his feet," that is for not giving full support to the demonstrations. He opposed starting the demonstrations; after they had begun and there were a number of arrests he failed to work as hard as some felt he should to secure bond for the students arrested; and he continued to bring pressure to end the demonstrations. His colleagues sought an explanation for his lack of support of direct action in this case, particularly surprising in light of his previous record of very aggressive (for Greenville) leadership. They learned that he had been told that the company supplying his service station with gasoline might cut off the supply if he became too closely identified with the sit-ins. Here then was a leader who had demonstrated his courage on numerous occasions in the past, who had protested against segregation in Greenville at times when few voices were heard, and who, in fact, enjoyed a considerable measure of economic independence since all his clients were Negroes; but who nevertheless was in a position of marginal vulnerability and in this case, when economic pressure was brought, felt obliged to bend. He apparently opposed his colleagues because he feared that he would lose his source of supply, something really quite unlikely in the urban South in 1960.

We are not able, largely because we are working with small numbers of leaders, to control for other variables such as class and status, which we believe influence the leadership style followed, and hence determine with some precision the importance of vulnerability as a determinant of style. Data from a large number of interviews with Negro leaders do indicate, however, that individuals whose occupational position makes them particularly vulnerable to economic sanctions from whites are very reluctant to follow a leadership style strongly opposed by whites—that is, the militant style. Moreover, the fact that only 10 per cent of all the Independents in Winston-Salem and 7 per cent of those in Greenville are Conservatives suggests that some Conservatives are not at all happy with the leadership role which they are performing, and are performing it only because they see no other role open to them in light of their economic position. On the other hand, many Independents—ministers, optometrists, dentists, and the like—may in fact find their economic position affected favorably by a more aggressive form of race leadership. They are not vulnerable to economic sanctions from whites, and their own community places a premium on more aggressive race leadership. At the least, the more militant leaders are better known. A young Negro dentist in Winston-Salem was quite frank on this point:

Look, as far as I'm concerned this [militant leadership] helps me. I don't think I'd have nearly the business that I have today were it not for the lead I've taken in the demonstrations. People are always coming in here and telling me, "We think you are doing a good job; keep it up!"

A final word should be added on the relationship between style of leadership and vulnerability. Vulnerability here has meant economic vulnerability, but it in fact should be defined much more broadly. We mean that some Negro leaders are psychologically unable to bear the kinds of harassment which frequently is the lot of the more militant leaders in the South. A Negro minister in Greenville who was active in the 1960 sit-ins in that city related that it was necessary for him to have his telephone number taken from the public listing because of a deluge of threatening phone calls. Some people simply cannot endure such conditions. They are unable to work under such threats as, "We are going to get your wife and kids!" Others seem to be able to do so. It would, of course, be quite inaccurate to dismiss this as simply evidence that some Negro leaders are "brave" and some are not. Our analysis has been limited to economic vulnerability because this is something that can be readily measured. But data from over three hundred detailed interviews with Negro leaders furnishes strong if impressionistic evidence that Militants are not as psychologically vulnerable to the various attacks and harassments which leaders on the "frontier area" of race relations must endure.

THE OUTSIDERS

Almost two-thirds of the top militant leaders in Winston-Salem are "outsiders"; that is, they are persons who were raised and educated, and/or who have lived for a considerable period of time, outside the South. Contact with the leadership styles operating in the more permissive race relations patterns of northern cities seems to have contributed to the formation of an approach considered quite "radical" in this North Carolina city. We are suggesting that the experience was of the variety, "How are you going to keep them down on the farm . . . ?" There are in Winston-Salem Negroes who were born, raised, and educated in the North who are not participating in race-advancement activity at all. Conversely, there are Militants who have never left their city of birth for more than forty-eight hours at a time. But our interviews indicate that contact with the more permissive race relations patterns of the North have influenced the style of a small group of leaders. While two out of three Militants in Winston-Salem are "outsiders," the ratio is one in three for Moderates and one in five for Conservatives. This data is summarized in Table 20.

TABLE 20

PERCENTAGE OF LEADERS WHO WERE RAISED AND EDUCATED, AND/OR WHO HAVE RESIDED OUTSIDE THE SOUTH BY STYLE OF LEADERSHIP, WINSTON-SALEM AND GREENVILLE

Style	Winston-Salem	Greenville
Conservatives	19	0
Moderates	33	12
Militants	64	22

None of the "outsiders" in Greenville are Conservatives, but it should be noted that a much lower percentage of all leaders in the South Carolina city have had extensive contact with the world outside the South. Winston-Salem, North Carolina, is a sufficiently congenial place for Negroes that northern Negroes on occasion move down to it. Winston Negroes educated outside the South consider seriously coming back home and indeed a few do return. This is not the case with Greenville. The South Carolina city is another world of race relations and very few who have escaped return.

AGE

Nearly a full generation separates militant and conservative leaders in the two cities. The "typical" Militant reached adulthood during World War II or the postwar period, the Conservative in the 1920's or 1930's. The median age of militant leaders in both Winston-Salem and Greenville is the late thirties. In contrast, the median age is the early fifties for Winston-Salem and Greenville Conservatives. It is forty-three for Winston-Salem Moderates, forty for the Greenville Moderates. When very young men (in their twenties) are found in positions of leadership it is virtually without exception as Militants.

Age is related to leadership style in the following ways. First, the pattern of race relations operative when the leader began participating as an adult seems to have importantly influenced his present approach to race relations. Expectations then created have continued to affect his style of race leadership. To put this very simply, a person who first began participating in race-advancement activity in the early 1930's in Winston-Salem usually cannot get quite as excited (although he may be just as resentful and concerned) about the failure of whites to accept certain kinds of integration as a young dentist who returned from professional school to Winston-Salem in the mid-1950's when the revolution was gaining momentum. Second, there seems to be with advancing years a greater disillusionment, or one might say realism, concerning the possibility for change and at the same time a greater stake in the existing system.

Referring to the groups and not to individual leaders we can say that Militants are the young leaders, Conservatives the old, and Moderates the middle-aged leadership. It should be noted, however, that the range of ages is much the same for the practitioners of each leadership style.[44]

We have identified here those biographical factors which seem to be of particular importance to an understanding of why leaders follow the styles they do. All of the correlations suggested here, it should be noted, were determined from interview data, and we do not claim that they have been statistically established. The data submitted in tabular form are only suggestive of factors also indicated in detailed interviews

[44] There are Militants as old as the conservative and moderate leaders. There are not, however, any moderate or conservative leaders in either Winston-Salem or Greenville in their twenties.

with Negro leaders in these cities. We should make clear that prediction as to whether any individual Negro leader will follow a militant, moderate, or conservative style is impossible on the basis of the kind of biographical data which can be gathered for large numbers of leaders. There are idiosyncratic or temperamental factors which can lead an individual to adopt a quite different style than we would expect from his biographical data.

CONCLUSION

Today all Negro political leaders in the urban South publicly profess opposition to segregation and discriminatory treatment in all forms—opposition, in short, to the old biracial system. We have seen over the last two decades a transition from a sharply polarized leadership continuum—with a large accommodating style accepting the biracial system at one end, and a weak protest style insisting on equal treatment at the other—to a more highly differentiated continuum structured by differences in approach to the common goal of full racial equality.

Most southern cities have followed a similar pattern in this transition. In the early period of the breakdown of the old biracial system the leadership continuum remained sharply polarized. All leaders then ostensibly opposed all forms of discriminatory treatment. But since Negroes were excluded from the political institutions in their respective cities, leaders had to choose between a role that appeared very much like the one of the old accommodationists, predicated upon securing the cooperation and approval of certain white leaders, and a role that reached outside the established channels for political action and relied on boycotts, picketing, sit-ins, and other forms of direct action. Greenville, South Carolina, is only now emerging from this first stage. The transition began earlier in Winston-Salem and progressed faster. At this time there is a significantly high level of integration of Negroes into the major political institutions of that city. Moreover, the big battles against gross exclusion from the city facilities and public accommodations have for the most part been fought and won. Negro leaders there must now turn their attention to the infinitely more subtle and complex problems which remain after gross exclusion has been ended. When a school system is totally segregated the solution for the Negro leader is relatively. clear: "Let's desegregate." But when Negro children are free to attend the school nearest their home as a matter of right, and yet when segregation is maintained by the existence of residential segregation, the problem is more complex and difficult and possible solutions are more varied. When the controversy involves the refusal of the owner of a cafeteria to serve Negroes, Negro leaders can get widespread agreement in their own community on the desirability of integrating the cafeteria. Differences center on such questions as whether to use direct action demonstrations. But when the issue is the larger position of the Negro in a society which dooms the Negro child to fewer years of school, and the adult to a lower paying job, a greater chance of being unemployed, and a shorter life, then the possible goals-orientation become again more varied. Negro leaders in Winston-Salem now must turn their attention to these new and, in a sense, much more difficult problems. The goal of full equality in the American democracy is an extraordinarily demanding taskmaster.

Gross exclusion problems will continue, of course, to "rock the boat" of race relations in many parts of the South— and on occasion in rim-South cities like Winston—for many years to come. But the passage of the Civil Rights Act of 1964 ended an era. Even now the attention of Negro leaders in the urban rim-South is being drawn to issue-areas in which solutions are infinitely more varied and complex. This already has been and will continue to be reflected in the continuum of race leadership styles. We may expect that the continuum will become more highly differentiated in the future.

Myrdal referred in his *Dilemma* to an interview with an urban deep-South Negro leader. The leader identified himself as the president of the local NAACP branch. He was then asked if there were other similar organizations in the city, and he said that there was also a League for Civic Improvement. The interviewer then asked why Negroes bothered with two organizations each having the same purpose of trying to improve the position of the Negro. The leader answered:

Sir, that is easily explainable. The NAACP stands firm on its principles and demands our rights as American citizens. But it accomplishes little or nothing in this town, and it arouses a good deal of anger in the whites. On the other hand, the League for Civic Improvement is humble and "pussy-footing." It begs for many favors from the whites, and succeeds quite often. The NAACP cannot be compromised in all the tricks that Negroes have to perform down here. But we pay our dues to it to keep it up as an organization. The League of Civic Improvement does all the dirty work.[45]

The interviewer then said: "Would you please tell me who is president of this League for Civic Improvement? I should like to meet him." "I am," the leader replied. "We are all the same people in both organizations." This is not, we should stress, the rule today. The factors which determine which style a given leader will follow are too compelling to permit it.

[45] Myrdal, *op. cit.*, p. 777.

CHAPTER V

Organizations for Race Leadership

IN the analysis of the styles of Negro political leadership in the preceding chapter, we omitted any consideration of the organizations which have been established to promote the cause of race advancement. This chapter is devoted, then, to an examination of the various race-advancement organizations operating in Winston-Salem and Greenville: the structure of these organizations, their effectiveness, the means they utilize to achieve race goals, and the style of leadership associated with each of the major types.

Broadly speaking, three types of organizations are involved in race advancement activity in the urban South. One type, the Welfare Organizations, include human relations councils, Urban League units, and various local welfare-oriented organizations such as Greenville's Phillis Wheatley Association. The number of organizations which engage at one time or another in welfare activity in the Negro community is, of course, much greater. The literally hundreds of Negro community clubs in every major southern city occasionally engage in limited race-advancement activity of a welfare nature. So do lodges like the Negro Masons and Elks. Negro YMCA's and YWCA's are similarly engaged. But in this chapter we are concerned with organizations which play a central role as pressure groups in freeing Negroes from various forms of discriminatory treatment and which provide both a forum and a source of organizational strength for Negro leaders. Organizations such as the Winston-Salem Urban League are referred to here as the Welfare Organizations because they work directly toward the realization of welfare goals such as the improvement of job opportunities for Negroes, within the discrimination framework. Welfare goals, of course, are a variety of race goals. The Welfare Organizations are trying to get better jobs, housing, schools, police protection, and the like, not for people in general but for Negroes who have been subjected to patterns of discriminatory treatment.

A second type is the Protest Organizations. The well-known national organizations—CORE, NAACP, SCLC, and SNCC—and their local affiliates and chapters fall in this category. Also included are the numerous local protest movements such as the Citizens Committee of Greater New Orleans, the Raleigh Citizens Association, and the Sumter County Movement (Americus, Georgia). Some of these, like the Durham Committee on Negro Affairs, are "peak" organizations which seek to integrate the various local race-advancement groups. The latter continue to maintain their own organizational identity. Others, like the Sumter County Movement, are formed through the initiative of national organizations (here the Student Non-Violent Coordinating Committee) as broad-based local protest movements. People from the national organizations frequently dominate such groups and friction with the "hometown leadership" is common. Still others like the Citizens Committee for Equal Education in Winston-Salem and the now largely defunct Greenville Committee on Social and Political Action are formed by local leaders who for some reason are dissatisfied with the existing race-advancement organizations.

The third type encompasses those organizations which

devote their attention primarily to the area of electoral politics. For convenience these will be referred to here as the Voting Organizations. The leaders who staff these organizations are the politicians. Voting Organizations are of three distinct varieties, each with a different purpose and hence with a different structure. The first variety works in areas where massive barriers still stand in the way of large-scale Negro voting and their efforts necessarily are concentrated on breaking down these barriers. The low rate of Negro voting and strong white resistance doom any attempts to win concessions from candidates and desired policies from city goverment. The Greenville Non-Partisan Voter Registration Committee, the Greenville City and County Voter Crusade, the Palmetto States Voters Association, and Mobile's Non-Partisan Voters League and its Coordinating Committee for Voter Registration are examples of this kind of Voting Organization.

The second variety operates in areas where significant numbers of Negroes are registered and voting. The task is not primarily that of registering Negroes but of manipulating the vote in behalf of certain race goals. These organizations screen candidates, withhold or bestow endorsements and work to elect favored candidates. They may urge Negroes to contest for elective office. Their politics is generally Democratic but they are not instruments of the Democratic party. They remain electoral pressure groups.[1] Atlanta's Negro

[1] These two types of Voting Organizations are highly unusual if not unique in American politics. They have not sought to become third parties because given the kind of electoral machinery which we have in the United States, a Negro third party could only go down to disastrous defeat. Nor are they arms of parent organizations turning to electoral politics to secure necessary governmental support for (generally) economic interests as both business and labor have done. They also differ from the kind of organization generally associated with ethnic politics in the United States. This is the case because from the death of the venture into fusion politics in the 1890's until very recently there was no political party in the South

Voters League, and Winston-Salem's West Winston Civic League Auxiliary and Democratic Voters Club are examples of this second type of Voting Organization. These vary greatly in structure, size, and effectiveness. Some, like the Negro Voters League in Atlanta, are large, well-organized electoral machines. The League has Republican and Democratic cochairmen. It generally has presented a united front in endorsing candidates. Its pyramidal organization, reaching down into every Negro precinct, is quite efficient and effective. Others, like the proliferation of voting clubs in Jacksonville, Florida, tend to be little more than the personal organizations of various Negro leaders. Some of these Voting Organizations are county-wide or city-wide; others limit their activity to a single Negro precinct. Where the first type of Voting Organization exists principally to register Negroes, the second works to organize and commit an existing electorate in behalf of race objectives.

The third category of Voting Organizations includes formal party organs controlled by Negro Democrats and Republicans. Like the second, this type is possible only in those parts of the South with relatively permissive patterns of race relations. These party organizations are almost always the last

---

seeking to organize and use Negro voters. Only in the last decade and then only in certain rim-South cities have the political parties made serious efforts to establish an organization in Negro precincts, and in general to begin integrating Negro voters into the party apparatus. These Negro Voting Organizations are not instruments of membership groups but of a reference group—Negro Americans. This reference group has been subjected to a pattern of discrimination more pervasive and deep-rooted in law and custom than any other which has existed in the United States. These Voting Organizations represent, then, recognition by southern Negroes of (1) the enormous stake which they have in electoral politics; (2) the futility of attempting to form a Negro party; and (3) the fact that white politicians will seriously consider Negro interests only when forced to, here by reason of the electoral strength of Negroes.

to appear, and are very new to the South indeed. They are not to be found in Mobile, Birmingham, or Greenville. They do exist in Atlanta, Richmond, Durham, and Winston-Salem. The party precinct organization is the basic unit here. Negro Democrats (and occasionally Republicans) are at once integrated into the formal party hierarchy and yet constitute a distinct faction. Negro precinct and ward units press for Negro interests within the party structure.

Race-advancement organizations, of course, do not always fit neatly into one of the above three categories. "Peak" community groups like the Durham Committee on Negro Affairs are in fact involved to some extent in all three areas: welfare, protest, and electoral politics. NAACP chapters are frequently very active in registering Negroes. Classification is determined by the central involvement of the organization.

Before beginning an analysis of these three categories of race-advancement organizations, the special position of the Negro Church in the South in the Negro's struggle for equality must be noted. The Church does not fall into one of our categories of race-advancement organizations, but its role in the struggle has been and remains of such importance that it must be given special recognition here. The Church we are speaking of is not, of course, the mystical, spiritual entity, but rather the buildings, ministers, and believers that make up the earthly organization. In one sense it is an occupational grouping like Negro lawyers or businessmen; and ministers, like lawyers and businessmen, are found in all three categories of race-advancement organizations. It is rare that city-wide ministerial fellowships play significant roles in race advancement. When groups of ministers do intervene in protest activity it is generally through a separate movement that does not have sectarian or theological connections such as, for example, the Southern Christian Leadership Conference.[2]

[2] "Christian" in the title of the Southern Christian Leadership Conference refers only to a commitment in a very general sense to

Still, Negro churches are playing a unique role which demands recognition beyond that which we will accord individual ministers and churches as they work through our three categories of race-advancement organizations.

The historically important position of the Negro Church in race leadership has been amply documented by Frazier, Myrdal, and others. The ministry was one of the few professions open to Negroes and—given the major spiritual, social, and communications functions which the Church performed—this made the clergy's assumption of a major role in race leadership inevitable.

In the last two decades the number of potential Negro leaders has increased dramatically throughout the South. There are more Negro dentists, lawyers, optometrists, and others with the academic background, skills, and economic independence necessary for effective race leadership. But the clergy continues to play a central role. This is indicated in the numerical importance of ministers in Negro leadership in Winston-Salem and Greenville. Of the forty-two top leaders in Winston-Salem, nine, or about 22 per cent, are ministers. The figures are seven out of twenty-five, or 28 per cent, in Greenville. In the South, of course, there are still many more Negroes in the ministry than in any professional category other than teaching. And Negro teachers are vulnerables while ministers really are not. Most of the Negro ministers interviewed in this study, whether they were in congregational churches like the Baptist or in churches where a hierarchy controls assignments like the AME (African Methodist Episcopal) or the AMEZ (African Methodist Episcopal Zion), agreed that vigorous participation in race-advancement activity is helpful rather than dangerous in career advancement.

---

certain values within the Christian tradition and to the fact that the leadership of the Conference is composed of ordained Christian ministers.

There has been a marked increase over the last two decades in the number of very well trained Negro ministers (the B.A. along with a B.D.) and this has further strengthened the position of the clergy.

We found a sharp difference of opinion among Negro ministers concerning their role in race advancement. Many older ministers in both Winston-Salem and Greenville see their jobs primarily as one of saving souls. But many of their younger (and often better trained) colleagues welcome involvement in politics on a regular and continuing basis.

As Table 21 shows, minister-leaders are predominantly Militants and Moderates.

TABLE 21

PERCENTAGE OF MINISTER-LEADERS BY STYLE OF RACE LEADERSHIP

Style	Winston-Salem	Greenville
Conservative	11	14
Moderate	33	57
Militant	56	29

The churches continue to perform important communications functions. Negroes are urged by ministers to vote and frequently are advised how to vote. NAACP membership drives are launched from the pulpits. In cities like Durham and Raleigh, where there are excellent Negro newspapers, the communications function of the Church is not quite as crucial. But in cities like Winston-Salem and Greenville, where there is no Negro press, it remains of the greatest importance. Negro churches are physically important as buildings where race-advancement organizations can meet. NAACP and CORE chapters in most southern cities, for example, regularly meet in church buildings.

In short, the well-trained cadre of Negro ministers convinced that talk of Heaven without work to meet the earthly problems of Negroes will make the Church "irrelevant" have used their positions as leaders in an institution which historically has played a central role in Negro community life, and the unparalleled (within the Negro community) communications possibilities of their profession, to maintain the Church's position in the struggle for race advancement. The Negro Church straddles the three categories of race-advancement organizations, but its particular importance demands this separate consideration. The increase in the numbers of Negro professional men outside the clergy is gradually reducing the clergy's numerical dominance in race leadership, but the impressive group of secularly oriented ministers are making certain that the Church continues to play a major role.

WELFARE ORGANIZATIONS

Welfare-oriented race-advancement organizations are active in both Winston-Salem and Greenville. In Winston-Salem an Urban League affiliate, one of the few in the South, has, since its inception in 1948, promoted under a Negro director the hiring of Negroes in downtown stores as clerks, in some of the city's major industries (above the janitorial level), and as deputy sheriffs, along with other traditional service work.[3] In Greenville an independent organization, the Phillis Wheatley Association, works on community service projects which, in the context of Greenville's race relations, parallel those of the Winston League. There is also a Human Relations Council in Greenville which, under a Negro president, has sought principally through discussion to break down patterns of discriminatory treatment.

[3] In January 1964, other southern cities with Urban League affiliates were: New Orleans, Louisiana; Jacksonville, Miami, and Tampa, Florida; Atlanta, Georgia; Little Rock, Arkansas; and Memphis, Tennessee. San Antonio and Dallas, Texas; Greensboro, North Carolina; and Nashville, Tennessee, had demonstrated some interest in having League affiliates established.

WHO ARE THE WELFARE LEADERS?

First, biographical data on the welfare leaders of Winston-Salem and Greenville which seem to be significantly related to the type of race leadership activity will be examined. Then we will discuss the pattern of leadership styles of the welfare leaders.[4]

As Table 22 shows, the welfare leadership in both cities contains a disproportionate number of economic vulnerables.[5]

---

[4] "Welfare leaders" here refers to, for Winston-Salem, the executive director and Negro members of the Board of Directors of the Winston-Salem Urban League; for Greenville, the executive director and the Negro members of the Board of Trustees of the Phillis Wheatley Association, and the officers of the Human Relations Council. The category includes, in short, the leadership of the major welfare-oriented race-advancement organizations in each city. The total number of welfare and protest leaders and politicians appearing in the statistics below exceeds the number of leaders (Conservatives, Moderates, and Militants) included in the analysis in Chapter IV. The criteria used in determining who were the top leaders are described in the Appendix. The criteria used here, however, are different. All members of the executive bodies of the Welfare Organizations are called the welfare leaders. Similarly, all members of the executive organs of the Protest Organizations are the protest leaders. Some of these people are not broadly recognized as leaders in the Negro subcommunity. But since they hold policy-making positions on the executive organs of the groups involved, they must be considered welfare leaders, protest leaders, or politicians. To put this another way, all members of the Board of Trustees of the Phillis Wheatley Association in Greenville must be considered welfare leaders; that is, leaders of this Welfare Organization. But some of them are not generally recognized as leaders of the subcommunity. There is also some overlapping membership; that is, some politicians are in positions of leadership in Protest Organizations, etc. This will be discussed further below.

[5] The distinction between those highly vulnerable, marginally vulnerable, and independent was developed at some length in the preceding chapter (see pp. 223–224).

The data in Table 22 take on greater significance when the vulnerability of the welfare leaders is compared to that of protest leaders. No protest leader in either Winston-Salem or Greenville has a highly vulnerable occupation.

TABLE 22

PERCENTAGE OF WELFARE LEADERS IN WINSTON-SALEM AND GREENVILLE
BY DEGREE OF VULNERABILITY OF OCCUPATION

Degree of vulnerability	Winston-Salem (N=11)	Greenville (N=15)
High vulnerability	36	40
Marginal vulnerability	36	27
Independence	27	33

As a group, welfare leaders are in a more fortunate socio-economic position than are their fellow race leaders. Defining class in terms of the amount and source of income within the context of the Negro population of Winston-Salem and Greenville, we have the distribution of the welfare leaders by class, as shown in Table 23.

TABLE 23

PERCENTAGE OF WELFARE LEADERS BY CLASS, WINSTON-SALEM
AND GREENVILLE

Class	Winston-Salem	Greenville
Upper-middle	36	27
Middle-middle and lower-middle	64	73
Lower	0	0

Comparable data on the protest leaders and the politicians will be discussed later in this chapter. Welfare leaders bring to their leadership positions relatively high status. In the context of the Negro community they are prestigious people. We will not attempt to be precise on this point, but the welfare leadership of both cities contains a disproportionately high number of those who derive high social status from income, occupation, education, associational memberships, social activities, and the like. Welfare leaders, to summarize, tend to possess the "scarce values" of income and status to a greater degree than do either politicians or protest leaders.

Welfare leaders as a group are older than either the politicians or the protest leaders. The median age for welfare leaders in Winston-Salem is fifty-one, in Greenville fifty-two. Finally, a relatively large segment of the welfare organization leadership in both cities is "home grown." "Home grown" means born, educated, and residing since birth in the South. Moreover, a high percentage of the welfare leaders are lifelong residents of Winston-Salem and Greenville respectively, and hence have a long association with their city's race relations and (though usually association at arms' length) with their city's white leadership. Few were educated or have lived outside the South. This information is summarized in Table 24.[6]

TABLE 24

PERCENTAGE OF WELFARE LEADERS BY TWO RESIDENCE VARIABLES; WINSTON-SALEM AND GREENVILLE

	Winston-Salem	Greenville
Life long residents	45	60
"Outsiders"	27	7

A considerably higher percentage of welfare leaders in Winston-Salem, it should be noted, have had contact with the

[6] The Term "outsider" was defined in Chapter IV, p. 227. Note that the percentage of lifelong residents and of "outsiders" does not total 100 for either city. There is, of course, a third category: those who have moved to Winston-Salem and Greenville from other parts of the South.

world outside the South. In general, the Winston-Salem welfare leaders are more cosmopolitan, better educated, more prosperous, and better equipped for leadership than their Greenville counterparts. In this the two groups of leaders reflect larger differences in the two Negro subcommunities, differences which have been discussed at length above.

This profile of the welfare leaders closely resembles that of the Conservatives. Each category of race-advancement organization is in fact characterized by a particular style of race leadership, and most welfare leaders in Winston-Salem and Greenville are Conservatives. But there is a significant representation of Moderates in the leadership of the welfare organizations. Better than one in four of the welfare leaders in Winston are Moderates, one in five in Greenville.

TABLE 25

PERCENTAGE OF WELFARE LEADERS BY STYLE OF RACE LEADERSHIP, WINSTON-SALEM AND GREENVILLE

Style	Winston-Salem	Greenville
Conservative	73	80
Moderate	27	20
Militant	0	0

The absence of Militants is not surprising. The organizations in the welfare category are bound by their structure, constituencies, programs, and procedures to recruit and attract the more conservative leaders.[7]

STRUCTURE AND FUNCTIONING

The welfare organizations in both Winston-Salem and Greenville have biracial leadership groups. Both the League in

[7] It should be noted that because of the different definition of leadership used here and the fact that not all welfare leaders are Conservatives, this analysis of biographical data of welfare leaders is not simply a restatement of the analysis of comparable data for Conservatives.

Winston-Salem and Phillis Wheatley in Greenville are United Fund organizations and hence dependent upon whites for financial support. Each welfare organization from its inception has been committed to the practice and procedure of biracial "cooperation." The leadership style associated with these organizations, and to a large extent their whole orientation follow from this.

The Winston-Salem Urban League has a white president and a white treasurer. A Negro is vice president. The League's only full-time professional employee, the executive director, is a Negro. Half the League's eighteen directors are Negroes. The National Urban League and its local affiliates are firmly committed to this kind of biracial organization. Hemen Sweatt, director of the League's Southern Regional Office, stated in an interview that the League has been approached by a number of groups from various southern cities seeking to establish League affiliates on other than this biracial basis:

We have had requests for all-white Urban League affiliates in some southern cities. We have also had requests for Leagues with only token white or token Negro representation. We have had requests for Leagues backed only by a small group of white Liberals, and hence which would lack widespread community support. We have said no to all of these. We maintain that for the League to do its job effectively it must enjoy the firm support and the recognition of both the white and the Negro community in its city of operation.

The position of the Winston-Salem Urban League as a United Fund agency is at once an enormous asset and a very serious liability. The United Fund is a source of significant financial support. At the same time, those interested in seeing the League continue its work cannot but be mindful of the fact that should its activities seriously antagonize a significant number of whites it could quickly find this source of funds cut off. After the 1954 *Brown v. Board of Education* decision, League affiliates in Jacksonville, New Orleans, and Little Rock were expelled by the United Funds of these three cities. The

League affiliates were in no way involved in the desegregation decision. But they were a convenient target for angry whites. The man who is currently executive director of the Winston-Salem Urban League, Samuel D. Harvey, is in fact dependent upon southern white men for his livelihood. Harvey emphatically denies, however, that this constitutes a serious impediment to the effective function of his organization.

Of course we are financially dependent upon whites. Specifically I am for my job. This means that we must be careful at times. But the entire program of the Winston-Salem Urban League is dependent upon our success in securing the cooperation of community leaders, white and Negro. If we fail to secure this cooperation, we fail completely, quite apart from the question of financial support. We believe that there is a place for an organization committed to effective biracial cooperation in such vital areas as jobs, education, and voting. This is what the League here and elsewhere tries to accomplish.

Hemen Sweatt noted that National Urban League programming in the area of voter education and registration began in certain southern cities in 1962 and 1963. In the early 1960's, for the first time, funds for effective activity in the field of voter registration became available in the South. The programs of the National Urban League and its local affiliates were conducted with grants from a voter education project administered by the Southern Regional Council. Sweatt candidly discussed the kinds of problems which confront the League as it moves into this area. He mentioned the "educational problems" with both Urban League boards and United Funds "in getting them to understand objectively the relationship of voter education among Negroes to the end product of all else in which the Urban League is involved program-wise." He described the voting and registration survey conducted by the Winston-Salem Urban League in 1963 in which over 10,000 Negroes were contacted as a "major breakthrough for voter education programming among Chest-supported Urban

Leagues of the South." To put the matter simply, the League has had great difficulties getting into an area in which it has great interest—voter education and registration. It has had those difficulties because whites on the boards of local League affiliates and the United Funds which finance these local affiliates have opposed League sponsorship of voter education projects. It has been necessary to "educate" these whites on the value of this kind of activity. League officials would say in reply to this that although they have not been able to move as quickly as they might like into voter registration projects, when they have been able to secure the backing of the local boards their work has been most impressive. The 1963 voting and registration survey in Winston-Salem was by far the most comprehensive ever conducted in that city.

The operations of the Winston-Salem League can best be described as "quiet negotiations." When things work as planned the League can be very effective indeed. In theory it operates to advance Negro interests in the following manner. First, it gathers on its executive board citizens who are highly respected and powerful, both economically and politically. Key executives of major industries figure prominently on the boards of local affiliates. In long and careful discussions these white leaders are persuaded that major modifications of the Negro's position in the community must be achieved. In southern cities at present these modifications center around job upgrading and the hiring of Negroes into positions from which they have been excluded. Having been persuaded of this need, the white leaders on the League boards then persuade their fellow executives, Chamber of Commerce associates, and others. Consensus is at last achieved and the action effected.

Certainly the Winston-Salem League follows the model in a number of ways. Leading Negro business and professional men and executives of the major industrial firms in Winston-Salem comprise its executive board. R. J. Reynolds, Hanes

Hosiery, and Western Electric are all represented by key executives. At the monthly meetings of the League, Negro board members continually "toss out" race-advancement suggestions for the consideration of the white members. At times interest is generated and through highly informal discussions and negotiations a particular project is advanced. The Winston-Salem Urban League does provide a group of Negro leaders with close contact and communication with leading whites. No other group of Negro leaders has comparable contact with top white business leaders. The Winston-Salem welfare leaders are able at regular monthly meetings to "rub elbows" with Winston-Salem's "economic dominants." Negroes present at these meetings agree that a high degree of cordiality is maintained at all times. Still there is every indication that the Negro board members do not, and in a sense cannot, exploit the opportunity this communications channel provides. It seems they are somewhat overawed by the economic power and high status of their white colleagues. They are inclined, moreover, to a fairly circumscribed approach to race advancement. Most are men who have worked long and hard to achieve their socioeconomic position and the degree of acceptance which membership on the League's executive body implies, and they are most reluctant to jeopardize this position. Moreover, they lack effective sanctions within the structure of the League. They are committed necessarily to a cooperative approach with the white leaders of the executive board.

The Winston League's accomplishments are at once impressive and limited. In areas where general agreement between whites and Negroes exists, the League has made slow but continuous progress. The League succeeded in 1962 in placing Negroes in positions from which they had previously been excluded in eleven Winston-Salem companies. It placed, for example, the first Negro salesclerk at the local Sears Roebuck store. The League helped with job upgrading and integration at the huge Reynolds plants. It promoted the hiring of highly trained Negro technicians and engineers at Western Electric's Winston plant. Yet even here only a few workers were involved. And certain failures in the job improvement sphere are notable. The Hanes family, owners of Hanes Hosiery, has been associated with the Winston League since its inception. James G. Hanes, retired head of the firm, was in 1963 Honorary Chairman of the Winston League. His son, now the president of the firm, is a member of the League's executive board. Yet it was not until late 1962 that Hanes Hosiery took its first very modest step to employ Negroes above the janitorial level. One Negro clerk-typist was hired.

The League's activities are not widely known or highly regarded by Winston Negroes. Only 2 per cent of those interviewed indicated knowledge of what the League is doing; only 2 per cent nominated the League's director as one of the city's outstanding Negro leaders.[8] The lack of visibility that these figures suggest is necessarily built into the League's operation. A Negro member of the board put it this way:

We can't very well walk out of negotiations with Reynolds and announce to the press, "Well, we made them give in on X, Y, and Z." They aren't going to take that. The one reason they will talk with us is that they feel sure the issues will be handled quietly. We simply can't do much to publicize our activities.

The Winston-Salem League is severely criticized by many militant Negro leaders and others in sympathy with the militant approach. The attack centers around the financial control of the organization by whites. Said one Militant of the League's director:

Did you see that $25,000 house he's building over there? Do you think he's going to do anything to make those fellows [white leaders on the League] mad? Not on your life.

Many Negro leaders in Winston appear not to under-

[8] See the Appendix for a description of the survey.

stand that the League is not solely a race advancement pressure group. It is that, but it is also a service organization. And it is committed to biracial cooperation. The Winston League's director put it this way:

I certainly agree that there is room for the NAACP approach. But there is for ours as well. We can do things they can't. There is enough work for all of us.

Militants rarely will concede this to the League. Phillis Wheatley encounters the same problem in Greenville. The director of the National League's Southern Regional Office observed:

We get that kind of thing everywhere. There is a clear lack of understanding of the purposes and possibilities of the League. We still believe strongly, however, that there is a place for our approach, resting as it does on the foundation of biracial cooperation.

Greenville's Phillis Wheatley Association has a similar organizational structure: a white president, a biracial board (twelve whites, twelve Negroes), and a Negro executive director; and its financial support is also drawn from white-controlled philanthropy (the United Fund). Like the Winston-Salem League, Phillis Wheatley can go no further than the white leaders on the Board want to go. It is committed to biracial cooperation. And the factors limiting its effectiveness are incomparably stronger than those operating in Winston-Salem. First, Phillis Wheatley cannot attract white leaders comparable in power and status to those serving on the League's board in Winston. The white members of Phillis Wheatley's board are respected citizens, but they are not top community leaders. White racial opinion in Greenville is such that association with Negroes even in a welfare-oriented organization is not wholly respectable. Many leading whites simply will not allow themselves to be attached in even the most peripheral manner. This is slowly changing, however, as is indicated by the willingness of many white community leaders to serve on the biracial committees established in Greenville in 1963. But any kind of race-advancement activity in Greenville remains highly suspect.

The race relations structure in Greenville has, moreover, made the position of welfare leaders there substantially weaker than that of their Winston counterparts. Not only do they lack access to white leaders, but opposition to projects such as job upgrading is much stronger. Given the relative inactivity of the moderate and militant leadership in the city, welfare leaders can bring few "positive inducements" to action in behalf of Negro interests. As a result, Phillis Wheatley has devoted its attention largely to service projects.

Greenville's Human Relations Council is a different kind of welfare organization. It promotes greater understanding between Negroes and whites, and fuller Negro political awareness. For this it relies on discussion and certain education projects. Financial support has not been a major problem because the financial commitments of the organization are limited. Its monthly meetings, devoted to explaining problems of the Negro community, are open to all interested persons. As an example of its education projects, in January 1963 the Council heard Mrs. Septima Clark, supervisor of the Teacher Training, Citizenship and Education program of the Southern Christian Leadership Conference. Plans were made for the Council to encourage well-educated Negro women in Greenville to go to SCLC's Dorchester Institute, a citizenship training school located near Savannah, Georgia. Upon returning to Greenville, they would teach adult classes in reading, writing, preparation for passing voting literacy tests, health, filling out tax forms, and the like. The Southern Christian Leadership Conference provided financial support.

The Council's work has been very limited, but it has provided a forum for biracial discussion. Whites participating in the Council discussions tend to be, however, the "town radicals," generally in sympathy with Negro welfare if not status demands. The benefits of the communication channel provided by the Human Relations Council of Greenville are thus somewhat limited.

To summarize, the chief claim of the Phillis Wheatley Association and the Human Relations Council as race-advancement groups is that they bring Negro and white leaders together for the discussion of problems confronting the Negro. The structure of race relations in Greenville prevents effective utilization of this communications channel. The association of whites with even this kind of race-advancement organization really is not considered wholly respectable.

RECRUITMENT

The goals of race-advancement organizations in this category are welfare goals; the means which they are required by their organizational structure to use—educating, informing, and persuading—are also those favored by conservative leaders. Welfare Organizations are committed to biracial cooperation; so are conservative leaders. It is not surprising, then, that Conservatives see the Welfare Organizations as good vehicles through which to work for race advancement. Conservatives frequently are unable and/or unwilling to participate in activity which brings upon the participants the strong hostility of whites. The Welfare Organizations provide opportunity for race leadership through an approved channel.

The Welfare Organizations themselves make certain that militant flies won't get in their ointment. Whites, of course, are involved in the selection of board members for both the Winston-Salem League and Phillis Wheatley. They simply will not accept militant Negro leaders, or even some of the more outspoken Moderates. A Negro member of the Winston League's executive board recalled how he had suggested a moderate leader for membership. He described the reaction of white board members:

They made it clear that they didn't want him on the Board. One said that he liked Bill but that Bill tended to go off "half cocked." He thought they needed people a little more "solid" and moderate. "We can't get any extremists here, you know," he said. "Our work is delicate and everything could be ruined if one of our members started 'popping off' a lot about discrimination."

In most cases the conservative Negroes working through the Welfare Organizations themselves want colleagues of a similar orientation.

PROTEST ORGANIZATIONS

Protest Organizations are those whose central thrust in race-advancement activity is through general public protest against discriminatory treatment. In this category in Winston-Salem are two NAACP branches, one the regular city branch with its auxiliary organizations, the other a branch on the campus of Winston-Salem State College; a chapter of the Congress of Racial Equality formed in the spring of 1963; the Citizens Committee for Equal Rights, which was organized as the Citizens Committee for Equal Education but which two weeks after its inception in March 1964 decided to expand its area of interest; and a unit of an NAACP youth group, the Commandoes, largely inactive since the 1963 protest demonstrations in Winston. Greenville's NAACP branch is the only Protest Organization presently operating in that city. Greenville in 1960 and 1961 had a chapter of the Congress of Racial Equality, but this was disbanded when, in the words of one of the chapter leaders,

I saw that the same people were running both [NAACP and CORE] organizations. That didn't make any sense. We were duplicating too much and spreading ourselves too thin.

WHO ARE THE PROTEST LEADERS?

No Protest Organization leader in either Winston-Salem or Greenville has an occupation which is highly vulnerable to white sanctions.[9] It is a basic fact of political life for Negroes in the South that one does not actively engage in the work of Protest Organizations unless he is secure from economic sanctions. It is by no means clear that a Negro schoolteacher in Winston-Salem would, upon assuming the presidency of the local NAACP branch, find his job in the public school system in jeopardy, but few have shown any inclination to take the chance.[10]

Data on the vulnerability of protest leaders in Winston-Salem and Greenville are summarized in Table 26:

TABLE 26

PERCENTAGE OF PROTEST LEADERS BY VULNERABILITY OF OCCUPATION,
WINSTON-SALEM AND GREENVILLE

Degree of vulnerability	Winston-Salem (N=28)	Greenville (N=16)
High vulnerability	0	0
Marginal vulnerability	18	25
Independence	82	75

[9] "Protest leaders" here are the officers and members of the executive boards of the Winston-Salem NAACP and CORE, and the Greenville NAACP. In April 1964 the Citizens Committee for Equal Rights in Winston-Salem was still a one-man organization. The Commandoes and the Winston-Salem State College NAACP are only sporadically active and both their membership and leadership are constantly changing.

[10] The wife of an NAACP leader in Winston has been and remains a teacher in the Winston-Salem school system. She has not experienced any difficulty. Nor has another woman teacher prominently associated with the Protest Organizations in that city.

Four professions—the ministry, law, dentistry, and optometry —account for slightly more than 60 per cent of the protest leadership of the two cities. These professional men with only Negro clients frequently find it to their economic advantage to be associated prominently with protest activity. They are in this respect in a markedly different position from the economic vulnerables.[11]

Protest leaders as a group have a lower class position than either welfare leaders or politicians. The "typical" protest leader is the young, somewhat underpaid Negro professional. He is of the Negro middle class but his occupational

[11] Vulnerability is of central importance in determining availability for race leadership and, as we noted above, extends beyond economic vulnerability. This was given an unusually cogent statement by a Winston-Salem minister. He accused certain of his colleagues of not providing effective leadership because they had, in his words, "sold out." Reminded that "selling out" is a harsh criticism and asked to be more explicit, the minister said:

"It is very natural for Negroes to want to maintain the friendship and the approval of influential whites. So they refrain from doing anything which would jeopardize their relationship. As a result they are appointed to committees and get an occasional affectionate pat on the back. We who say what we think and do what we believe must be done pay the price in terms of fewer contacts with white leaders, the absence of approval, and in general being on the outside. But I am willing to pay that price. I am not beholden to any white man. I own no property. The church, all Negroes, pay my salary. If I should have to leave here, the Methodist Conference will place me. I seek only the approval of my own community."

Clearly this sense of complete independence from white-imposed sanctions is unusual, but it is a necessary part of availability for the most militant forms of race leadership. We have referred here only to economic vulnerability. But as we noted above and as the statement of the Winston-Salem minister so well points out, there are other dimensions to vulnerability, including the need for white approval, which cannot readily be obtained for large numbers of leaders.

position does not yet provide him with either economic security or a really comfortable income. The class position of the protest leaders is summarized in Table 27.[12]

[12] We noted in Chapter IV, pp. 219–220, that the term *class* as used here includes what C. Wright Mills has called "gradations" (the amount of income) and "sources" (whether salaried, self-employed, wage earner, and the like). (See Mills' essay, "The Social Life of a Modern Community," reprinted in Irving Louis Horowitz [ed.], *Power, Politics and People: The Collected Essays of C. Wright Mills* [New York, 1963], p. 41). Here perhaps we should say more about how we determined the class position of the leaders. The 1960 census showed the income of nonwhite families in Winston-Salem and Greenville to be:

	Winston-Salem (percentage of families)	Greenville (percentage of families)
Under $1,000	12.6	16.5
$1,000 to 1,999	15.5	23.6
2,000 to 2,999	16.6	24.0
3,000 to 3,999	20.4	17.0
4,000 to 4,999	13.1	9.7
5,000 to 5,999	7.0	5.0
6,000 to 6,999	5.7	1.9
7,000 to 7,999	3.2	0.9
8,000 to 8,999	1.9	0.4
9,000 to 9,999	1.3	0.2
10,000 and over	2.3	0.4
Median Income	$3,248	$2,410

We classified Negro leaders in Winston-Salem in the following manner: (1) Salaried and self-employed persons with a family income of $7,500 or above, upper-middle class; (2) salaried and self-employed persons with an income of $3,250 to $7,500, and certain wage earners (census category, Craftsman, Foreman, etc.) with an income of $4,000 to $7,500, middle-middle and lower-middle class; (3) salaried and self-employed persons with a family income of under $3,250, or wage earners with a family income under $4,000, lower class. This classification is by no means satisfactory for all purposes of analysis. Quite obviously there is a very significant difference between wage earners

TABLE 27
PERCENTAGE OF PROTEST LEADERS BY CLASS; WINSTON-SALEM AND GREENVILLE

Class	Winston-Salem	Greenville
Upper-middle	4	0
Middle-middle and lower-middle	67	75
Lower	29	25

Protest leaders, like leaders in general, are a group of a much higher class position than the subcommunity as a whole. But among their fellow race leaders their class position is relatively low. Similarly, protest leaders are, in comparison to other race leaders, low-status people. The "typical" protest leader is not the well established M.D., but the struggling young optometrist. Protest leaders are not members of Negro "society." [18] They generally are single-purpose leaders and do not bring to their race leadership records of community service or philanthropic activity.

Protest leaders in Winston-Salem and Greenville are as a group younger than either the welfare leaders or the politicians. The median age in Winston-Salem falls in the late thirties; it is forty in Greenville. A very large majority of the

with an income of $3,999 and those earning under $1,000 per year. The very poor, however, do not enter into our analysis. They simply do not provide leaders. All of our lower-class leaders are earning over $2,600 per year. Approximately the same income levels apply in designating class in Greenville and we will not repeat them here. Income levels for each class are slightly lower in Greenville, reflecting the generally lower income levels of Negroes in the South Carolina city.

[18] E. Franklin Frazier's statement that "many Negro professional men and women take more seriously their recreation than their professions" does not apply to the protest leader. (See Frazier, *Black Bourgeoisie* [Collier Books; New York, 1962], p. 171.)

protest leaders in Winston moved there from other communities. A majority are "outsiders." Protest leaders in Greenville, however, differ little in these residence variables from their welfare colleagues. No Protest Organization leader in Greenville has ever lived for any period of time outside the South; the only "outsider" went to college in the North.[14] The move-

TABLE 28

PERCENTAGE OF PROTEST LEADERS BY TWO RESIDENCE VARIABLES;
WINSTON-SALEM AND GREENVILLE

	Winston-Salem	Greenville
Lifelong residents	25	50
"Outsiders"	57	6

ment of northern Negro professional men into rim-South cities like Winston-Salem is now fairly common. They do not move, however, into such deep-South cities as Greenville.[15]

No protest leader in either Winston-Salem or Greenville is associated with the conservative style of race leadership. Most are Militants, but a significant number are Moderates. A very high percentage of Conservatives are not leaders of the

[14] If a leader was raised in one of our two cities, left to attend a Negro college *somewhere in the South,* and then returned to his home community, he is here considered a "lifelong resident." On the other hand, if a leader was born in one of our two cities, went North for his education, and then returned home, he is considered an "outsider."

[15] An African Methodist Episcopal Zion (AMEZ) minister in Winston-Salem said that he had the choice of taking a church in Harlem or in Winston-Salem. He chose Winston-Salem. A number of Negro professional men who have lived in the North told the author that they prefer the rim-South environment to that of the northern ghetto. None, however, indicated that they had considered moving to a deep-South city. This is further indication that Negroes perceive sharp differences between the rim-South and deep-South patterns of race relations.

welfare-oriented race-advancement organizations, but virtually all militant leaders in Winston-Salem and Greenville occupy

TABLE 29

PERCENTAGE OF PROTEST LEADERS BY STYLE OF RACE LEADERSHIP; WINSTON-SALEM AND GREENVILLE

Style	Winston-Salem	Greenville
Conservative	0	0
Moderate	29	19
Militant	71	81

formal leadership positions in the Protest Organizations. Many Conservatives in Winston-Salem work through the Voting Organizations. Others are able to operate informally without an organizational base. Militants, on the other hand, need organizational support for the sanctions—"negative inducements"—which are essential to their promotion of race goals.

The distinction made by Louis Lomax between the older, more firmly established, and somewhat more conservative leadership of the NAACP and the newer, hungrier, and more militant leadership provided by organizations such as CORE and SNCC cannot be applied universally to southern protest leadership.[16] In many parts of the South the NAACP remains the only organized protest movement and as such has a monopoly on militancy. But in an increasing number of southern cities the newer protest movements have organized and have pushed the NAACP from its long-time position as the most militant race advancement organization. This is reflected not surprisingly in the leadership styles associated with the Protest Organizations. Comparing the styles of the leaders of the Winston NAACP with those of the leaders of the Winston CORE chapter, we find significant moderate representation on the former but none at all on the latter (see Table 30).

[16] Louis Lomax, *The Negro Revolt* (New York, 1962), p. 101 ff.

TABLE 30

PERCENTAGE OF NAACP AND CORE LEADERS BY STYLE OF RACE
LEADERSHIP; WINSTON-SALEM

Style	NAACP	CORE
Conservative	0	0
Moderate	47	0
Militant	53	100

STRUCTURE AND FUNCTIONING

The philosophy and program of the Welfare Organizations require that they be biracial. Protest Organizations in both Winston-Salem and Greenville, however, are all-Negro in leadership and membership. Very few whites are to be found in southern cities, to be sure, who want to work through Protest Organizations. But most protest leaders are not uphappy over this. They welcome white support, but really prefer that the support remain *outside* their organizations. In fact, the Winston NAACP has on two occasions refused membership to whites, partly it seems for ethnocentric considerations and partly for self-protection. An officer of the Winston NAACP described one case:

We had a white fellow request membership last year. He even sent his membership fee—for gold card membership. We had a big hassle over whether or not to accept him and finally decided to return his money. He didn't give up easily, said he wanted to help our work, but we couldn't take a chance. We have to be careful that we don't get a Communist on our membership list. They [whites in general] would murder us if that ever happened.

We pointed out to him that the NAACP national office accepts practically anyone into membership, no questions asked. We also suggested that there are, even in the South, a number of whites who want to help race-advancement organizations like the NAACP out of wholly honorable motives. He replied:

Well, that's what we told the fellow, that he should write the National. Let them handle it. We are down on the firing line and can't take a chance. The fellow may have been all right but it seems a little strange that he was so anxious to join our branch.

Other members of the branch disagreed with this position and felt that membership should have been extended.

Contact with whites on the local level in the South, particularly from the perspective of a protest leader, naturally breeds suspicion of the motives of whites. It does seem, however, that protest leaders as a group would score a little higher on an ethnocentrism scale, if such a test were given, than would their welfare colleagues. However this may be, to appeal to ethnocentrism clearly is the politic thing to do within Protest Organizations. Welfare Organizations are established on the assumption that a vehicle for biracial cooperation is necessary. Some whites at least must be viewed as friends or as potential friends. Protest Organizations in contrast predicate much of their work on the assumption that the white man will not give the Negro any more than he has to give. Whites are seen, if not as devils, at least as basically and fundamentally antagonistic to Negro interests.

Protest Organizations are mass membership organizations, and in this they differ again from their welfare counterparts. Welfare leaders have no followers within their organizations. These organizations consist of officers and board members. Guilds attached to them play no part in leadership selection or in the determination of policy. Both the NAACP and CORE, however, seek to enroll rank and file Negroes in their branches. Leaders of the Welfare Organizations are formally selected by a process of co-optation. In Protest Organizations the formal selection process requires election by the members of the branch. We know, of course, that branch leaders are in fact generally chosen by informal co-optation. The existing leadership decides whom it wants on the executive board, reports this through a nominating committee to the branch, and has its choices ratified. Branch meetings are used by the leadership, not for policy determination, but to inform the rank and file and to gain their support and financial backing, and to demonstrate to whites and Negroes broadly based support. Decisions, however, are usually made in as oligarchical a manner as in the Welfare Organizations. But this should not be interpreted to mean that the formal organizational demands are without significance. Protest leaders are committed to considerable interaction with the Negro rank and file. Many of the Negroes attending branch meetings are lower-class persons. Occasionally protest leaders must defend themselves before mass meetings. This factor, that Protest Organizations are mass membership groups while Welfare Organizations are really only leadership vehicles, helps explain differences in the kinds of leaders which these two groups of organizations recruit.

The Winston-Salem NAACP branch presently has more than 700 members. Membership over the last decade has fluctuated from a high of more than 1000 to a low of 450. The biggest factor determining the size of branch membership seems to be the way in which membership drives are conducted. In some years very little work is put into the drives and membership suffers. At other times highly ambitious drives are conducted and membership increases significantly. At one time in the mid-1950's the Winston-Salem branch was one of the largest in the South, and was the largest in North Carolina. The newly formed CORE chapter in Winston-Salem has fewer than 200 members but many of these are very active. The Greenville NAACP branch has never had a membership greater than 309, and in 1963 the membership was only 232. In both cities, however, many more Negroes regularly support the programs of the Protest Organizations.

Each Protest Organization, we noted, is in fact controlled by a relatively small group of leaders. Branch meetings are very poorly attended. There are usually fewer than twenty-five persons at meetings of the Winston-Salem NAACP branch. The Protest Organizations are financed primarily by the portion of membership dues which they are permitted to retain. A number of businesses and social organizations, and a few individuals, take out life memberships which for $1,000 give the purchaser a very nice plaque and membership in perpetuity. During major racial protests, as for example the 1960 sit-ins in Winston-Salem, special contributions are solicited. Some money is collected through the sale of Christmas seals and the like.

The Protest Organizations in Winston-Salem and Greenville, and indeed throughout the South, suffer from enormous amounts of internal controversy. One of the incorrect assumptions made by many southern whites is that protest leaders are as one in program and race values. Negroes, of course, recognize that serious divisions exist. Lack of unity was cited as the major weakness and failing of race-advancement organizations by Negroes interviewed in surveys in Winston-Salem and Greenville. Protest leaders themselves lament that "Negroes can't work together." The stake which Negroes have in race advancement is so great, and the sanctions which the various protest leaders have over their peers is so insubstantial that a high level of division is to be expected. That it is not greater is due only to the presence of the common enemy, the white man. As patterns of race relations become more permissive, divisions frequently become more numerous because protest leaders find themselves with more options and the reasons for unity become less pressing.

The Greenville NAACP branch was almost ruined in 1960 by an internal struggle. Sit-ins in that city were started on the initiative of a visiting white divinity student and several younger members of the local branch. There were a series of demonstrations and some Negro students (fewer than 200 in all) were arrested. The branch was convulsed by charges and countercharges. One group, the "Young Turks," accused the "Old Guard" of not giving enough support to the sit-ins. The Old Guard countered with the accusation that it was pernicious to continue to send young people to jail when funds for getting them out had been exhausted. Two aspects of the division are common to most internal controversies in southern Protest Organizations.

(1) A basic ideological difference ran through the controversy. One group argued that protest demonstrations are good in themselves. They "prick" the consciences of whites. The greater the number of people arrested, the more the plight of the Negro is dramatized and the more the whites are inconvenienced. The second group accused the former

of putting kids in jail without any money to get them out. I was as much in favor of sit-ins as they were, but I simply could not support sending young people to jail when I knew we were out of funds for bail.

The second group insisted that it had approached the question of continuing demonstrations pragmatically. The point had clearly been made that Negroes were strongly opposed to lunch counter segregation. Discontent had been dramatized. There was no point, it was argued, in putting more people in jail. Other values such as the safety and security of Negroes were being jeopardized. This same ideological division appeared prominently and dramatically in the demonstrations in Birmingham, Alabama, in the spring of 1963. When the Martin Luther King group began demonstrations they encountered the opposition of a significant segment of the established leadership. Only when hoses and dogs were turned on Negro youths in the streets of Birmingham was a high degree of unity among protest leaders and a high level of community involvement realized. It is very doubtful that the serious ideological division in the Birmingham protest leadership over the content, timing, and extent of direct action demonstrations would have been resolved had it not been for the atrocities perpetrated by whites.

(2) The "ins" in the Greenville NAACP—in 1960 the Old Guard—saw in the demonstrations a threat to their position of leadership. They saw very clearly that several younger leaders were emerging from the demonstrations with enhanced prestige. They denounced the Young Turks as publicity seekers:

All they were after was headlines. They didn't care what happened to the kids involved. They didn't run this thing for the people but just to get their names in the papers.

The vehemence of the denunciation can be understood only if we recognize that two battles were going on during the sit-in demonstrations. The first was between whites and Negroes, the second *within the protest leadership* for influence in the Negro community. In virtually any political situation, of course, incumbents try to maintain their positions, but for reasons discussed in Chapter III race leaders are particularly insecure. Moreover, the status values that go along with leadership are more scarce in the Negro subcommunity than in the white.

Protest Organizations throughout the South frequently find themselves facing in several directions at the same time, with different leaders holding positions which are mutually contradictory. In this situation certain protest leaders individually initiate demonstrations which, if they gain significant public support, are then, after the fact, adopted by the Protest Organization. There is often so much internal division that the Protest Organizations are not effective agents for planning protest activity. This was the situation with the "wade-ins" at the Reynolds Park pool in Winston-Salem in the summer of 1962. The executive board of the Winston NAACP was deeply divided over the desirability of having "wade-ins" and as a result there was little coordinated planning. A small group of NAACP leaders and some college students integrated the pools and presented the branch with a *fait accompli.* It had no choice but to give its endorsement. Once demonstrations have begun and racial incidents (police brutality, arrests, demonstrations, and the like) have forced highly ethnocentric responses, the Protest Organizations become relatively cohesive. A Winston-Salem protest leader observed:

> The NAACP is an organization which thrives on protest. It lives on conflict. It is strongest when it is protesting something. In periods of relative quiet it finds it hard to stop everyone from flying off in all directions.

It is generally true in both Winston-Salem and Greenville that even the Protest Organizations have been able to achieve a high level of internal cohesion on sensitive race goals only when they have had a strong assist from whites. When the response of whites is fairly flexible, Protest Organizations often find themselves badly divided. In Winston-Salem in the spring of 1963 demonstrations were begun by those who believed that the city's Goodwill Committee, with which the local NAACP had allied itself, had not moved fast enough to eliminate discrimination. A Congress of Racial Equality chapter was formed and through the spring, summer, and fall of 1963 the chapter sponsored occasional picketing, sit-ins, and protest marches. Through all of this, however, police brutality was absent. Arrests were at a minimum and sentences were moderate. The city's biracial committee continued to put pressure on merchants to desegregate. The local NAACP branch remained deeply divided as to what posture it should take with respect to the demonstrations, and as a result played a very small part. Even the leadership of the CORE chapter was frequently divided on whether to accede to requests of the biracial committee that demonstrations be halted for a period. This is not to say that adroit "rolling with the punch" by white leaders can necessarily prevent significant direct action demonstrations. Indeed the divided CORE chapter was able to mount quite impressive demonstrations. But it *is* to say that sharp disagreements in the protest movement will almost certainly occur when the response of whites is conciliatory. These divisions constitute a very serious problem for the Protest Organizations, necessarily curtailing their activity and reducing their effectiveness.

The Protest Organizations in Winston-Salem have sought to be the city's conscience in the area of race relations. Over the last five years they have engaged in a wide variety of public protests. (1) Letters have been written to public officials and local newspapers urging desegregation of public facilities, the hiring of more Negroes in city government jobs, and so on. (2) Petitions have been presented urging city officials to act in behalf of various Negro interests; in 1962, for example, 2,500 signatures were collected on a petition calling for the appointment of two more Negroes to the city's school board. (3) Sit-in demonstrations, wade-ins, skate-ins, and drive-ins (at outdoor motion picture theaters) have been initiated by local protest leaders. (4) Attempts have been made on two occasions to organize boycotts of merchants found to be discriminating against Negroes in hiring practices. ("We don't call it a boycott, we call it selective buying," the NAACP president said.) (5) Voter registration drives have been conducted on an annual basis. In April 1964 the local NAACP and CORE organizations jointly sponsored a voter registration project and brought Martin Luther King to the city to give impetus to the drive. (6) Pressure has been put on merchants and industrial establishments to hire more Negro workers and to upgrade the Negroes already working. Activity here has been sporadic and poorly coordinated, however, and its effectiveness cannot easily be determined. (7) Protest Organizations have operated to raise public protest in virtually every area where discriminatory treatment is suspected, from the refusal of an annual fair to admit Negroes, to the failure of the school board to extend integration, to mistreatment of Negro violators by police.

Until 1963, except for one brief period, the Winston-

Salem NAACP branch held a monopoly on militancy in that city. Its one challenge occurred in the 1960 sit-ins. The main impetus for the sit-ins in Winston came from students of the all-Negro Winston-Salem State Teachers College (now Winston-Salem State College). The branch was criticized for not providing the students with sufficient moral, financial, and physical support. After the sit-ins ended, however, the branch recouped its position. The 1963 revolt seems to have created a leadership organization more militant than the NAACP. It was a revolt of the young. The 1963 demonstrations were led by people between twenty-five and thirty-five years of age. The NAACP branch, whose name only a year before was synonymous with militancy, suddenly found itself accused of "Uncle Tom-ing." Its leaders committed themselves in the spring of 1963 to cooperation with the city's biracial committee (on which six of them served). The biracial committee achieved impressive gains, removing barriers to the use by Negroes of most hotels, motels, cafeterias, restaurants, and theaters in Winston-Salem. Confronted with pressures from the city's white leadership to support the committee and oppose demonstrations, and the demands of a large group of young Negroes organized in the CORE chapter and the NAACP Commandoes who said that direct action demonstrations were necessary, the branch floundered. A few of its leaders gave full support to CORE; others sought to straddle the fence. The majority continued to support the biracial committee. In a series of joint meetings in 1963 the NAACP and CORE organizations sought to "paper over" their differences, and the name "CORE-NAACP" was affixed to the sponsorship of most demonstrations. But leadership of the demonstrations came from CORE. The local NAACP leaders were not enthusiastic about the demonstrations, although they did not, indeed could not, repudiate them. And the issue was not an easy one. Demonstrations were clearly embarrassing since the biracial committee had achieved more desegregation of public facilities in three months than had been achieved in the preceding half-century. Whites were asking: "What incentive is there for us to cooperate when we get demonstrations just the same?" But it was equally true that it was demonstrations which had made whites willing to act, and discriminatory treatment had by no means been banished from the city.

The Winston-Salem chapter of the Congress of Racial Equality and an NAACP youth group, the Commandoes, were formed in the spring of 1963 in Winston-Salem, because, as one leader put it, "The adult NAACP group here isn't doing anything. Winston-Salem has all kinds of segregation and they are sitting on their hands."

Demonstrations, chiefly picketing of K&W cafeterias which had not desegregated, continued throughout much of the year. Groups of several hundred marched on City Hall protesting arrests. Petitions were presented to city officials. The chapter drew up a list of demands, calling for, among other things, the assignment of school children without regard to race and a city ordinance banning segregation in public facilities.

The NAACP-CORE conflict in Winston-Salem was rooted primarily in age differences. The students who provided the majority of demonstrators were anxious to join their fellow students who were marching in Greensboro, High Point, Durham, Charlotte, and many other southern cities. There was no yearning for bourgeois respectability, for a "clean" record. The Negro college student is quite different from his white counterpart. Most NAACP branch leaders were not willing to march. The NAACP in Winston-Salem is an established organization. It has a number of Moderates among its leaders and these in particular opposed direct action. Moreover, many of the militant leaders had achieved some measure of acceptance through the biracial committee and were reluctant to jeopardize this new position. The kind of status division we noted between the welfare leaders and the protest leaders existed on a smaller scale within the protest movement itself, between the young professional men of the NAACP and the student-dominated CORE.

The Greenville NAACP branch has operated in essentially the same areas as has the Winston-Salem branch, but has done much less. The absence of a Negro college in the Greenville area, the general scarcity of human resources, the much more rigid pattern of segregation, and sharp internal disagreement have limited protest activity. Although NAACP leaders periodically threaten demonstrations there have been none of any size since the 1960 sit-ins. The branch has engaged in the following activities. (1) It has applied pressure on city officials to integrate the Greenville school system. In the summer of 1963 two branch leaders, one a lawyer, petitioned the school board to permit their children to attend all-white schools nearer to their homes than the Negro schools to which they were assigned. The requests were denied and litigation was begun. (2) The branch gave divided support to the city's one major series of direct action demonstrations—the 1960 sit-ins. In addition, branch leaders have initiated direct action protests at a number of other facilities: a read-in at the public library, serve-ins at public tennis courts, and a skate-in. (3) It has periodically concerned itself with voter registration. (4) The two lawyers among the branch leadership have handled all civil rights litigation. (5) Much of the branch's work has consisted of pressures informally applied by individual leaders on city officials and owners of businesses. It has kept the flag of protest flying.

It should be noted that the above represent NAACP branch activities only in a limited sense. The branch's executive body rarely participated as a unit in planning and execution. It is true, of course, that individuals, not organizations, are actors. But the Greenville branch has had a particularly tenuous existence. It has simply provided an umbrella under which individual leaders or small groups of leaders have worked in the interest of race advancement.

Among the assets of the Protest Organizations in Winston-Salem and Greenville is the high level of visibility of their actions. Our surveys indicated that the major activities of the Protest Organizations are well known and generally applauded by Negroes.[17] Moreover, appeals for direct action demonstrations to promote race goals cannot easily be opposed by other race advancement organizations.

The Protest Organizations in Winston-Salem are better organized and better financed than their Greenville counterparts. Participants for demonstrations can be found more readily in Winston than in Greenville for a number of reasons, not the least of which is the fact that sanctions applied by whites are far less formidable in the upper-South city. With little money, few members, overworked leaders, lower expectations among the rank and file, and few citizens willing to risk the penalties which confront participants in direct action, the Greenville protest movement has been and remains feeble. Still, the Protest Organizations must be credited for much of the very little which has thus far been accomplished. They have achieved partial desegregation of city parks, have opened up tennis courts to Negro players, have helped to integrate the city school system, have opened the public library to Negroes, and have contributed to the integration of some lunch counters and restaurants.

The effectiveness of Protest Organizations in both cities suffers from the relatively low repute in which their leaders are held by whites. Any attempt to remedy this, however— for example, the cooperation of the Winston-Salem NAACP with the city's biracial committee in 1963—leads to an alienation of part of the old constituency, and involves perhaps an abdication of the protest function. The hostility which the

[17] Fifty per cent of the respondents in Winston named an accomplishment of the Protest Organizations as *the greatest single achievement* made toward equal treatment in the last few years. Sixty-seven per cent did the same in Greenville.

Protest Organizations generally arouse makes communication with white leaders difficult. Mutual suspicion is high. Cooperative ventures are usually impossible.

The inability of the Protest Organizations to achieve biracial cooperation and the inability of the Welfare Organizations to adequately articulate Negro opposition to all forms of discrimination and in so doing to light fires under recalcitrant whites is, of course, one reason why the two kinds of organizations exist. It is also true, however, that neither the white nor the Negro citizens of a southern city can be expected to generally appreciate the necessity of balancing the two approaches. Demonstrations at the wrong time and directed at the wrong people have on occasion set back biracial cooperation (that is cooperation that really does achieve goals sought by Negroes); but little can be accomplished without some direct action.

Perhaps the greatest problem confronting Protest Organizations arises because their major weapon—direct action demonstrations—cannot be finely regulated. At times when there is need to flood a city with protests, they are only able to sprinkle it. Most Americans, and this includes Negro-Americans, are not easily aroused by demonstrations, particularly when such demonstrations carry with them threats to other values such as comfort and security. At other times when the flow of demonstrations should be restricted, the dynamics of movement created at such time and expense carry the demonstrations on and on and seriously jeopardize other race values. Despite all this, the Protest Organizations provided the prod without which little would have been accomplished in many areas. White America doesn't like demonstrations and often will pay a good price for peace.

RECRUITMENT

The philosophy and structure of the Protest Organizations commit them to a type of race-advancement activity most attractive to Militants. They were established to raise public protests against all forms of discriminatory treatment. Moreover, being in the forefront of protest in the sensitive areas, they have recruited Negroes able to operate under strong disapproval of whites, exposed to pressures and sanctions from police, courts, business enterprises, and on occasion the mob. The criteria for success in leadership of Protest Organizations are quite different than for welfare leadership. Welfare leaders stand or fall on their ability to persuade white leaders that their approach to race advancement is legitimate. For this reason, high social status granted for the kinds of achievements considered significant within the white community—public service and economic success—is important. The welfare leader really must conform to the demands of middle-class style and values. Negro acceptance of the decisions of welfare leaders is necessary, but the active support of the subcommunity is not. Protest leaders, in contrast, must be able to mobilize mass support in protest actions designed to force white compliance. Negroes have made it clear (see Chapter III) that they generally will not permit the transfer of social prestige to the political realm. The cause of race advancement is so vital that the definition offered by the leader-candidates of the proper role of race leadership alone dominates the selection process.

Welfare leaders must be temperamentally able to endure long periods of quiet negotiations when the tangible results are few. They must somehow present race demands in a manner which maximizes the possibility of effective biracial cooperation. Protest leaders on the other hand must transmit an impatience that can bring crowds to the streets. To do this they must pose Negro-white conflict in its most evocative form. They must drain from racial issues the last measure of capacity to mobilize protest over the powerful inertial forces constantly operating. In brief, the welfare leader must be adept at the techniques of manipulation and persuasion in small groups; the protest leaders in techniques of mass appeal. The different programs, methods of operation and constituencies of these two varieties of organizations have made it necessary for them to recruit persons with quite different skills and interests.

Welfare Organizations attract Negroes who have arrived at the summit of their careers. After years of effort these Negroes want to relax. Instead of angry protests they want quiet discussions. Instead of rejection they want the acceptance into the white man's world to which their talents so obviously entitle them. Very successful Negroes, although subject to all kinds of indignities, still have attained some stake in the existing situation. They have achieved certain values which they are reluctant to jeopardize. Protest Organizations, in contrast, attract young men for whom a reputation acquired in protest work can be an important asset. Race leadership is seen as an instrument for social and economic advance.

To summarize, Protest Organizations (the same can be said for Welfare and Voting Organizations) are, by their very structure and reason for being, committed to certain kinds of race goals, advanced by certain kinds of means. These in turn make necessary certain leadership skills and interests. The activities of Protest Organizations offer rewards and create problems which attract (and repel) particular types of leaders. This determines what we here call the recruitment process for the organizations of race leadership. Leaders recruited in a certain image, of course, assure that the organization will perpetuate that image.

VOTING ORGANIZATIONS

The Voting Organizations are those race-advancement groups which are primarily concerned with the task of enlarging, organizing, and/or manipulating the Negro vote in the interest of race advancement. The leaders of the Voting Organizations are called the politicians. Negroes holding elective office or serving in policy-making capacities on city and county boards and commissions (such as a school board or a recreation commission) are also included in the category "politicians," whether or not they have formal positions in any Voting Organization. The appointive or elective positions provide them with the opportunity to make politically relevant decisions for the Negro subcommunity.[18] While politicians share a common involvement with the Negro vote as an instrument for advancing the race, their jobs are quite different. The chairman of the Greenville City and County Voters Crusade, for example, is concerned with the task of creating a substantial Negro electorate, and hence plays a quite different role from the Negro alderman in Winston-Salem who holds office because of a large Negro vote and who is, at least formally, inside the structure of city government.

Discussions of Negro political leadership in the South are generally discussions of the leadership of Protest Organizations. There is a tendency for friends to praise and foes to

[18] The inclusion of appointed officials is justified first because the appointment of Negroes to policy-making boards in city and county government is generally a bow to Negro political power. As such, it is but another manifestation of the heightened Negro activity in electoral politics which produces the elected official, the party worker, and other leaders. Second, although whites can at times afford to appoint a man to, for example, the school board solely on the basis of technical qualifications, appointments of Negroes to such boards anywhere in the South are too few and access is too recent for this to be possible or desirable when the Negro appointee is involved. He will necessarily be judged by both whites and Negroes primarily on his style of race leadership. Specifically, included as politicians here for Winston-Salem are: (1) the chairman of each Democratic and (where they exist) Republican precinct organization and those Negroes at higher levels in the party organization; (2) the officers of two voting clubs, the West Winston Civic League Auxiliary and the Democratic Voters Club; and (3) all Negroes holding elected or appointed office in city and county government. In Greenville the politicians are the officers and members of the boards of the two Voting Organizations: the Greenville Non-Partisan Voter Registration committee, and the Greenville City and County Voters Crusade.

blame protest leaders for virtually all Negro effort directed at realizing race goals. There is good reason for this. The activities of these organizations are of the kind that commands attention. And one cannot question the importance of the leadership provided by such national figures as King, Lewis, and Farmer, and by the hundreds of local protest leaders throughout the South. This general fascination with the protest leader, however, has prevented a necessary examination of the Negro politician and the Voting Organizations, and the new type of race leadership which they are providing. At the end of World War II there were really no Negro politicians in the South. Today their numbers are rapidly increasing in the states of the rim South and in certain parts of the deep South. In the last two decades there has been an enormous expansion of the Negro vote in the South (see Table 31). This expansion of the Negro vote has not occurred evenly across

TABLE 31

NUMBER AND PERCENTAGE OF VOTING AGE NEGROES REGISTERED, FOR SELECTED YEARS, 1940–1964; THE ELEVEN SOUTHERN STATES *

Year	Number of Negroes registered	Percentage of voting-age Negroes registered
1940	250,000	5
1947	595,000	12
1952	1,008,614	20
1960	1,414,052	28
1964 (February)	1,751,813	35
1964 (November)	2,250,014	45

* Source: Data on Negro registration from 1940 to 1960 was compiled by Donald Matthews and James Prothro, "Social and Economic Factors and Negro Voter Registration in the South," *The American Political Science Review*, LVII (March 1963), 27; the 1964 figure is an estimate released by the Southern Regional Council on February 15, 1964. The estimates for November 1964 were released by the National Association for the Advancement of Colored People. The estimates for November 1964 given by the Southern Regional Council were approximately the same.

276

the South. It has been much greater in the cities of the rim South than in those of the deep South. Negro voter registration data for Winston-Salem and Greenville and the counties in which they are located are compared in Table 32. The

TABLE 32

NEGRO VOTER REGISTRATION IN WINSTON-SALEM AND GREENVILLE, THE
COUNTIES AND STATES IN WHICH THEY ARE LOCATED, AND THE SOUTH,
NOVEMBER 1964 *

	Number of Negroes registered	Percentage of voting-age Negroes registered
South	2,250,014	44.9
North Carolina	276,000	50.1
Forsyth County	15,600	62.4
Winston-Salem	14,300	62.5
South Carolina	181,050	48.7
Greenville County	7,975	43.3
Greenville	5,400	52.4

* Source: Data for the South, North Carolina, and South Carolina were furnished by the NAACP. The city and county data were compiled by the author.

14,300 Negro voters in Winston-Salem constitute 30 per cent of the total electorate and are a major force in the city's politics. The size of the Negro electorate both reflects and assures a relatively permissive pattern of race relations. The 5,400 Negroes registered in Greenville in November 1964 represent a substantial numerical increase over the 2,750 registered a year before; but because the vote is a recent acquisition, because Negroes lack leadership and are confronted with a denial by whites of the legitimacy of their electoral participation, and because they make up little more than one-quarter of the city's voting-age population and at the same time are severely disadvantaged in education and other socioeconomic characteristics, their position in electoral politics continues to be weak.

A situation has developed in Winston-Salem and in other major cities of North Carolina which permits active Negro electoral participation. The major constituents of this situation are (1) unrestricted Negro access to the ballot box; (2) a relatively high socioeconomic differentiation of the Negro population, and the development of a sufficiently large middle class with enough skills and education to furnish effective leadership; and (3) a pattern of race relations which brands as legitimate in both the Negro and white populations the kind of interchange between Negro and white which occurs when Negro politicians contest for and gain office in government and manipulate a Negro vote that not infrequently is decisive. There has been Negro representation on the Board of Aldermen in Winston-Salem since 1947. Negroes are serving as members of the school board, the planning board, the recreation commission, and other local government bodies, and on the Democratic and Republican county executive committees. The position of Greenville Negroes in electoral politics lags far behind. No Negro holds elective office in Greenville, nor is it likely that one will in the near future. There is no Negro representation on any city board or commission, and no white candidate has yet made a serious effort to woo Negro voters in the city.

WHO ARE THE POLITICIANS?

The greater acceptance of participation by Negroes in electoral politics in Winston permits Negroes in particularly vulnerable positions to work as politicians. The relative absence of the Greenville vulnerables from election activity is shown in Table 33. Six of the politicians in Winston-Salem, for example, are public-school teachers. The decision of one of these to run for alderman in the spring of 1963 is indicative of the change in white attitudes and in the political position of Negroes in this North Carolina city. When World War II ended there were 300 registered Negro voters in Winston.

TABLE 33

PERCENTAGE OF POLITICIANS BY VULNERABILITY OF OCCUPATION,
WINSTON-SALEM AND GREENVILLE

Degree of vulnerability	Winston-Salem (N=28)	Greenville (N=12)
High vulnerability	21	8
Marginal vulnerability	54	25
Independence	25	67

Now there are over 14,000. Negro participation in all phases of electoral politics has been accepted by whites. In Greenville vulnerables remain considerably more hesitant about participating in electoral activity, but it is now possible for Negro leaders to promote Negro registration and voting without fear of sanctions. The change is recent and is not wholly reflected in the level of vulnerability of the politicians in the city. Only in the last two years have those in positions of high and marginal vulnerability moved into the leadership of the Voting Organizations. A 1964 voter registration drive in Greenville received adequate coverage in the local newspapers. The fact that Greenville Negroes will never constitute more than a quarter of the city's electorate, even if the percentage of voting-age Negroes going to the polls is as high as that of voting-age whites, is partial explanation for the breakdown of white resistance: Negroes really are not a threat.

Negro politicians in both cities are drawn primarily from the middle-middle and lower-middle class. No politician in either city is lower class and only a small percentage are of the very prosperous.

Politicians in Winston-Salem and Greenville do not differ significantly from welfare leaders or protest leaders in the two residence variables referred to in Tables 24 and 28. A much higher percentage of politicians in Winston-Salem than in

TABLE 34
PERCENTAGE OF POLITICIANS BY CLASS, WINSTON-SALEM AND GREENVILLE

Class	Winston-Salem	Greenville
Upper-middle	18	8
Middle-middle and lower-middle	82	92
Lower	0	0

Greenville have had contact outside the South. This fact is shown in Table 35.

Politicians in general are a much more disparate group than are either welfare or protest leaders. We are able to say that the welfare leadership in Winston and Greenville contains a preponderance of high-status persons, whereas protest leaders bring to their race leadership relatively low prestige. Politicians as a group cannot be identified in terms of this variable. The spread is too great. The median age for politicians in Winston-Salem is forty-six, in Greenville forty-seven. The spread is such, however, that this tells us very little.[19] In general, politicians in our two cities are as a group less readily identifiable.

This is explained by the fact that the organizational posi-

TABLE 35
PERCENTAGE OF POLITICIANS BY TWO RESIDENCE VARIABLES;
WINSTON-SALEM AND GREENVILLE

	Winston-Salem	Greenville
Lifelong residents	50	42
"Outsiders"	36	8

[19] It should be noted, however, that no politician in either Winston-Salem or Greenville is under thirty-five years of age. The young who have achieved positions of leadership have done so solely through the Protest Organizations.

tion of the politician "types" him much less than does that of either welfare or protest leaders. The politician can be belligerent or quiet. He can work in the very sensitive areas of race relations or can concentrate on such broad community goals as greater voter awareness and participation. He can operate (in Winston-Salem and increasingly in Greenville) with white approval, or he can initiate activity which will bring him the strong support of his own community over the strenuous objections of whites. And the point is, of course, that he can do this in a way consonant with the demands of his leadership position and the expectations of his constituents. The "typical" politician is a racial Moderate, but it should be noted the factors determining this are somewhat less compelling than those requiring that the Protest Organizations be vehicles for militant leadership and the Welfare Organizations for the Conservatives.

TABLE 36

PERCENTAGE OF POLTICIANS BY STYLE OF RACE LEADERSHIP,
WINSTON-SALEM AND GREENVILLE

Style	Winston-Salem	Greenville
Conservative	36	8
Moderate	50	59
Militant	14	33

Two years ago a majority of the politicians in Greenville were Militants, but today a majority are Moderates. This is indicative of the greater acceptance of Negro electoral participation in this deep-South city, a change which is spreading throughout urban areas in the deep South. To be sure, significant differences in the styles of leadership of the politicians in the two cities remain. Militant representation is limited among Winston politicians, but more than a third are Conservatives. In Greenville it is the conservative style which is marginally represented while Militants remain prominently associated with the Voting Organizations. Participation in electoral politics in Winston-Salem is largely by the Conservatives and Moderates. It is still something of a frontier area of race relations in Greenville. But this pattern is changing. Limited Negro participation through voter registration drives and related electoral activity does not now encounter nearly as much opposition from whites in Greenville and many other deep-South cities as it did in 1960. With this measure of grudging acceptance the tone and function of the Voting Organization has changed somewhat, and along with this has come a change in the personnel of leadership.

Having considered at length biographical data on the leaders of the three categories of race-advancement organizations, we must now examine briefly the extent to which the leadership of these three types of organization overlaps. The overlap, as Table 37 shows, is quite extensive and is somewhat greater in Greenville than in Winston. The protest leader–welfare leader combination is an unlikely one. It is not surprising that only one leader in the two cities is available for these two disparate leadership roles. Almost half of the politicians in Greenville are protest leaders. With the 17 per cent

TABLE 37

PERCENTAGE OF THE LEADERSHIP OF EACH CATEGORY OF RACE-ADVANCEMENT ORGANIZATION WORKING IN POSITIONS OF LEADERSHIP IN OTHER RACE-ADVANCEMENT ORGANIZATIONS

	Winston-Salem	Greenville
Protest leaders who are:		
Welfare leaders	4	0
Politicians	18	31
Welfare leaders who are:		
Protest leaders	9	0
Politicians	46	13
Politicians who are:		
Welfare leaders	18	17
Protest leaders	18	42

who are welfare leaders a clear majority of the politicians are active in other types of race-advancement organizations. This indicates the shortage of race leaders in the South Carolina city, and in the case of the politician–protest leader combination, the fact that electoral politics remains a kind of frontier area in race relations. Electoral participation has yet to make the full transition from the status to the welfare area. In addition to this, the significant numbers of politicians in both cities who are at the same time holding positions of leadership in the other types of race-advancement organizations is further indication that the Voting Organizations provide a framework for more varied approaches to race advancement than do either the Protest or the Welfare Organizations.

STRUCTURE AND FUNCTIONING

The two Voting Organizations in Greenville, the Greenville Non-Partisan Voter Registration Committee and the Greenville City and County Voters Crusade, are of a type found throughout urban areas of the deep-South. They exist to create a Negro electorate of sufficient size so that it can "count" in city, county, and state politics. They seek to replace the enervating belief that "there isn't any use for Negroes to try to vote" with the confident expectation that Negroes *can* become a "balance of power" bloc in city politics. They struggle to overcome the enormous electoral liability imposed by the very low socioeconomic position of Greenville Negroes. They encourage Negroes to make the effort to surmount the very real obstacles which confront them in registering and voting.

In Winston-Salem the scope of Negro electoral activity is much broader, and this is reflected in the different kinds of race-advancement organizations. Voter registration activity remains important. All the Voting Organizations and a number of other race-advancement groups like the NAACP, CORE, and the Urban League are periodically active. But since a large Negro electorate already exists, the manipulation

283

of the vote in the interest of race objectives assumes the highest priority. The Democratic Party organizations in Negro precincts and the informal organizational support of a number of influential Negro Democrats are of the greatest importance here.[20] Also involved in promoting a cohesive Negro vote and gaining concessions from candidates in exchange for electoral support are two political clubs: the West Winston Civic League Auxiliary and the Democratic Voters Club.[21]

The loyalties of Winston Negroes in local, state, and national politics are overwhelmingly Democratic. Well over 90 per cent refer to themselves as Democrats. The rise of Goldwater Republicanism in the Winston-Salem area and throughout the South has blotted out the bits of loyalty to the party of Lincoln that survived the New Deal. The Republican candidates in state and local elections in North Carolina and South Carolina have regularly driven Negro voters into the arms of Democratic politicians whom the Negroes really did not like, but who were clearly the best of a bad lot. Although much of the organizational structure is formally or informally linked with the Democratic party, it should be made clear that Negro Democrats are Negroes first and Democrats second.

Judged solely in terms of the cohesiveness of the Negro vote, the Voting Organizations in Winston have achieved impressive success. In a number of closely contested races of great importance to Negroes over the last decade, Winston Negroes have voted for the chosen candidate by majorities not infrequently in excess of 9–1. Tables 11 and 12 (pages 104–105) show that in four successive mayoralty elections between 1957 and 1963, Negro voters gave 96, 92, 83, and 91 per cent of their votes to the preferred candidate, while no more than 58 per cent of the white voters were able to agree

[20] Republican organization in Negro precincts exists with few exceptions only on paper.

[21] The Voting Organizations were described in some detail in Chapter I. See pp. 97ff.

on a candidate in any of these four elections. This same level of cohesiveness was achieved in numerous other contested elections—local, state, and national—over the last decade. (See Table 38).

TABLE 38

COHESION OF WINSTON-SALEM NEGRO VOTE IN SELECTED LOCAL, STATE, AND CONGRESSIONAL ELECTIONS, 1953–1963

Election	Year	% of Negro vote received by candidate winning majority of Negro vote	Party of candidate	% of total vote in Winston received by candidate*
Mayoralty (primary)	1953	86.4	Democrat	53.7
Gubernatorial	1956	64.2	Republican	39.9
Mayoralty (primary)	1957	97.5	Democrat	58.3
Gubernatorial	1960	93.0	Democrat	47.7
Mayoralty (primary)	1961	68.7	Democrat	52.0
National House of Reps. (primary)	1962	86.2	Democrat	52.1
Aldermanic (North Salem ward)	1963	95.6	Democrat	61.3
Aldermanic (South Salem ward)	1963	94.6	Democrat	55.1
Aldermanic (North Salem primary)	1963	83.8	Democrat	57.4

* The 39.9 per cent of the total vote received by the Republican candidate in the 1956 gubernatorial election was of the *total county* rather than the city vote.

The cohesiveness of the Negro vote in Winston-Salem is attributable less, it seems, to organizational effectiveness than to the fact that (1) Negro Americans bring to the act of voting agreement on the criteria which should determine the choice; and (2) one candidate has generally been clearly preferable in terms of these criteria. The lower level of cohesiveness of the white vote in Winston-Salem (and other areas) is a product of three factors. (1) white voters generally do not have as great a stake in the outcome of local elections. There is no issue as important to whites as a group as race advancement is to Negroes. (2) A number of lesser issues—taxation, education, and the like—assume approximately equal weight in many elections for white voters. These secondary issues rarely permit a ready distinction between the two parties or anything approaching unanimous agreement on which candidate's position is preferable. Indeed, it is the function of the candidates and the parties to so structure their response to these issues that they can attract a majority of voters. And, in the absence of strong issue-orientation, candidate-orientation or party-orientation become of greater importance. (3) Whereas all candidates and/or parties must make a serious effort to win a majority of the white vote if they are to be successful, it is still tempting for many politicians to appeal to white voters unhappy about overtures made by opposing candidates to Negro voters. In short, the choice is often less clear-cut for white voters.

Many Negro Americans have become remarkably attuned to the most subtle differences in approach of various candidates to racial issues. The cause of race advancement is so vital that Negroes are naturally sensitive to even marginal differences. Occasionally the "pro-Negro" and the "anti-Negro" candidates define themselves with strokes so broad that no one could be confused. The Terry Sanford–I. Beverly Lake gubernatorial contest in North Carolina in 1960 is an example of this. But the same cohesiveness can be observed in elections in which the positions of rival candidates are not nearly as sharply differentiated. This cohesiveness is all the more notable in view of the generally low political awareness and sophistication of many southern Negroes. The "typical" Winston Negro voter ranks low in all the socioeconomic variables associated with the level of political skill and awareness.[22]

We can now generalize about those conditions which affect the ability of the Voting Organizations to determine the direction and cohesiveness of the Negro vote. If a candidate is well known to Negroes, the Voting Organizations can do little. Occasionally Negro politicians attempt to convince their followers that a politician who has established an unfavorable image has had a change of heart and should be supported. These attempts generally result in ignominious failure even when impressive organizational work goes into the campaign and even when the Negroes backing the candidate are prestigious persons. Race advancement is so important that views once formed generally are strongly held and hence the vote is not subject to manipulation. There are, however, many elections in which the positions of the various candidates for an office are not well known or are not obviously different. Whites, of course, are confronted with a similar situation, but the generally low level of political awareness of southern Negro voters does intensify the problem. When in such elec-

[22] Donald Matthews and James Prothro of the University of North Carolina in a survey administered by the Survey Research Center of the University of Michigan sought to measure, among other things, the level of awareness of matters political of southern Negroes. They asked such questions as: "Who is the governor [of this state] now?" and "About how many years does a United States senator serve?" There was a very high correlation of knowledge of the subjects raised by these questions with socioeconomic position, and the relatively low socioeconomic position of southern Negroes was reflected in the inability of most participants in this survey to answer these and similar questions correctly.

tions the Negro politicians are able to agree upon an endorsement their designation can and frequently does determine the direction of the Negro vote and assure a high level of cohesiveness. The death of the white alderman in Winston-Salem's North Salem ward, for example, brought into the 1963 Democratic primary three candidates not well known to the ward's large (25 per cent of the total) Negro electorate. The dominant group in the Winston-Salem Democratic party (which we have identified as relatively liberal on racial terms) supported one of these candidates. He was also acceptable to Negro leaders in the Columbia Heights (Negro) precinct of that ward.[23] These precinct leaders then passed the word that "Schultz is the best choice for Negroes" by means of a limited door-to-door campaign, in transporting voters to the polls, and through informal discussions. They secured for Schultz 84 per cent of the Negro vote in this three-way race. Schultz ran second in the white precincts of the ward, gaining only 35.7 per cent of the vote. Moreover, Negro voters comprised 45 per cent of the turnout in this primary election although they constituted only 25 per cent of the ward's registered voters. Schultz was nominated. Negroes gave him 95.6 per cent of their vote in the general election, when he faced a Republican opponent.

The situation was comparable in the 1961 mayoralty primary in Winston. The city's Democratic leaders (the "ins") wanted John Surratt to succeed six-term mayor Marshall Kurfees. Five candidates entered the primary and of these two were able to seriously challenge Surratt. Surratt was a virtual unknown in city politics while two of his opponents were

---

[23] There was no advanced discussion. The Democratic leaders did not "clear" the candidate in advance. These leaders were racial moderates and hence looked favorably upon a candidate who was moderate in his racial views. They also were aware of the necessity of maintaining the coalition which has been so successful in municipal elections.

former mayors. Kurfees used his considerable prestige among Winston Negroes to convince most Negro politicians that Surratt would be their best choice. Negro support was also solicited on the grounds of party loyalty.[24] Although John Surratt was for Negro voters a completely unknown quantity, he won 62 per cent of the combined Negro vote for all but one of the Negro precincts. The other four candidates collected 38 per cent of the vote. Surratt's margin over his leading challenger in these precincts was better than 3 to 1. But in one large Negro precinct the Negro politicians were divided. The Democratic precinct leaders backed Surratt. The West Winston Civic League Auxiliary, however, backed another candidate. The Auxiliary's activity is limited largely to this one precinct, Kimberley Park. It had followed its usual practice and had invited each mayoralty candidate to appear at a meeting to answer questions. The president of the Auxiliary expressed her group's reaction in this way:

Both Surratt and Goodale spoke at the meeting. We didn't like the way Surratt handled some of the questions. Goodale sounded better to us so we decided to back him.

Although Surratt averaged for the other Negro precincts 62 per cent of the five-candidate vote, he received only 47.2 per cent of the five-candidate vote in this precinct. He gained 425 votes to 382 for Goodale. The vote for Surratt and his leading challenger in Kimberley Park and in the other Negro precincts are compared in Table 39. The only variable distinguishing Kimberley Park from the other Negro precincts was cohesiveness of the Negro leadership structure. It was the only pre-

[24] The chairman of one of the Negro precincts told the author: "I thought Goodale sounded a bit better and our precinct committee agreed to support him. But then I got a call from Gallaher [the county Democratic chairman] saying 'The party wants Surratt.' He said that Surratt would continue Kurfees' liberal policy toward Negroes. So we decided to go along with Surratt."

TABLE 39

Two-candidate vote, Negro precincts in Winston-Salem;
1961 Democratic Mayoralty Primary

Candidate	Kimberley Park precinct	Other Negro precincts
Surratt	52	76
Goodale	48	24

cinct in which Negro voters received divided counsel from their leaders.

The Negro vote in the South in state and local elections usually is highly cohesive. There are, of course, important exceptions. Attempts are frequently made to divide the Negro vote. "Anti-Negro" candidates try to enlist the support of a few prestigious Negroes. They do not, however, make a serious effort to win Negro support. Rather, by attaching a few prestigious names to their cause they hope to confuse the issue sufficiently to divide the vote. Such stratagems seldom work. If the subcommunity is able to recognize one candidate as "better" on racial questions, the endorsement of another by a few prestigious persons will swing few votes. In the early 1950's in Winston-Salem several attempts were made to defeat Marshall Kurfees by securing the support of a few prominent Negroes. On one occasion Kurfees' opponents tried to persuade a Negro to run for Mayor. They hoped that such a candidacy would siphon off some of the Negro votes that Kurfees would otherwise get and hence bring about his defeat. This attempt failed because the Negro subcommunity would not accept it. In the 1964 runoff primary to select the Democratic candidate for governor in Louisiana between deLessups Morrison and John McKeithen, a number of Negro politicians and a Voting Organization called the Louisiana Advancement Organization worked in behalf of McKeithen even though he ran as an ardent segregationist. It is not clear why these Negroes supported McKeithen over Morrison (who sounded much better on racial questions).[25] But their endorsement did not help McKeithen. An examination of the vote in all-Negro precincts indicates that deLessups Morrison received 95 to 97 per cent of the Negro vote. The choice for Negroes was, at least superficially, clear-cut, and the Negro vote could not be split.

Outright attempts to buy Negro support have been unsuccessful in the last decade, if we understand by "buying support" the proffering of cash, jobs, and the like to Negroes in exchange for their support for a candidate whose racial views are not as acceptable to Negroes as are those of an

[25] Earl Amedee, a Negro lawyer in New Orleans long active in electoral politics, insisted that:

"McKeithen is a true successor and disciple of the political philosophy of the late Earl K. Long, and Long never was a hater of the people. . . . We should like to allay any fears Negroes have that McKeithen will be a race-hater and race-baiter as governor. . . . We feel that the Honorable John J. McKeithen, Democratic nominee for governor, who organized and waged the most brilliant campaign in modern Louisiana political history . . . ⌈will not allow race baiting⌉ to hamper his efforts to make Louisiana a Great Governor." (*The Louisiana Weekly*, January 25, 1964).

Morrison was looked upon by many northern Liberals as another Stevenson. Most Louisiana liberals would tell you that he was not. They considered him slick and not to be trusted. McKeithen has been more liberal on economic terms than Morrison, whose appeal was great in areas that went heavily for Eisenhower in 1956. McKeithen was a disciple of Earl Long, and Long, in a contest with Morrison in 1956, received over 90 per cent of the Negro vote. The Longs, almost alone among twentieth-century southern demagogues, did not resort to race-baiting. Earl Long was the master of skirting the issue with crude-sounding but effective statements like "The nigger is my friend." McKeithen took the easier road and race-baited. Most close Louisiana observers still insist that McKeithen is no Wallace or Barnett but is in the context of Louisiana politics a racial moderate. But the fact remains that in this campaign he ran on an anti-Negro platform.

opponent. Buying votes was possible two decades ago when candidates were indistinguishable on racial grounds and expectations that significant changes in the pattern of race relations could be effected were low. Today Negroes throughout the South expect dramatic change, generally see real differences among candidates, and vote for those candidates who they believe will do the most for their race. We found in a survey of a large number of recent elections in the South that Negro voters are rarely incorrect in their assessment of the candidates.

When sharp divisions in the Negro vote do occur it is generally because the choice between the candidates is not clear. The candidates either have not made their positions on racial matters known, or if the positions are known it is hard to tell which is better. The incumbent mayor, Hayden Burns, opposed John Lanahan in the 1963 Democratic mayoralty primary in Jacksonville. Both candidates had the support of a number of Negro politicians. It was very hard to say which candidate would do more for Negroes. Burns, in winning the primary, gained 40 per cent of the Negro vote.

Virtually all the Voting Organizations in Winston-Salem —the party precinct organizations, the organizational support of influential Negro politicians, and the voting clubs—are linked formally or informally with the Forsyth County–Winston-Salem Democratic party. This is a marriage of convenience. County Democratic leaders are "Sanford" Democrats—relatively liberal on racial matters. Negroes have a stake in keeping this group in power. They act as a pressure group within the party working for liberal policies and liberal candidates. They rarely are consulted before the choice of candidates is made. It is also unusual for them to receive specific promises of action to be taken (such as they did receive in the 1963 mayoralty campaign when one candidate said in effect: "Vote for me and I will appoint a biracial com-

mittee to bring about further integration of public facilities.")
Instead, it is a more general posture of certain candidates that
attracts Negro electoral support. The local Democratic leadership recognizes that if it fails to meet certain minimum
demands, it will lose Negro support. If it does not offer candidates relatively liberal on racial policies, it cannot expect to keep
the strong Negro backing which it has needed so often in the
past.[26] In return for their electoral support Negro Democrats
get liberal candidates and (again relatively) liberal policies,
and they get access. Negro politicians in Winston-Salem down
to the precinct chairman level are able to meet with the mayor
and other city officials without difficulty. They are assured
of at least a polite reception.

It is not now equivalent to a "kiss of death" for white
politicians to receive formal Negro support in Winston-Salem.
It was possible in certain parts of the South in the pre-*Brown
v. Board of Education* period for white candidates to solicit
the support of the very small Negro electorate without
jeopardizing their position with white voters. Whites understood that no candidate would make any concessions threatening the structure of the old biracial system. Supporters of
candidates for state and local office would seek to secure some
Negro votes through the exchange of money or promises to
meet some pressing welfare need, or would simply remind
Negroes that he had "always tried to be a friend of your
people." In this period the small Negro vote was without ideological direction and frequently was splintered. With the

[26] Negro electoral support is important—if at times posing major
problems as well—to the liberal wing of the North Carolina Democratic party, the faction led by former governor Terry Sanford,
Richardson Preyer, and Bert Bennett. The Negro vote can be counted
on in a number of issue-areas where race is not directly involved; for
example, in voting on bond issues for schools and hospitals and for
measures to increase the representation of the populous counties at the
expense of rural counties having small populations.

increase in racial tensions in the late forties and early fifties, white candidates in the South who had significant numbers of Negro constituents often found themselves in a squeeze. In his study of the Negro in Florida politics, H. D. Price noted that

the opening of Florida's Democratic primaries to a growing number of Negro voters has put the average candidate in a difficult position. . . . If the candidate's constituency contains a sizeable Negro vote and a large number of race-conscious whites, any overt appeal to either group is likely to turn the other group against him.[27]

Certainly an appeal to Negro voters anywhere in the South is going to cost the candidate some white support, but in rim-South cities like Winston-Salem, where the patterns of race relations are relatively permissive, candidates can make certain overtures without fear of being repudiated by large numbers of white voters. Even in the immediate post-*Brown* period Marshall Kurfees was able to win elections in Winston although he was clearly linked to the Negro vote. Kurfees regularly appeared before Negro groups and his bids for support were hardly clandestine. He was able to retain the support of the city's business elite who wanted Negro discontent siphoned off in the interest of a good business climate. He did lose the support of many lower-class and lower-middle-class whites. Kurfees was known as "the niggers' mayor" in lower-class white precincts. Today it is possible in Winston for a white candidate to receive the full public support of the Negro Voter Organizations and still win the support of the majority of whites. The 1963 mayoralty race (see page 105) is a case in point. In this contest a genuinely attractive white candidate received full Negro support while running against a candidate who was making an overt appeal for the votes of disenchanted whites. The election was held in

[27] H. D. Price, *The Negro and Southern Politics* (New York, 1957), p. 59.

the spring of 1963, a time of serious racial tension. The Democratic mayoralty candidate lost some white support but this was more than offset by gains among Negroes. Moreover, many whites in Winston will reject a candidate who is not "moderate" on racial questions. A white candidate still is putting his chance for election in jeopardy if he becomes too closely identified with Negro interests and support. He easily can destroy himself by yielding too much. But he can go much further and indeed if he is to win perhaps *must* go much further in recognizing Negro interests than did his counterpart in Winston a decade ago, or than do politicians today in the deep South. The fact that he has Negro electoral support and that his opponent is opposed by most Negroes will not in itself significantly lessen his appeal if otherwise he looks attractive to the white majority. A candidate who runs on a mild segregationist platform in Winston (for no one assumes a George Wallace posture) is writing off the large Negro electorate and the growing number of whites who want a moderate.

Were there a Negro newspaper in Winston-Salem, Voting Organizations like the Democratic Voters Club would publish endorsements before elections as do their counterparts in Durham, Miami, Jacksonville, and other rim-South cities. In the absence of a Negro newspaper, endorsements are transmitted to the subcommunity through other channels. Endorsed candidates occasionally appear before the Voting Organizations making the endorsement. Such appearances are noted in the *Winston-Salem Journal* without comment. The most efficient and least dangerous way of transmitting endorsements remains the distribution to Negro voters of cards bearing the names of the annointed. For reasons which are not clear, the endorsing organizations in Winston rarely identify themselves by name on the endorsement card.[28] Democratic precinct committees in primaries usually simply distribute literature

[28] Voting Organizations in many other southern cities distribute cards with their names and information telephone numbers prominently displayed.

supplied by the favored candidates. The voting clubs generally print cards identifying themselves by a phrase or slogan.
Figure 4 shows the card with endorsed candidates handed out
by the Democratic Voters Club in the 1960 general elections.[29] The club identifies itself with the phrase, "The Peo-

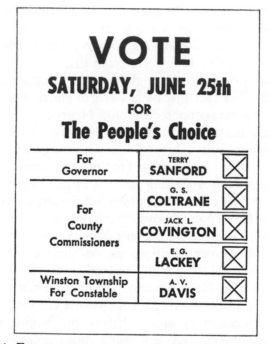

FIGURE 4. ENDORSEMENT CARD OF THE DEMOCRATIC VOTERS CLUB,
WINSTON-SALEM, N.C., FOR 1960 NORTH CAROLINA GENERAL ELECTION.

[29] The club is led by a Negro union official. His local, which
includes taxi and bus drivers, is the only all-Negro local in Winston.
The union leader has been active in electoral politics for more than
a decade. Technically the Democratic Voters Club was not organized
until 1963. In fact, the 1963 action simply gave a new name to the
union leader's organization. He recently has been undecided whether
to call the organization the Democratic Voters Club, the East Winston
Democratic Voters Club, the East Side Democratic Voters Club, the
East Winston Voters Club, or the All-American Voters Club.

ple's Choice." White candidates not endorsed have on occasion printed similar cards bearing the same endorsements for all but one race. In that one race the candidate substitutes his name for that of his endorsed opponent. But the club's people stationed at the polling places have been able to thwart those attempts. The purpose of cards of whatever source is to give the voters the full list of favored candidates in a convenient form for reference in the voting booth.

Endorsed candidates usually are asked to bear the costs of the electoral activity of the precinct organizations and voting clubs. Negro politicians in Winston and other southern cities are acutely sensitive to the charge that they can be bought, but they have no other source of funds. The cost of conducting a campaign in a precinct with 3,300 voters is considerable. The biggest expense is hiring workers to transport voters to and from the polls. The Winston politicians try to get as much volunteer help as possible. The door-to-door surveys conducted by the leaders of the Columbia Heights precinct in which voters are (1) told of the endorsed slate, (2) urged to vote, and (3) offered transportation and other help are, for example, done with volunteer labor. But transportation and literature require cash. There is no indication, however, that endorsements are determined by the availability of funds. Endorsements are made, and if the favored candidates then fail to supply enough money, campaign activity simply is limited. The county Democratic party distributes funds to the precinct committees for general elections. In the primaries funds come from supporters of individual candidates.

Of the various techniques used in promoting candidates favored by Negroes, one of the most controversial is the "single-shot" vote. This does not refer to the diminishing tendency of Negro voters to vote only in the one or two election contests on the ballot in which they see important differences between candidates on racial matters. The "single-shot" as an electoral weapon can be used in contests in which the voter is to choose two or more representatives—for example, a primary contest for the three Democratic nominations to the North Carolina House of Representatives from Forsyth county. Usually, seven or eight candidates are entered for the three positions. The three who receive the most votes become the party's nominees and hence are virtually assured of election. Negroes often are very interested in one candidate but do not care who gets the two other nominations. But more than that, knowing that many whites will not vote for the candidate favored by Negroes simply because he is a Negro or considered strongly "pro-Negro," Negroes have real incentive not to give their two remaining votes to candidates who thereby might gain sufficient strength to displace their candidate. The following hypothetical example will make clearer why the "single-shot" is used. Let us assume that there are seven candidates contesting for the three Democratic nominations to the North Carolina House of Representatives from Forsyth county. Candidate B (Table 40) is a Negro. Candidates A, C, and B were nominated. Although the 4000

TABLE 40

WHEN THE "SINGLE-SHOT" VOTE CAN BE EFFECTIVE

Distribution of votes	Candidates						
	A	B	C	D	E	F	G
Negro	103	4,000	308	85	23	70	107
White	9,000	2,500	7,200	6,300	6,000	1,000	1,000
Total	9,103	6,500	7,508	6,385	6,023	1,070	1,107

Negro voters had 8000 additional votes to distribute among the six other candidates after voting for their favorite, they in fact cast only 696. Most Negroes, in short, voted for candidate B and then simply did not use their two remaining votes. If all 4,000 Negroes had voted for two additional candidates, it is almost certain that either candidate D (fourth place) or candidate E (fifth place) would have displaced Negro candidate B.

On two occasions in Winston-Salem the "single-shot" has

worked just this way, nominating a candidate who undoubtedly would not have been nominated had Negroes used all of their votes. In 1960 Dr. Lillian Lewis gained the Democratic nomination for a position on the county school board. Nine candidates sought the five nominations and Dr. Lewis came in fifth. Her 10,623 votes were 811 more than the total received by the candidate who finished sixth. Most Negroes used the "single-shot." In one Negro precinct, for example, Lewis received 1,000 votes, her nearest opponent 62. Without "single-shot" voting Dr. Lewis almost certainly would have come in sixth and hence would not have been nominated. In 1962 Lewis was renominated, by an even narrower margin. She again ran fifth in a field of nine candidates. She received only 81 votes more than the sixth-place candidate. The 3,500 Negro voters cast only 2,132 votes for the other eight candidates when they could have cast 14,000. Had they all used all their votes, candidate G almost certainly would have beaten Dr. Lewis for the fifth nomination (see Table 41).

TABLE 41

DISTRIBUTION OF NEGRO AND WHITE VOTES, 1962 DEMOCRATIC
PRIMARY, SELECTION OF PARTY NOMINEES FOR
FORSYTH COUNTY SCHOOL BOARD

Distribution of votes				Candidates				
	Lewis	A	B	C	D	E	F	G	H
Negro	3,500	219	299	383	240	120	242	286	343
White	3,565	5,532	4,757	7,923	7,144	3,028	7,623	6,698	7,397
Total	7,065	5,751	5,056	8,306	7,384	3,148	7,865	6,984	7,740

The use of the "single-shot" is not without risks for Negroes. Negro block voting alarms many whites and the "single-shot" seems like a particularly sinister kind of bloc voting. Use of the weapon, then, invites retaliation. It is particularly dangerous for the Negro candidate himself publicly to urge his followers to "single-shot." In the same 1962 primary in which Dr. Lewis won, another Negro candidate seeking the Democratic nomination to the North Carolina House of Representatives was defeated. He ran fourth in a field of six for the three nominations from Forsyth County. This candidate, the Reverend William R. Crawford, was an experienced politician. He had served five terms as alderman from the South Third (Negro) ward in Winston-Salem. First elected in 1951, he served through 1961, when he was defeated by another Negro Democrat. Crawford was respected in Forsyth Democratic circles. When he decided to run for the North Carolina House, he was the third vice-president of the Forsyth Democratic county committee. He is a responsible leader and his talents are very great indeed. His candidacy to establish himself as the first Negro to serve in the North Carolina legislature since Reconstruction was a serious one. Crawford decided to urge his followers to use the "single-shot." On the Sunday before the primary election many Negro ministers in Winston urged their congregations to vote only for Crawford. The reaction to this from white Winstonians was immediate and adverse. Some white Democratic leaders professed to feel that Crawford was not playing the game correctly. To whites suspicious of Negroes anyway, the plea from the pulpit for a "single-shot" was further evidence of sinister machinations. But perhaps as damaging as anything whites had to say was a letter printed in the local newspaper, written by an influential Negro lawyer. The author of the letter attacked the call for the "single-shot" on moral grounds and for reasons of expediency. Negroes seeking to be treated like everyone else must not discriminate themselves. On the practical level, if one "single-shots" and loses he has nothing. There is no one his vote helped elect.[30]

In the same primary in which Dr. Lewis won, Reverend

[30] *Winston-Salem Journal*, May 26, 1962. The letter probably was written for political revenge. Crawford and the writer were political enemies.

Crawford was defeated. The 3,798 Negro voters gave 1,925 votes to the five white candidates, although they could have given (while still voting for Crawford) 7,600 votes. The

TABLE 42

DISTRIBUTION OF NEGRO AND WHITE VOTES, 1962 DEMOCRATIC PRIMARY; SELECTION OF THREE NOMINEES FROM FORSYTH COUNTY FOR THE NORTH CAROLINA HOUSE OF REPRESENTATIVES

Distribution of votes	Lewis (from Table 39)	Candidates					
		Crawford	A	B	C	D	E
Negro	3,500	3,798	551	457	198	264	455
White	3,565	2,110	8,477	8,719	3,947	6,559	4,688
Total	7,065	5,908	9,028	9,176	4,145	6,823	5,143

following can be said in evaluation of Crawford's use of the "single-shot": (1) If he had received as many votes from whites as Lewis did, he would have won. (2) He did get 300 more votes in Negro sections, but this gain was marginal. (3) Although Crawford urged the "single-shot" and Lewis did not, fully as many Negroes voted for white candidates in the House of Representatives election as voted for white candidates in the school board election. But the appeal for the "single-shot" was not the failure the above might indicate. Two of the white candidates for the North Carolina house were incumbents, fairly well known to Negro voters and considered not unfriendly. The school board candidates, in contrast, were not well known. Moreover, the county board did not control the city schools where most Negro students were in attendance. White voters probably were less willing to send a Negro to the legislature than to the county school board. Finally, Dr. Lewis is light-skinned and it seems certain that a number of whites (how many cannot be determined) simply did not recognize her as a Negro. It is doubtful, in short, that Crawford's public campaign for "single-shot" voting actually cost him the support of many whites.

This conclusion is substantiated by Crawford's experience in the 1964 Democratic primary in which he again sought nomination for a house seat—this time successfully. Table 43 shows that Crawford did even more poorly with white voters in the 1964 primary—when he and his supporters did not publicly encourage "single-shot" voting—than in the 1962 primary. Although 19 per cent of the white voters in 1962 gave Crawford a vote, only 18 per cent did so in 1964. He won in 1964 because the Negro community was united behind him and turned out in fairly substantial numbers. But even in the 1964 primary, Negro turnout in behalf of a fairly popular Negro candidate was not impressive. Slightly less than 50 per cent of the registered Negro voters in the county went to the polls in the 1964 primary, and Negroes constituted 29 per cent of the electorate—about their percentage of the total number of registered voters.

TABLE 43

DISTRIBUTION OF NEGRO AND WHITE VOTES, 1964 DEMOCRATIC PRIMARY; SELECTION OF THREE NOMINEES FROM FORSYTH COUNTY FOR THE NORTH CAROLINA HOUSE OF REPRESENTATIVES

Distribution of votes	Candidates					
	Crawford	A	B	C	D	E
Negro	7,000	1,120	725	300	510	350
White	3,128	13,216	8,889	6,643	11,523	5,722
Total	10,128	14,336	9,614	6,943	12,033	6,072

The Negro vote is an issue-oriented vote and cannot be maintained for one candidate, a group of candidates, or a party if Negroes see more favorable positions on racial matters presented by others. As an issue-oriented vote it is potentially highly fluid. Although the Voting Organizations in Winston are formally or informally linked to the Democratic party, the Negro Democrats are Negroes first and Democrats second. James Wilson noted the extraordinary phenomenon of Chicago Negroes voting for a white Democrat over a Negro Republican.[31] The effectiveness of the Negro vote in that city has been partially destroyed by having been thus wedded to the machine. The structure of Negro politics in Winston is vastly different. It would be wrong to see Negroes so wedded emotionally or organizationally to the party of Roosevelt and Kennedy that the Republicans have no chance.

We will have much less to say about the Voting Organizations in Greenville because their activity has been much more modest. The Greenville Non-Partisan Voter Registration Committee and the Greenville City and County Voters Crusade are the latest in a series of organizations which have sought to create a Negro vote large enough to "count" in city and county politics. We have already referred to the kinds of problems which these organizations encounter. The Negro vote in Greenville county has been so small that white candidates have seen no reason to seek Negro support. Negroes are systematically excluded from the Republican and Democratic party organizations in Greenville. No Negro has ever held elective office and there is no Negro serving in any policy-making capacity in Greenville city or county government. Negroes can register without difficulty. In fact, Harrison Reardon, chairman of the Greenville City and County Voters Crusade, was quoted as saying in March 1964,

We have received excellent cooperation from everybody, Senator Morrah on down. . . . Registration is not a matter of race. It is a matter of getting all people to register and vote as part of the democratic way of life.

But many Negroes in Greenville have seen little incentive to vote. All of the candidates look the same; that is, all look equally hostile. Moreover, the low socioeconomic position of

[31] James Q. Wilson, *Negro Politics: The Search for Leadership* (Glencoe, Ill., 1960), p. 51.

Greenville Negroes imposes very formidable limitations on the size of the Negro electorate. Negroes constitute only 30 per cent of the population in Greenville and even less of the voting-age population (because of the lower life-expectancy and larger families). Without access to party councils and not holding policy-making positions, Negro politicians try to make themselves "count" by increasing the size of the Negro electorate.

The Greenville Non-Partisan Voter Registration Committee was formed in the summer of 1962. The Committee received limited funds from the Voter Education Project of the Southern Regional Council, administered in the Greenville area by the Southern Christian Leadership Conference. It also sent letters to a hundred prominent Greenville Negroes asking each to give ten dollars to help support the Committee's work. It collected sixty-eight dollars. With the funds at hand it hired a college student to ring doorbells and urge those who had not registered to do so. The "field worker" also was to provide information on the registration process and to arrange transportation for those indicating a desire to register. A skeleton volunteer organization was set up in two wards which have large Negro populations. This 1962 registration campaign did not significantly increase Negro registration. In fact, very little work was done. The Committee never made any endorsements, on the grounds that it was necessary to register the voters before urging them to cast their ballots for particular candidates.

The Greenville City and County Voters Crusade was formed in late 1963 as the Non-Partisan Voter Registration Committee lost momentum. The leaders of the Committee simply had been unable to generate much interest among Greenville Negroes. They were further disheartened by their inability to secure further and more substantial funds from the Voter Education Project. The Voters Crusade is a quite different kind of organization from the Committee or its predecessors. First, only one of the Crusade's leaders had been involved in the work of Protest Organizations in Greenville (although most had been active previously in race leadership). Most of the leaders of the earlier Voting Organizations were Militants; the Voters Crusade leaders are Moderates. They represent, then, in one sense, a second generation of politicians. They are people who moved into voter registration work at a time when white opposition to Negro participation in electoral politics in Greenville was on a sharp decline.

The Voters Crusade faced at the outset the task of maintaining the existing level of registration, quite apart from increasing it. Ward and precinct lines were redrawn in Greenville in 1963. As a result many voters found themselves in different wards and precincts than those listed on their voting certificates, and were required to reregister. Perhaps as many as one-half of the Negro voters in Greenville were thus affected. At the outset the Voters Crusade made a serious attempt to recruit workers and in general to establish an organization able to carry out the extremely time consuming task of registering significant numbers of people. It set for itself the goal of 10,000 registered Negroes in Greenville County, more than double the number registered at the time it began work. In the first months of the project in 1964 workers met on a weekly basis with the organization's leaders. A car pool was established to provide transportation. Provisions were made to furnish minimum instruction to enable those interested in registering to do so.

The Voters Crusade enjoyed considerable success in 1964. About 3,500 Negroes were added to the 4,500 previously registered in the county. In the city itself, where the Crusade concentrated its efforts, the Negro electorate reached 5,400 for the November 3 election—which meant that it had doubled in a year's time. In March 1964 a Greenville Negro leader, Donald James Sampson, filed for one of Greenville county's eleven house seats—the first time since Reconstruction that a Negro had filed for the General Assembly from the county.[32] Sampson lost badly because of three factors: (1) the Negro electorate in the county is still very small; (2) large numbers of Negro-cast ballots were invalidated through the application of the South Carolina full-slate law (see the discussion in Chapter II, page 94); and (3) only one white voter in ten would give him a vote. (In Forsyth county in 1964 about one white voter in five voted for Crawford, the Negro candidate for one of the Democratic nominations for the North Carolina House.) Still, the far higher level of participation made possible by the registration activity of 1964 has provided the basis for the transformation of Greenville Negroes from political blanks to participants who must at least be considered by white politicians.

THE NEGRO CANDIDATE

H. D. Price observed in his study of the Negro in Florida politics that the possibility of electing a Negro to local office is a major spur to Negro political interest and participation.[33] The presence of a Negro candidate in the race for alderman in the South Third ward in Winston-Salem in 1947 provided impetus for Negro registration. The Greenville Negro leader who ran for the South Carolina House of Representatives in 1964 did so without expectation of victory. He knew that his candidacy would give area Negroes a reason for registering and voting. For the first time in county elections, they would have a choice that was meaningful.

The Negro candidate also appeals to race pride. His position on the ballot is indicative of an increase in status and power. If he loses, nonvoting Negroes can be castigated for

[32] Eleven other Negroes in two other South Carolina counties filed for seats in the state House of Representatives. None were successful.

[33] Price, *op. cit.*, p. 781.

"letting the race down." ("If 3,000 more had voted he would have won!")

The Winston-Salem Negro alderman has had one advantage over his counterparts in many other rim-South cities. A Winston alderman is elected only by the residents of the ward he represents and the South Third is a Negro ward. The Negro alderman in Winston-Salem has only Negro constituents. He does not need to worry about offending white voters. More often in the urban South, aldermen are designated as representatives of the wards in which they reside but are elected at large. In Greensboro, Raleigh, and Jacksonville, for example, where there is at-large election, Negro candidates have had to secure significant numbers of white votes in order to win and this has not been easy to do. The Negro businessman who ran for alderman from Ward 2 (a largely Negro ward) in Jacksonville in 1963 gained 15,000 votes in the Democratic primary. Despite the fact that he ran well ahead in Ward 2,[34] he was defeated by a white candidate who received 19,000 votes. The task of trying to satisfy two constituencies with such different expectations is frequently too much for those Negroes who succeed in getting elected in city-wide voting. In the 1963 municipal primary election in Greensboro the three-term Negro alderman was defeated. His share of the white vote was as large as it had been in his previous victories. But disgruntled Negroes had entered two other candidates who siphoned off a sufficient number of Negro votes to drop the incumbent from the general election ballot. These Negroes felt that the incumbent had not been zealous enough in promoting their interests. He was "squeezed"

[34] Jacksonville councilmen were elected by wards until 1947 when Negroes narrowly missed electing one of their number. At the first session of the Florida legislature after this election a local bill was passed amending the Jacksonville city charter to have councilmen elected by the city at large.

between the demands of Negro and white constituents. In Raleigh in April 1963 the Negro councilman was bitterly denounced by the city's militant leaders for "Uncle Tom-ing it" with white politicians. Part of the charge was that the councilman, dependent upon whites for electoral support, had become too solicitous of white interests. Negro aldermen in Winston, dependent only upon Negro constituents, have had much less trouble with the charge of "selling out."

Record numbers of Negro candidates entered municipal elections in the states of the southeast in 1963. Many were defeated, but Negroes are now serving on city councils in such cities as Portsmouth and Port Royal, Virginia; Winston-Salem, Raleigh, Durham, and Chapel Hill, North Carolina; Nashville, Tennessee; and Atlanta, Georgia. No Negro has ever held elective office in city government in a major city of South Carolina, Mississippi, Alabama, or Louisiana.

Problems become much greater when Negroes seek county-wide office.[35] Negroes generally have a harder time voting and seeing that their votes are counted in rural areas than in the cities. Moreover, in counties in the industrial rim-South (where Negroes have their best opportunities) the rural areas and small towns outside the central cities have a lower percentage of the population Negro than do the central cities. Negroes have sought county-wide office in Forsyth county (Winston-Salem) on seven occasions. They have been successful on two (the same candidate was elected and then re-elected to the county school board). A decade ago these candidacies did little beyond increasing Negro interest and involvement in electoral politics. The Negro candidate was badly defeated. In 1952, a Winston NAACP leader ran for the state House of Representatives. He finished sixth in a field of seven for the three nominations. In that same year a Negro businessman lost his bid for a Democratic nomination for county commissioner.

[35] State-wide office simply is not within the reach of Negroes at present in any southern state.

He was seventh among eight candidates seeking the five nominations. In 1958 a Negro businessman failed to get the Democratic nomination for the county school board. He came somewhat closer (in numbers of votes), and placed seventh among nine candidates for five nominations. Then in 1960 and 1962, Dr. Lillian Lewis won nomination and election to the county school board, and in 1962 the Reverend William Crawford was defeated by a relatively small margin in his bid for the state House of Representatives, running fourth among six candidates for three nominations.

Finally, in 1964, Crawford succeeded in getting the Democratic nomination for a House seat. This improvement in the position of Negro candidates came largely from increased voting by Negroes, rather than from a greater willingness of whites to vote for Negroes. The Negro candidate for the House seat in 1952 got as many votes (2,400) from whites as Crawford did in 1962. And in the 1964 primary Crawford was unable to get the support of more than one out of five white Democrats; he did not do quite as well in fact as he had done in 1962. Support from one white Democrat in five is all Negro candidates in Forsyth county primaries can count on —or at least all they have so far been able to get, even with substantial Democratic party support. Given this, "single-shot" voting is necessary, offering the only opportunity for success.

The hopes raised among Negroes and their allies by Crawford's primary victory were short-lived. He was defeated by a Republican opponent in the general election, and the manner of his defeat was devastating. His two Democratic colleagues won their seats by substantial margins (about 5,000-vote pluralities out of 56,000 votes cast); and the Republican winning the third House seat was the only member of his party to win in the county. Crawford ran about 1,100 votes ahead of his Democratic colleagues in Negro precincts and 5,600 votes behind them among white voters. Twenty-five per cent of the white Democratic voters—otherwise loyal to their party—substituted a Republican for Crawford or simply voted only for the two white Democrats. A plan to substitute had been promoted for several months by some Republicans and Democrats unhappy about the prospects of having a Negro represent them. The plan was opposed by most of the regular Democratic leaders. That 25 per cent of the white Democrats would refuse to support a Negro Democrat with a long record of party loyalty, and that 15 per cent would give their votes instead to a Republican candidate points up the great difficulties facing Negro candidates for county office, even in an area where race relations are relatively permissive and where the Negro electorate is unusually large.

Crawford could have won in spite of these defections, however, if significant numbers of Negro voters had not made a technical error in casting their ballots. Crawford received 2,500 fewer votes from Negroes than did President Johnson, and since he was not opposed by any group of Negroes only one explanation for this exists: many Negroes pulled the voting machine lever for the national ticket and thought that they had voted for everyone. They then walked out without having pulled a separate lever for the county ticket. Straight ticket voting required pulling two master levers rather than one. Since Crawford lost by only 1,774 votes, had he received only as many votes from Negroes as Johnson received he would have won by a margin of about 725 votes. Approximately 80 per cent of the registered Negroes in Forsyth county went to the polls—far surpassing the previous high—and they gave better than 98 per cent of their votes to the Democrats. Yet the proportion of the total vote cast by Negroes did not exceed the 30 per cent which has been the rule since 1958, because of the comparable expansion of the white electorate. This, together with the defection of a quarter of the white Democrats and the technical error made by 20 per cent of the Negro voters spelled defeat for Crawford, and the loss of an unusually good opportunity to send a Negro to the legislature —not done since Reconstruction. So numerous are the obstacles confronting a Negro candidate for county office that victory—even in relatively fortunate circumstances—frequently remains just beyond reach.

In the Negro ward in Winston-Salem competition among Negro candidates has become the rule. In the first decade in which Negroes were elected from the South Third ward, the aldermanic candidate was not challenged. The goal of Negro representation was so recently achieved that competition *among Negroes* seemed unnatural and undesirable. The important thing was securing Negro representation. Winston Negroes now have moved into a second stage of political involvement. Representation is no longer a novelty but rather an accepted right, and a normal kind of political rivalry and conflict has emerged. The incumbent alderman was successfully challenged in 1961, and in 1963 two challengers waged unsuccessful but spirited contests.

The Negro candidate is now part of the political scene in Winston-Salem. He has just begun to make an appearance in Greenville.

THE POLITICIANS AND RACE ADVANCEMENT

Negro politicians in upper-South cities like Winston-Salem operate from positions of strength, and are now playing a major role in race-advancement activity. The size of the Negro electorate makes white recognition of the politicians unavoidable. If, as Samuel Lubell has argued, the top position to which a minority group member can be elected or appointed is a good index of the minority's political acceptance, then the position of Negroes in police and fire departments, on school boards and planning commissions, and on city councils in Winston-Salem and the other major North Carolina cities indicates both how far Negroes have come in the last decade and how far—since these positions represent the highest open to Negroes—they have yet to go.[36] The sheer electoral

[36] Samuel Lubell, *The Future of American Politics* (New York, 1952), p. 77.

strength of Negroes in the cities of the rim South is both a reflection and a cause of their greater acceptance.

The position of the politicians in Winston combines access and acceptance with visibility, subcommunity approval, and the possession of sanctions. The work of the politicians is highly visible. They get headlines. They speak publicly. They can be heard defending Negro interests in public meetings. Politicians have an arsenal of "negative inducements"— sanctions—with which to promote Negro interests. At the same time, because of the kinds of people attracted to electoral politics and because politicians work through the formal, constitutional channels centered around voting (which frightens whites much less than direct action), Negro activity in electoral politics has come to be regarded by whites as "moderate" race-advancement activity, and politicians are able to maintain access to white leaders and achieve a large measure of acceptance. Moreover, they do not need to sacrifice the approval of their own community for white acceptance. Our survey in Winston-Salem indicates that the activities of the politicians are both well known and warmly applauded. The four leaders receiving the most nominations as the "outstanding leaders" in the city are politicians. Negro participation in electoral politics in Greenville has begun to assume a similar position.

Negro politicians frequently find themselves squeezed between the expectations of their constituents and the demands of their office. In one sense, of course, the same observation is valid for whites. But the problem is somewhat more acute for Negroes holding elective or appointed office. If an alderman is to be effective, he must establish some kind of rapport with his colleagues.[37] But a race leader frequently cannot establish

[37] A number of studies of the national Congress have noted the same requirement for legislative effectiveness. (See William White's *Citadel* [New York, 1957] for a discussion of the "Senate type.") The dissent from this position found in Huitt's article on the "outsider's"

rapport and at the same time satisfy his constituents that he is performing his protest function adequately. In the spring of 1963, for example, conflict broke out among Winston Negroes over the question whether they should demonstrate or cooperate with the biracial committee. At a particularly tense meeting of the parties to the dispute (protest Negroes, cooperation Negroes, and white leaders) the mayor called upon the Negro alderman, Carl Russell, for his comments on the controversy. When elected, Russell had been considered an "outspoken" Negro leader. In his first two years he was very much an outsider on the Board of Aldermen, much more than his predecessor had been. But he had gradually established a working arrangement with his colleagues. He had learned to vote with Alderman X on an issue dear to the latter's heart in return for support on another. In particular, he had established a working relationship with the mayor who as a party leader could give things Russell wanted for his constituents in return for support. Politics in Winston-Salem is not like politics in Chicago, where the Dawson machine is firmly enmeshed in the Democratic party organization and hence reluctant to see certain kinds of race demands arise because these tend to be disruptive.[38] Still, when Russell was called upon he did not feel able to repudiate the mayor. He answered that he had faith in the mayor's committee and that dramatic progress had been made. Negroes did not, to be sure, have everything they wanted, but that was why the Goodwill

role in the Senate (Ralph Huitt, "The Outsider in the Senate: An Alternative Role," *American Political Science Review*, LV [September 1961], 566–575) is particularly relevant to an evaluation of the effectiveness of the Negro officeholder. He does, however, find himself under strong pressure to compromise, to bargain, to indulge in political give and take.

[38] Wilson, *op. cit.*, p. 117. Dawson and his associates worked to stop a school boycott planned by protest leaders in February, 1964. The word went out to the precinct levels, "Stop it" (see the *New York Times*, February 5, 1964).

Committee was still operating. He committed himself to opposing demonstrations at that time. For this Russell was roundly denounced. Militant leaders at the meeting continued to berate him, and his political position in the Negro community was weakened. Had he moved the other way, however, the channels open to him within the Democratic party might well have been closed.

In Raleigh, Negro councilman John Winters encountered a similar problem. Raleigh Mayor W. G. Enloe was the owner of a segregated theater which Negroes were picketing. After a long period of demonstrations and name-calling the mayor announced his intention to resign and secure an injunction to prohibit the demonstrations. He said he could be dissuaded only if the demonstrators curtailed their activities somewhat. Winters became convinced that the resignation of the mayor would be detrimental to Negro interests. The mayor, he felt, might become a martyr in the eyes of white segregationists. More than this the resignation might intensify racial conflict and strengthen the hand of the extreme segregationists in the Raleigh Democratic party. Channels which Winters had painstakingly built might be destroyed. So he and some of his associates urged the organizations conducting the demonstrations—the Raleigh Citizens Association and the Raleigh NAACP—to reduce the scope of their demonstrations. These organizations finally agreed to his appeal. Winters informed the mayor of this decision minutes before the council session at which the mayor was to tender his resignation. Enloe then announced to a crowded council chamber that because of an intercession for more restraint by the pickets he would not resign. He referred to Winters as "John." Because of this, which indicated to some that the councilman was "Uncle Tom-ing it," Winters was subjected to a particularly intense campaign of vilification. He offered his resignation but was finally persuaded to withdraw it by a number of leaders who rallied to his side. But his position was weakened. These conflicts created by the two dimensions of their role—race leader and party leader—frequently plague southern Negro politicians.

Despite this, the Negro politician is firmly established in the urban rim-South and is beginning to make an appearance in the cities of the deep South. Sustained by a Negro vote that is constantly expanding and which frequently holds the balance of power, the Negro politician should pay an increasingly important role in the next decade.

RECRUITMENT

We have noted that positions of leadership in the Welfare and the Protest Organizations tend to type those occupying them—that the functions to be performed are prescribed and really quite uniform. White reactions to protest and welfare leaders are similarly clear and predictable and do not admit of differences within each category. Welfare leaders and protest leaders are as a result relativly homogeneous groups in terms of the variables (such as degree of economic vulnerability) which are directly related to the performance of their leadership roles. There is much greater diversity in the functions being performed by politicians. The chairman of the Voters Crusade in Greenville is a politician. So is the Democratic precinct worker in Winston-Salem. So is the Negro member of the City-County Planning Board. Politicians are, then, a more heterogeneous group. Moreover, the position of an individual politician is generally much more flexible. Neither his role nor white expectations concerning that role are as rigidly determined.

But if his position types him less than does that of welfare and protest leaders, it does make certain demands and provides for certain approaches to race advancement. And in Winston, Greenville, and other southern cities examined more cursorily, the "typical" politician is a Moderate. There are both Conservatives and Militants among the politicians (more of the former in more permissive race relations situations and more of the latter when patterns of segregation are more rigidly enforced). But the center of gravity is on ground occupied by Moderates. Three general considerations explain the recruitment of Moderates. First, the activities incumbent upon the politician in the performance of his work as politician are often pedestrian, demanding discussion and compromise and offering little chance for dramatic gain. Getting cars to carry voters to the polls on election day and arguing with fellow school board members to obtain a higher expenditure for books for the libraries of Negro high schools do not excite the more militant leaders. Politicians are not prevented from promoting status goals, but the stuff of politics is welfare. Moderates, more interested in welfare goals, have found this part of the politician's work quite acceptable.

Second, southern whites continue to exercise influence over many positions occupied by the politicians. Any Negro running for city-wide or county-wide office generally must get a good number of white votes if he is to win. The only Negro in a county-wide office in Forsyth county, for example, gained about half of her votes from whites in the 1962 Democratic primary. The Militant simply can not get white votes. Negroes serving on the school board, the planning board, and the housing commission in Winston-Salem were approved by a white board of aldermen. White leaders recognize that they cannot now get away with appointing only Conservatives to these positions. A large segment of the sub-community simply will not accept this. Compromise, then, leads to the selection of Negro leaders who are generally acceptable to both parties—the Moderates.

The third factor, and we must admit that here the argument gets somewhat circular, is that Negro participation in electoral politics has been given the stamp of legitimacy by whites in Winston-Salem and the other rim-South cities. It attracts vulnerables who are seeking maximum opportunity for vigorous and effective race leadership within the limits of acceptable conduct. A Negro precinct chairman in Winston-Salem who is both forceful and particularly sensitive to patterns of racial discrimination observed:

"I have a lot of white clients [he is a painter]. Some tell me I'm the best in town. They often talk about my work as precinct leader but I'm sure I wouldn't get their business if I worked with the NAACP."

A fourth factor explaining the moderate style of Negro politicians differs from the first three, which maintain that electoral politics draws racial Moderates; it also appears that this form of political participation *makes* Moderates. James Wilson described the organizational constraints operating on politicians in Chicago:

The machine proceeds by intra-party haggling and trading; public attacks and outspoken antagonisms only "rock the boat." Issues are obstacles to be overcome, not opportunities to be sought; open controversy is anathema.[39]

There is no Negro "machine" in Winston-Salem. Party politics is a much more occasional and loosely structured affair. But it does require a kind of give and take that Negro politicians quickly learn. There are a growing number of Negro politicians, moreover, who feel a vested interest in the Democratic party and its success, and who will at times subordinate immediate race goals to party needs. A politician who is reputed to be a "race man" recently spoke at a rally in support of a segregationist who happened to be a Democratic candidate. (The Republican candidate was, from the Negro viewpoint, just as bad.) He did this because in his words, "I am a party man." A Negro school board member said:

[39] Wilson, *op. cit.*, p. 117.

There are six whites on the board and only one Negro. You're not going to get anywhere by making them mad at you. You've got to gain their respect.

Another politician felt that it had taken him his first two years in office to appreciate the importance of knowing the right people and being able to work with them:

After a while I was able to call up the right man when something popped, and get things done.

Politics, even on the modest scale practiced in middle-sized cities like Winston-Salem, offers incentive to the Negro politician to modify his race demands to the point where the whites with whom he works find them tolerable, although by no means necessarily fully acceptable.

The criteria for success in leadership of the Voting Organizations are a blend of those which we noted for the other two categories of race-advancement organizations. The politician must be able to persuade white leaders that he is a legitimate person with legitimate goals, but he must retain active rank-and-file support and be able to mobilize his community for such action as voting. The politician must be temperamentally able to operate in the interminable haggling of government boards and of the party organization. He must be able to compromise, but he still must be willing and able to dramatize race demands. He must be adept at both private manipulation and public exhortation. Inevitably he achieves something less than all of each, but it is a composite of these that maximizes his effectiveness.

Postscript:

The Revolution Moves On

IN this study leadership has been seen as a response to particular societal situations. This is not to say that what leaders do is unimportant, but rather to insist that they cannot escape certain basic givens—the problems to be solved and the resources available for solving them. One becomes particularly aware of the importance of the leadership setting in a study of Negro political leadership and the evolution of patterns of leadership. Race relations in the American South have been undergoing profound and rapid change, and this has made necessary very basic changes in the structure of race leadership.

Two decades ago, when the old biracial system was intact, the southern Negro was without effective political power. The dominant form of race leadership in the South in this period— that of the "Uncle Tom"—is testimony to that powerlessness. The classic Uncle Tom has disappeared because the situation which produced him no longer exists. Three basic modifications of the structure of race leadership which have resulted from the gradual collapse of the old biracial system and the concomitant strengthening of the political position of Negroes should be noted here. First, there has been a marked increase in the number of Negro leaders. Southern Negroes remain a deprived group, but they are much less so now than they have been. Educational opportunities have improved. The number of Negro professional men has increased. In general, the pool of leadership talent has been expanded in every southern city. (The importance of the size of the reservoir of leadership talent was pointed out in Chapter II, where differences between Winston-Salem and Greenville in this regard were noted.) The incentives for active participation in politics have also become much greater.

Second, there has been an increasing differentiation of the race leadership structure. Two decades ago only two responses by Negro leaders were possible or recognized: acceptance of the biracial system and protest against it. The former was dominant and the latter but a feeble gesture. Today Negro leaders are united in opposition to all remnants of the old biracial system, and they have infinitely greater options in terms of objectives and means. Negroes were, for example, really without the franchise in most of the South until the end of World War II. Now formal barriers to registration and voting have been removed in almost all major southern cities, and in some, principally rim-South cities, Negroes have been integrated into the local Democratic coalitions. In such cities there is a wide variety of organizations working to enlarge the Negro electorate and to manipulate it in the interests of race advancement. Two decades ago NAACP branches stood as lonely sentinels protesting against segregation. Today in many southern cities second generation (e.g., CORE) and third generation (e.g., SNCC) protest organizations are struggling against the white man, and against each other for the loyalty of the subcommunity.

Third, The Negro Revolt in the South (as in the North) has not yet reached Thermidor. It is still moving always to the left. Negro leaders—holding their positions because the subcommunity accepts their definitions of how the race should be advanced—could not resist, even if they wanted to, the demands that the revolution be pushed to its conclusion. Any demand recognized as more militant than the previous one will find a hearing among Negroes because their problems are so pressing and solutions to these problems not at hand. The content of the continuum of leadership styles changes, then, in the following manner: new goals-means-rhetoric combinations, recognized by Negroes and whites as more militant, supplant those previously at the militant end of the continuum, and everyone on the continuum moves slightly toward the conservative pole. The continuum expands, and certain goals-means-rhetoric combinations may no longer have sufficient subcommunity support to remain on the continuum. Changes in the content of the continuum may be effected by the addition of new people or by a part of the existing leadership taking up the new demands.

Negro leaders operate under extraordinary pressures. They face strong white opposition whenever they attempt to achieve significant changes in the Negro's position. They are charged with working in an area in which their constituents' most vital interests are continuously involved. Moreover, since the whole area of race advancement is caught up in such rapid change, Negro expectations, the techniques for promoting race goals, and the resources available are constantly evolving. These pressures are especially strong on those leaders—principally protest leaders and some politicians—who are most in the limelight. More often than not race leaders are swept along by the revolution. A Winston-Salem leader recognized this when he said:

They asked me to cooperate and call a halt to the pool integration. I told them that I didn't want to, that what was being done was right. But, hell, man, I couldn't have stopped that anymore than you could have. There are plenty waiting to take my place if I falter.

Operating from weak institutional and status positions, possessing few sanctions with which to secure the compliance of their followers, and dealing with issues which involve the deepest and most vital political interests of Negroes, race leaders are exceedingly vulnerable. Hence the fluidity potential of race leadership will remain high.

In deep-South cities such as Greenville, the old gross exclusion battles are still being fought and only now beginning to be won. It was not until late April 1964, for example, that a federal court ordered the Greenville county school district —which with 53,000 students is the largest in South Carolina —to end its policy of complete school segregation. Thus the first battle in the long struggle for school integration was not won in Greenville until a decade after the *Brown* decision. Greenville's Negro leaders will continue for some time to be preoccupied with removing the formal barriers which stand between Negroes and the use of various public facilities.

But even in deep-South cities like Greenville with the passage of the 1964 Civil Rights Act many of these battles have been won. In more fortunate rim-South cities such as Winston-Salem, all major public facilities have *really* removed the big "keep out" signs that greeted Negroes for so long. In the urban rim-South the old biracial system—which dictated one place for Negroes and another for whites—no longer exists. Discrimination does, of course, but not the biracial system. Negro pupils in Winston-Salem now can attend the school nearest their homes. All public recreation facilities are open to Negroes, and they have easy access to all good motels, hotels, and related public accommodations in the city. The major employers of Winston have subscribed to an equal employment opportunities statement:

The employers of Greater Winston-Salem believe that all people must have equal opportunity to seek and receive employment commensurate with their qualifications and ability. . . . These employers of Greater Winston-Salem wish to make it known that they recruit, hire, assign, train, upgrade, promote, transfer and pay employees on the basis of merit without discrimination because of race, creed, color or national origin.

Many problems remain but they are not those of gross exclusion. Negro leaders in Winston and its sister cities of the rim South must now begin to turn their attention to the problems that remain after gross exclusion has been ended. Their northern counterparts already are embroiled in these problems.

The old gross exclusion problems really were quite simple and certainly were straightforward. When school segregation meant that a Negro high school student in Forsyth county who lived only five hundred yards from a white high school was required to travel twenty miles (a two-hour school bus ride) across the county to an all-Negro school, both the injustice and the remedy could easily be seen. But when, as in Winston-Salem today, school segregation results primarily from residential segregation rather than from a formal policy, and when residential segregation is perpetuated by the weaker economic position of Negroes which in turn is ultimately a product of the after-effects of two centuries of slavery and another century of deprivations and discriminations, it becomes much harder to find a remedy. When discrimination in the economic sphere meant that Hanes Hosiery Company refused to hire Negroes in anything other than janitorial capacities, the abuse was flagrant and the remedy at hand. But when Negroes are excluded from jobs because they do not have the training which they lack because of problems of education and motivation which go all the way back to the very core of what it has meant to be black in white America, then easy answers simply are not to be found.

As Negro leaders move from the straightforward problems of gross exclusion to the newer and infinitely more subtle and complex problems involved in trying to make "equality of opportunity" more than a slogan, they will have to experiment. Solutions are not as simple or as self-evident. Stall-ins and the like will come to the South. In the experimentation both Negroes and whites undoubtedly will resort to silly and even pernicious actions. In 1975 Americans will look back on the 1940's, 1950's, and early 1960's in the South as a time when the civil rights battles were quite simple and clear-cut.

We are witnessing today a nationalizing of the politics of desegregation. Historically most Negro-Americans have resided in the South, where until about two decades ago, Negroes were without political power. The battles which Negro leaders were fighting were to break down the barriers by which they had been excluded *in toto* from the major institutions—political, social, economic, and educational. Northern whites, unlike their southern brethren, were never wedded strongly to total segregation. Today, however, a majority of Negro-Americans (and this trend is continuing) live outside the old Confederacy. The power positions of northern and southern Negroes, once at opposite poles, have been brought closer and closer together. And though the attitudes of northern and southern whites on gross exclusion are quite different, they are essentially the same on the problems beyond gross exclusion. Thus, as the Revolution moves on, the politics of desegregation in the cities of the South comes more closely to resemble that in the cities of the North.

Appendix: Methods of Study

THE LEADERSHIP SAMPLE

WE sought to interview all Negroes in Winston-Salem and Greenville who were, potentially, in a position to influence significantly the realization of race goals. At the beginning of our research in each city an attempt was made to get an overview of the structure of race relations, past and present. Local newspapers (back to 1954) were scanned for race news. City and area histories were examined. Informants were located and were asked to discuss, in a general way, race relations and the leaders and organizations involved in race-advancement work. Thus, we were able to determine which organizations in the subcommunity were centrally involved in the civil rights struggle. A preliminary list of race leaders was then compiled to include the following: the officers and members of the executive bodies of the various race-advancement organizations and persons holding elective and appointive office in city and county government. There are relatively few of these positions. Competition for them is sufficient to ensure that occupants generally are persons with political influence within at least a segment of the subcommunity. Moreover, the possession of a leadership position in one of the race-advancement organizations provides a base from which the advancement of various race goals can be influenced.

Each person on this list when initially interviewed was shown the names of the others and asked (1) to add to the list any persons not included whom he considered to be leaders; (2) to delete from the list persons whom he did not consider to be leaders; and (3) to name the ten "top leaders" in the subcommunity. We asked each interviewee to think of leaders as those "able to make decisions significantly effecting the resolution of racial problems in this city." Only four persons in Winston-Salem and three in Greenville not on the lists received more than one nomination. These names were added. No name was deleted by a leader involved in the same area of race-advancement activity; that is, no person involved in the activity of the Welfare Organizations suggested the deletion of a colleague in welfare organization activity. Some names, however, were regularly deleted by persons working in other areas of race advancement; for example, protest leaders deleted the names of certain welfare leaders. Without exception those thus deleted were not nominated as "top leaders" by any other leaders. They were not well known in the subcommunity at large.

Sample surveys were conducted in the Negro subcommunities of Winston-Salem and Greenville. Respondents were asked to identify those whom they considered to be the "five most outstanding Negro leaders in this community." A few not on the list received one nomination but none received more than one. Moreover, in the course of our research over a period of three months in each city, we attended numerous meetings of race-advancement organizations, interviewed many whites and Negroes, and carefully examined the process by which race goals are promoted. We concluded that the initial list accurately identified those Negroes who were political leaders. Those possessing political influence in the subcommunity find their way into decision-making positions in one or more of the race-advancement organizations. Race leaders, moreover, need a position in a race-advancement organization from which to promote race objectives. In the highly fluid situation of Negro politics, leader-candidates can easily form their own organizations if they are dissatisfied with the existing ones.

In later trips to the two cities, changes in the personnel of race leadership noted in newspaper accounts and from correspondence were carefully examined. Additional interviews were conducted and the necessary changes in the list of race leaders were made.

The somewhat haphazard way in which the list of race leaders was compiled seems to have presented no serious problems. We are satisfied that our final list includes all those who played, at the time of writing, leading roles in race-advancement work in the two cities. Compiling the list from those holding formal organizational positions proved to be generally reliable. Fifty-eight Negroes were identified as leaders in Winston-Salem, thirty-six in Greenville. All of these were interviewed at least once; most were interviewed two to four times. Interviews were semistructured. In the initial interview certain biographical data were obtained. Interviews varied in length from thirty minutes to more than five hours. The average length was two hours.

In the course of our research in each city it became clear that some of those on the leadership list could be considered leaders only because they held positions in race-advancement organizations which enabled them to play a part in committing the organizations to particular forms of race advancement. They were well known by those immediately involved in the work of the given organization, but were not generally recognized as leaders either by rank and file members of the subcommunity or by leaders of other race-advancement organizations. On the other hand, some leaders were generally recognized as such by individuals outside their own area of race advancement. They were well known throughout, and associated with projects involving, the entire subcommunity. Their role in race advancement was more extensive and more significant than that of the former group. This distinction was brought into part of our analysis. In the sections in Chapter

V, "Who are the Welfare Leaders?" etc., all of the leaders on the final total list were included. All were prominently associated with at least one race-advancement organization. The three categories, Welfare Organizations, Protest Organizations, and Voting Organizations, were designed to include the entire spectrum of race-advancement activity. But in the statistical section of Chapter IV, "Who are the Conservatives, the Moderates, the Militants?" only those more broadly recognized as race leaders were included. It was felt that the statistical information on Conservatives, Moderates, and Militants would in one sense provide a truer picture if it included only those more prominently associated with race-advancement activity in the subcommunity and playing a generally more significant role; and excluded those whose names appeared on our total list of leaders only because their positions on the executive bodies of race-advancement organizations enabled them to influence the policy of those organizations.

SUBCOMMUNITY SURVEY INTERVIEWS

To obtain a stratified sample of the subcommunity in each city, Negro residential districts were mapped according to class. This was done in the following manner. First, each block in the Negro neighborhoods of Winston-Salem and Greenville was visited by automobile. Each was assigned a class designation (upper-middle, middle-middle and lower-middle, and lower) on the basis of these observations. We were concerned with such things as the size and general condition of the houses, the kind of repair which they were in, the amount of yard space, sanitary conditions, and general desirability.[1] Second, we used the census data on the character-

---

[1] See M. Elaine Burgess, *Negro Leadership in a Southern City* (Chapel Hill, N.C., 1962), pp. 213–14; and Lloyd Warner, *et al.*, *Social Class in America* (Chicago, 1949), pp. 143–154, for descriptions of methods of block rating.

istics of housing units by blocks: the percentage of owner-occupied units, average number of rooms per unit, average dollar value of the properties or the average contract rent, and so on. From these two sources of data a class rating was assigned to each block and to each neighborhood.

Sample blocks were selected and interviewers were instructed to interview an adult resident in every fourth house within the selected blocks. Second and third follow-up calls were made when necessary to find a party at home. When contact still was not made after a third call or when the party refused to answer questions, a resident of an adjoining house was interviewed. One hundred and fifty interviews were completed in each city. Forty were in upper-middle blocks in each city, sixty in middle-middle and lower-middle blocks, and fifty in lower-class blocks. Biographical data permitting a determination of class were requested from each respondent. The class positions determined on the basis of this data coincided in most instances with our previous designation of the block.

Questions were asked in the surveys (1) to obtain information on registration and voting (whether the respondent had tried to register, problems encountered in seeking to register if any, etc.); (2) to get an evaluation of the activities of the various race-advancement organizations operating locally; (3) to gain general information on the levels of political awareness of Negroes in the two cities and on their racial attitudes; (4) to obtain subcommunity evaluation of what areas of race advancement are most important and deserve the immediate attention of race leaders; and (5) to get subcommunity judgment on who are the outstanding local race leaders.

COMPARATIVE SOUTH-WIDE DATA

It was considered essential that a narrowness so easily occurring with the community study approach be avoided here; that we be able to generalize about patterns of race leadership on a firmer basis than the two community studies alone could have afforded. In addition, hypotheses on which this study was based required further validation. Can one profitably view the rim South and the deep South as constituting two distinct "worlds" of race relations for the purpose of analyzing patterns of race leadership in the urban South? And are the two communities selected for detailed analysis in fact broadly representative of the basic race relations structure of their respective subregions? To meet these objectives the following research plan was devised and followed.

(1) At the outset a number of published studies and unpublished reports on various aspects of race relations in a number of major southern cities were reviewed. Some of these, such as the study of Durham, North Carolina, by M. Elaine Burgess, *Negro Leadership in a Southern City*, were particularly useful. We consulted with a number of scholars who were competent to discuss patterns of race relations in the South. Professors Donald Matthews and James Prothro of the University of North Carolina, and Allan Sindler, then of Duke and now of Cornell, were particularly helpful. In addition, the author had made personal contacts on a more casual basis, in a number of regional cities. Census data for all major southern cities (defined here as cities over 50,000 population) were carefully analyzed. We were concerned with such variables as income, education, and occupation for the Negro and white populations of these cities, and with patterns of residential segregation.

(2) Eleven major southern Negro newspapers were regularly reviewed during the research period. (The names of these newspapers and the issues covered are found in the Bibliography.) Articles relevant to this study were clipped and filed. Many of the better Negro weekly newspapers are far better chroniclers of Negro politics in their cities of pub-

lication than are the mass circulation daily papers of white politics. The mass media have confronted southern Negroes with a conspiracy of silence, and the Negro weekly was established to cover precisely those things that the mass media would not touch. One of these things is political activity *within* the Negro subcommunity.

(3) Trips were made to fourteen other major cities in the Southeast during the research period and informants in each were consulted. The informants were asked about general features of race relations in their communities, and were asked specifically about patterns of race leadership. We were aware that reliance on limited numbers of informants and on interviews covering a wide range of subjects in a relatively cursory manner could only provide data that is at times sketchy, impressionistic, and incomplete. But the exercise was not one in futility. To ask five key Negro leaders in Columbia, South Carolina, to comment on precisely drawn generalizations, after having accumulated substantial amounts of information on Negro politics in that city—and to duplicate this in thirteen other regional cities—is to provide the basis for setting the two communities selected for intensive analysis in a larger world of race relations.

Even with this rather extensive gathering of comparative data, we proceeded with the greatest caution whenever we moved beyond the data yielded by the more systematic research in our two communities. But at a minimum the methodology here appears adequate for establishing the validity of the basic hypotheses on which this study was developed. The utility of blending the specificity of the community study approach with a more general and less systematic type of region-wide analysis also seems clear.

A FINAL NOTE ON THE NATURE OF EVIDENCE

The leader interviews were the basic source of data on race leadership in Winston-Salem and Greenville. These interviews were semistructured and ranged widely over subjects relating to race relations in each city. Conclusions advanced about the opinions of race leaders were in most cases derived directly from the interview data. Since these conclusions stand on the basis of detailed probing in the interview situation, we decided that in many cases it would be at best misleading to affix a percentage to them: "63 per cent of the leaders believed . . ." For the percentage would conceal the subtle distinctions that the depth interview made possible. But in all such cases the conclusions were advanced only after the most careful analysis of nearly 3,500 pages of recorded interview data.

Bibliography

BOOKS

Allport, Gordon W. *The Nature of Prejudice*. Boston: Beacon Press, 1954.

Aptheker, Herbert. *American Negro Slave Revolts*. New York: Columbia University Press, 1943.

Ashmore, Harry S. *The Negro and the Schools*. Chapel Hill: University of North Carolina Press, 1955.

Baldwin, James. *Nobody Knows My Name*. New York: Dell Publishing Company, 1962.

Bardolph, Richard. *The Negro Vanguard*. New York: Rinehart and Company, 1959.

Bendix, R., and S. M. Lipset. *Class, Status and Power*. Glencoe, Ill.: Free Press, 1953.

Boykin, James H. *The Negro in North Carolina Prior to 1861*. New York: Pageant Press, 1958.

Brink, William, and Louis Harris. *The Negro Revolution in America*. New York: Simon and Schuster, 1964.

Brinton, Crane. *The Anatomy of Revolution*. New York: W. W. Norton and Company, 1938.

Buckmaster, Henrietta. *Let My People Go*. New York: Harper and Brothers, 1941.

Burgess, Margaret Elaine. *Negro Leadership in a Southern City*. Chapel Hill: University of North Carolina Press, 1962.

Campbell, Angus, Warren Miller, and Donald Stokes. *The American Voter*. New York: John Wiley and Sons, 1960.

333

Carter, Hodding. *The South Strikes Back*. Garden City, N.Y.: Doubleday and Company, 1959.

Carter, Wilmoth A. *The Urban Negro in the South*. New York: Vantage Press, 1961.

Cash, Wilbur J. *The Mind of the South*. New York: Alfred A. Knopf, 1941.

Conrad, Earl. *Harriet Tubman*. Washington, D.C.: The Associated Publishers, 1943.

Cox, Oliver C. *Caste, Class, and Race; A Study in Social Dynamics*. Garden City, N.Y.: Doubleday and Company, 1948.

Dahl, Robert. *Who Governs?* New Haven: Yale University Press, 1961.

Davis, Allison, and John Dollard. *Children of Bondage*. Washington, D.C.: American Council on Education, 1940.

Davis, Allison, Burleigh B. Gardner, and Mary R. Gardner. *Deep South: A Social Anthropological Study of Caste and Class*. Chicago: The University of Chicago Press, 1941.

DeGrazia, Sebastian. *The Political Community*. Chicago: University of Chicago Press, 1949.

Dollard, John. *Caste and Class in a Southern Town*. New Haven: Yale University Press, 1937.

Drake, St. Clair, and Horace R. Cayton. *Black Metropolis: A Study of Negro Life in a Northern City*. New York: Harcourt, Brace and Company, 1945.

DuBois, W. E. B. *Black Reconstruction*. New York: Harcourt, Brace and Company, 1935.

——. *The Negro in Business*. Atlanta: Atlanta University Press, 1899.

——. *The Negro Problem*. New York: James Pott and Company, 1903.

——. *The Souls of Black Folk*. Chicago: McClurg and Company, 1903.

Dykeman, Wilma, and James Stokely. *Neither Black nor White*. New York: Rinehart and Company, 1957.

——. *Seeds of Southern Change*. Chicago: University of Chicago Press, 1962.

Franklin, John Hope. *The Free Negro in North Carolina*. Chapel Hill: The University of North Carolina Press, 1943.

Franklin, John Hope. *From Slavery to Freedom.* New York: Alfred A. Knopf, 1956.

Frazier, E. Franklin. *Black Bourgeoisie.* New York: Collier Books, 1962.

—— (ed.). *The Integration of the Negro into American Society.* Washington, D.C.: Howard University Press, 1951.

——. *The Negro Family in the United States.* Chicago: The University of Chicago Press, 1939.

——. *The Negro in the United States.* New York: The Macmillan Company, 1957.

Gerth, H. H., and C. Wright Mills (eds.). *From Max Weber: Essays in Sociology.* New York: Oxford University Press, 1946.

Ginzberg, Eli. *The Negro Potential.* New York: Columbia University Press, 1956.

Gosnell, Harold F. *Negro Politicians.* Chicago: The University of Chicago Press, 1935.

Gouldner, Alvin W. (ed.). *Studies in Leadership.* New York: Harper and Brothers, 1950.

Greenberg, Jack. *Race Relations and American Law.* Boston: Little, Brown and Company, 1959.

Harris, Abram L. *The Negro as Capitalist.* Philadelphia: The American Academy of Political and Social Sciences, 1936.

Herskovits, Melville J. *The Myth of the Negro Past.* New York: Harper and Brothers, 1942.

Hoffer, Eric. *The True Believer.* New York: New American Library, 1958.

Horowitz, Irving Louis (e.). *Power, Politics and People: The Collected Essays of C. Wright Mills.* New York: Ballantine Books, 1963.

Hughes, Langston. *Fight for Freedom: The Story of the NAACP.* New York: W. W. Norton and Company, 1962.

Hunter, Floyd. *Community Power Structure.* Chapel Hill: University of North Carolina Press, 1953.

——. *Top Leadership, U.S.A.* Chapel Hill: University of North Carolina Press, 1959.

Johnson, Charles S. *Growing Up in the Black Belt.* Washington, D.C.: American Council on Education, 1941.

335

Johnson, Charles S. *The Negro College Graduate*. Chapel Hill: The University of North Carolina Press, 1938.

——. *Patterns of Negro Segregation*. New York: Harper and Brothers, 1943.

—— et al. *Statistical Atlas of Southern Counties*. Chapel Hill: The University of North Carolina Press, 1941.

Kardiner, Abram, and Lionel Ovesey. *The Mark of Oppression: A Psychological Study of the American Negro*. New York: W. W. Norton and Company, 1951.

Key, V. O. *Southern Politics in State and Nation*. New York: Alfred A. Knopf, 1950.

Killian, Lewis, and Charles Grigg. *Racial Crisis in America*. Englewood Cliffs, N.J.: Prentice-Hall, 1964.

King, C. Wendell. *Social Movement in the United States*. New York: Random House, 1956.

King, Martin Luther, Jr. *Stride Toward Freedom*. New York: Ballantine Books, 1960.

Larkins, John R. *Patterns of Leadership Among Negroes in North Carolina*. Raleigh: Irving-Swain Press, 1959.

Lasswell, Harold D. *Politics: Who Gets What, When, and How*. New York: McGraw-Hill Book Company, 1936.

Lewinson, Paul. *Race, Class and Party*. New York: Oxford University Press, 1932.

Lewis, Edward E. *The Mobility of the Negro*. New York: Columbia University Press, 1931.

Lewis, Hylan. *Blackways of Kent*. Chapel Hill: University of North Carolina Press, 1955.

Lincoln, Eric. *The Black Muslims in America*. Boston: Beacon Press, 1962.

Lipset, S. M. *Political Man*. Garden City, N.Y.: Doubleday and Company, 1960.

Locke, Alain (ed.). *The New Negro*. New York: A. and C. Boni, 1925.

Logan, Rayford W. (ed.). *What The Negro Wants*. Chapel Hill: University of North Carolina Press, 1944.

Lomax, Louis E. *The Negro Revolt*. New York: Harper and Row, 1962.

——. *The Reluctant African*. New York: Harper and Brothers, 1960.

Lynd, Robert S., and Helen M. Lynd. *Middletown in Transition.* New York: Harcourt, Brace and Company, 1937.

Mays, Benjamin E., and Joseph W. Nicholson. *The Negro's Church.* New York: Institute of Social and Religious Research, 1933.

McGill, Ralph. *The South and The Southerner.* Boston: Little, Brown and Company, 1964.

Merton, Robert K. *Social Theory and Social Structure.* Glencoe, Ill.: Free Press, 1949.

Mills, C. Wright. *The Power Elite.* New York: Oxford University Press, 1957.

Moon, Henry Lee. *Balance of Power: the Negro Vote.* Garden City, N.Y.: Doubleday and Company, 1948.

Muse, Benjamin. *Virginia's Massive Resistance.* Bloomington: Indiana University Press, 1961.

Myrdal, Gunnar. *An American Dilemma.* New York: Harper and Brothers, 1944.

Nolan, William. *Communism Versus The Negro.* Chicago: Henry Regnery, 1951.

North Carolina Manual, 1963. Raleigh, N.C.: Office of the Secretary of State, 1963.

Petrullo, Luigi, and Bernard M. Bass (eds.). *Leadership and Interpersonal Behavior.* New York: Holt, Rinehart and Winston, 1961.

Pierce, Joseph A. *Negro Business and Business Education.* New York: Harper and Brothers, 1947.

Price, Hugh. *The Negro and Southern Politics.* New York: New York University Press, 1951.

Quint, Howard H. *Profile in Black and White.* Washington: Public Affairs Press, 1958.

Record, Wilson. *Race and Radicalism.* Ithaca: Cornell University Press, 1964.

Reddick, L. D. *Crusader Without Violence.* New York: Harper and Brothers, 1959.

Redding, J. Saunders. *The Lonesome Road: The Story of the Negro's Part in America.* Garden City, N.Y.: Doubleday and Company, 1958.

——. *On Being Negro in America.* New York: Bobbs Merrill, 1951.

337

Rohrer, John H., and Munro S. Edmondson (eds.). *The Eighth Generation.* New York: Harper and Brothers, 1960.

Rowan, Carl T. *Go South To Sorrow.* New York: Random House, 1957.

Thompson, Daniel C. *The Negro Leadership Class.* Englewood Cliffs, N.J.: Prentice-Hall, 1963.

Tindall, George Brown. *South Carolina Negroes, 1877–1900.* Columbia: University of South Carolina Press, 1952.

Truman, David. *The Governmental Process.* New York: Alfred A. Knopf, 1955.

Tumin, Melvin M. *Desegregation: Resistance and Readiness.* Princeton, N.J.: Princeton University Press, 1958.

Tussman, Joseph. *The Supreme Court on Racial Discrimination.* New York: Oxford University Press, 1963.

United States Bureau of the Census. *Negro Population, 1790–1915.* Washington, D.C.: U.S. Government Printing Office, 1918.

——. *Negroes in the United States, 1920–1932.* Washington, D.C.: U.S. Government Printing Office, 1935.

—— *Sixteenth Census of the United States: 1940.* Washington, D.C.: U.S. Government Printing Office, 1943. *passim.*

——. *Seventeenth Census of the United States: 1950.* Washington, D.C.: U.S. Government Printing Office, 1952. *passim.*

——. *U.S. Census of Housing: 1960.* Washington, D.C.: U.S. Government Printing Office, 1961. *passim.*

——. *U.S. Census of Population: 1960.* Washington, D.C.: U.S. Government Printing Office, 1962. *passim.*

United States Commission on Civil Rights. *Civil Rights U.S.A.: Public Schools North and West, 1962.* Washington, D.C.: U.S. Government Printing Office, 1962.

——. *Civil Rights U.S.A.: Public Schools Southern States, 1962.* Washington, D.C.: U.S. Government Printing Office, 1962.

——. *Equal Protection of the Laws in North Carolina.* Report of the North Carolina Advisory Committee. Washington, D.C.: U.S. Government Printing Office, 1962.

——. *Equal Protection of the Laws in Public Higher Education, 1960.* Washington, D.C.: U.S. Government Printing Office, 1960.

——. *50 States Report; Reports of the State Advisory Commit-*

tees. Washington, D.C.: U.S. Government Printing Office, 1961.

——. *Freedom to the Free.* Washington, D.C.: U.S. Government Printing Office, 1963.

——. *1959 Report.* Washington, D.C.: U.S. Government Printing Office, 1959.

——. *1961 Report.* 5 vols. Washington, D.C.: U.S. Government Printing Office, 1961.

Warner, Robert A. *New Haven Negroes.* New Haven: Yale University Press, 1940.

Warner, W. L., and Associates. *Democracy in Jonesville.* New York: Harper and Brothers, 1949.

Washington, Booker T. *The Story of the Negro.* 2 vols. New York: Doubleday, Page and Company, 1909.

Weatherford, W. D. *Negro Life in the South.* New York: Young Men's Christian Press, 1910.

Weaver, Robert C. *The Negro Ghetto.* New York: Harcourt, Brace and Company, 1948.

West, J. *Plainville, U.S.A.* New York: Columbia University Press, 1945.

Wharton, Vernon L. *The Negro in Mississippi 1865–1890,* Vol. 28 in the *Sprunt Studies in History and Political Science.* Chapel Hill: University of North Carolina Press, 1947.

White, William. *Citadel.* New York: Harper and Brothers, 1957.

Wilson, James Q. *Negro Politics: The Search for Leadership.* Glencoe, Ill.: Free Press, 1960.

Woodson, Carter G. *A Century of Negro Migration.* Washington, D.C.: The Associated Publishers, 1918.

——. *The History of the Negro Church,* 2nd ed. Washington, D.C.: The Associated Publishers, 1922.

——. *The Negro Professional Man and the Community.* Washington, D.C.: The Association for the Study of Negro Life and History, 1934.

Woodward, C. Vann. *Origins of the New South, 1877–1913.* Baton Rouge: Louisiana State University Press, 1951.

——. *The Strange Career of Jim Crow.* New York: Oxford University Press, 1955.

Woodward, C. Vann. *Tom Watson, Agrarian Rebel*. New York: The Macmillan Company, 1938.

Wright, Richard. *Black Boy*. New York: Harper and Brothers, 1945.

——. *Native Son*. New York: Harper and Brothers, 1957.

NEWSPAPERS

Atlanta World, January 1963–January 1964.

Birmingham World, January 1963–January 1964.

Carolina Times [Durham, N.C.], July 1962–April 1965.

Carolinian [Raleigh, N.C.], October 1962–April 1965.

Florida Star [Jacksonville], December 1962–March 1964.

Greenville [S.C.] *News*, January 1954–April 1965.

Greenville [S.C.] *Piedmont*, January 1954–April 1965.

The Herald [Savannah, Ga.], July 1962–April 1964.

Journal and Guide [Norfolk, Va.], March 1963–March 1964.

Louisiana Weekly [New Orleans], December 1962–March 1964.

Mobile Beacon and Alabama Citizen [Mobile-Tuscaloosa, Alabama], December 1962–April 1964.

New York Times, January 1960–April 1965.

Weekly Review [Augusta, Ga.], December 1962–April 1964.

Wilmington [N.C.] *Journal*, January 1964–April 1964.

Winston-Salem [N.C.] *Journal*, January 1954–April 1965.

ARTICLES

Angell, Robert C. "The Social Integration of American Cities of More than 1,000,000 Population," *The American Sociological Review*, XII (June 1947), 335–342.

Baldwin, James. "The Dangerous Road Before Martin Luther King," *Harper's Magazine*, CCXXII (February 1961), 33–42.

Barth, Ernest A. T. and Baha Abu-Laban. "Power Structure and The Negro Sub-Community," *The American Sociological Review*, XXIV (February 1959), 69–76.

Bierstedt, Robert. "An Analysis of Social Power," *The American Sociological Review*, XV (December 1950), 730–738.

The Crisis, January 1946–March 1964, *passim*.

Farris, Charles D. "The Re-Enfranchisement of Negroes in Florida," *Journal of Negro History*, XXXIX (1954), 259–283.

Fleming, Harold C. "Resistance Movements and Racial Segregation," *The Annals,* CCCIV (March 1956), 44–52.

Frazier, E. Franklin. "The American Negro's New Leaders," *Current History,* XXVIII (April 1928), 56–59.

——. "Garvey: A Mass Leader," *The Nation,* CXXIII (August 18, 1926), 147–148.

——. "Negro Harlem: An Ecological Study," *The American Journal of Sociology,* XLIII (July 1937), 72–88.

"How Whites Feel About Negroes: A Painful American Dilemma," *Newsweek,* LXII (October 21, 1963), 44–57.

Huitt, Ralph. "The Outsider in the Senate: An Alternative Role," *The American Political Science Review,* LV (September 1961), 566–575.

Johnson, Guy B. "Negro Racial Movements and Leadership in the United States," *The American Journal of Sociology,* XLIII (July 1937), 56–72.

Killian, Lewis, and Charles U. Smith. "Negro Protest Leaders in a Southern Community," *Social Forces,* XXXVIII (March 1960), 253–257.

Matthews, Donald R., and James W. Prothro. "Political Factors and Negro Voter Registration in the South," *The American Political Science Review,* LVII (June 1963), 355–367.

——. "Social and Economic Factors and Negro Voter Registration in the South," *The American Political Science Review,* LVII (March 1963), 24–45.

"The Negro in America," *Newsweek,* LXII (July 29, 1963), 15–36.

Phylon, The Atlanta University Review of Race and Culture (January 1946–January 1964), *passim.*

Polsby, Nelson W. "Three Problems of Community Power Analysis," *The American Sociological Review,* XXIV (December 1959), 796–803.

Rossi, Peter H. "Community Decision Making," *Administrative Science Quarterly,* I (March 1957), 415–441.

Speier, Hans. "Social Stratification in the Urban Community," *The American Sociological Review,* (April 1936), 193–202.

Strong, Donald S. "The Rise of Negro Voting in Texas," *The American Political Science Review,* XLII (1948), 500–510.

UNPUBLISHED MATERIALS AND PAMPHLETS

"Changing Patterns in the New South." Atlanta: Southern Regional Council, 1955.

Collins, LeRoy. "The South and the Nation." Atlanta: Southern Regional Council, 1960.

Dabbs, James M., *et. al.* "A Hundred Years Later." Atlanta: Southern Regional Council, 1962.

"Greenville's Big Idea." Greenville, S.C.: Community Council of Greenville County, 1950.

"The North Carolina Good Neighbor Program." Raleigh: North Carolina Good Neighbor Council, 1963. (Mimeographed.)

Patrick, Clarence H. "Lunch-Counter Desegregation in Winston-Salem, North Carolina." A report issued at Winston-Salem, N.C., July, 1960.

Pettigrew, Thomas. "Epitaph for Jim Crow." New York: Anti-Defamation League of B'nai B'rith, 1964.

Price, Margaret. "The Negro and the Ballot in the South." Atlanta: Southern Regional Council, 1959.

——. "The Negro Voter in the South." Atlanta: Southern Regional Council, 1957.

Reif, Jane. "Crisis in Norfolk." Richmond: Virginia Council on Human Relations, 1960.

Rudwick, Elliott M. "The Unequal Badge." Atlanta: Southern Regional Council, 1962.

Sindler, Allan P. "Aspects of Durham Politics: White and Negro." To be a chapter in a forthcoming volume on the history of Durham, N.C., 1964.

"The Student Protest Movement: A Recapitulation." Atlanta: Southern Regional Council, 1961.

Winston-Salem [N.C.] *Urban League Annual Report.* 1961, 1962, 1963.

Zinn, Howard. "Albany: A Study in National Responsibility." Atlanta: Southern Regional Council, 1962.

Index

Atheneum Paperbacks

STUDIES IN AMERICAN NEGRO LIFE

THE ADAMS PAPERS

THE NEW YORK TIMES BYLINE BOOKS

Atheneum Paperbacks

HISTORY—AMERICAN

Atheneum Paperbacks

HISTORY

HISTORY—ASIA

ECONOMICS AND BUSINESS

Atheneum Paperbacks

LAW AND GOVERNMENT

DIPLOMACY AND INTERNATIONAL RELATIONS

Atheneum Paperbacks

Atheneum Paperbacks

Atheneum Paperbacks

THE WORLDS OF NATURE AND MAN

LITERATURE AND THE ARTS